Distinguished Studies in

American Legal and Constitutional History

Edited by
Harold Hyman
William P. Hobby
Professor of History
Rice University

A Garland Series

Distinguished Studies in American Legal and Constitutional History

1. Gary J. Aichele. *Legal Realism and Twentieth-Century American Jurisprudence: The Changing Consensus.*
2. Kenneth R. Bowling. *Politics in the First Congress, 1789–1791.*
3. Steven R. Boyd. *The Constitution in State Politics: From the Calling of the Constitutional Convention to the Calling of the First Federal Elections.*
4. Martin J. Costello. *Hating the Sin, Loving the Sinner: The Minneapolis Childrens' Theatre Company Adolescent Sexual Abuse Prosecutions.*
5. Richard S. Eckert. *The Gentlemen of the Profession: The Emergence of Lawyers in Massachusetts, 1630–1810.*
6. C. Ashley Ellefson. *The County Courts and the Provincial Court in Maryland, 1733–1763.*
7. James C. Foster. *The Ideology of Apolitical Politics: Elite Lawyers' Response to the Legitimation Crisis of Liberal-Capitalism, 1870–1920.*
8. Patrick M. Garry. *The American Vision of the Free Press: An Historical and Constitutional Revisionist View of the Press as a Marketplace of Ideas.*
9. Robert M. Goldman. *'A Free Ballot and a Fair Count': The Department of Justice and the Enforcement of Voting Rights in the South, 1877–1893.*
10. James W. Gordon. *Lawyers in Politics: Mid-Nineteenth Century Kentucky as a Case Study.*
11. Frederick K. Grittner. *White Slavery: Myth, Ideology, and American Law.*
12. Walter T. Hitchcock. *Timothy Walker: Antebellum Lawyer.*
13. Wythe Holt. *Virginia's Constitutional Convention of 1901–1902.*
14. John W. Johnson. *The Dimensions of Non-Legal Evidence in the American Judicial Process: The Supreme Court's Use of Extra-Legal Materials in the Twentieth Century.*
15. John M. Lindley. *'A Soldier is Also A Citizen': The Controversy over Military Justice in the U. S. Army, 1917–1920.*
16. Lester G. Lindley. *The Impact of the Telegraph on Contract Law.*
17. W. Ray Luce. Cohens v. Virginia *(1821), The Supreme Court and State Rights: A Reevaluation of Influences and Impacts.*
18. Stephen Middleton. *Ohio and the Antislavery Activities of Attorney Salmon Portland Chase, 1830–1849.*
19. Stephen M. Millett. *The Constitutionality of Executive Agreements: An Analysis of* United States v. Belmont.
20. Samuel N. Pincus. *The Virginia Supreme Court, Blacks, and the Law, 1870–1902.*
21. H. D. Rosenthal. *Their Day in Court: A History of the Indian Claims Commission.*
22. Peter E. Russell. *His Majesty's Judges: Provincial Society and the Supreme Court in Massachusetts, 1692–1774.*
23. Keith R. Schlesinger. *The Power that Governs: The Evolution of Judicial Activism in a Midwestern State, 1840–1890.*
24. Stephen K. Shaw. *The Ninth Amendment: Preservation of the Constitutional Mind.*
25. John M. Spivack. *Race, Civil Rights, and the United States Court of Appeals for the Fifth Judicial Circuit.*
26. Beverly Zweiben. *How Blackstone Lost the Colonies: English Law, Colonial Lawyers, and the American Revolution.*

COHENS V. VIRGINIA (1821)

The Supreme Court and State Rights, a Reevaluation of Influences and Impacts

W. Ray Luce

Garland Publishing, Inc.
New York & London
1990

Library of Congress Cataloging-in-Publication Data

Luce, W. Ray.
Cohens v. Virginia (1821) : the Supreme Court and state rights : a reevaluation of influences and impacts / W. Ray Luce.
p. cm. — (Distinguished studies in American legal and constitutional history)
Thesis (Ph. D.)—University of Virginia, 1978.
Includes bibliographical references.
ISBN 0-8240-2765-5 (alk. paper)
1. Federal government—United States—History. 2. State rights—History. 3. Judicial review—United States—History. 4. United States. Supreme Court—History. 5. Government liability—Virginia—History. 6. Virginia—Constitutional history. I. Title. II. Title: Cohens versus Virginia (1821). III. Series.
KF4600.L83 1990
342.73'042—dc20 [347.30242]
90-19172

Printed on acid-free, 250-year-life paper.
Manufactured in the United States of America.

For Kay
for all the reasons

TABLE OF CONTENTS

ACKNOWLEDGMENTS

The author is indebted to numerous individuals and institutions in the preparation of this study. Richard Ellis has shown continued patience, support, and criticism. Bernard Mayo and Robert Brugger offered direction and insights. The Special Collections and Interlibrary loan staffs of Alderman Library, University of Virginia, were particularly helpful as were library staffs at Virginia State Library, the Library of Congress, the National Archives, William and Mary Library, Pierpont Morgan Library, Maryland Historical Society, Virginia Historical Society, Duke University Library and the University of North Carolina Library. Special thanks go to fellow graduate students who offered suggestions and camaraderie, and to my family who sacrificed much that this study might be completed. Additional thanks to Mary Barbash and Tom Cinadr for assistance in the preparation of the Garland edition.

PREFACE TO THE GARLAND EDITION

This study was completed as a Ph.D. dissertation in history at the University of Virginia. An explosion of writings about the United States Constitution has occurred since the completion of my study of _Cohens v. Virginia_ in 1978. These studies, many written in response to the Bicentennial of the Constitution in 1987, have provided additional background for the case and its impact. They have not, however, provided significant new material on the case itself.

Two recent books provide particularly important background material related to the _Cohens_ case. The first is Boyd Clifton Rist's dissertation: "The Jeffersonian Crisis Revived: Virginia, the Court, and Appellate Jurisdiction Controversy" (Unpublished Ph.D. dissertation, University of Virginia, 1985). Rist places Virginia's struggle against the Supreme Court, especially in the cases of _Martin v. Hunter's Lessee_, _McCulloch v. Maryland_, and _Cohens v. Virginia_ into a larger historical background, and traces the cases' impact, and state rights thought forward to 1900. Rist made extensive use of the current study along with other secondary works on the controversies. The second study, David P. Currie's _The Constitution in the Supreme Court 1789-1888_, Chicago, 1985, discusses the Court in terms of cases and is particularly useful in tracing specific issues decided in the Cohens case both forward and backward relative to other judgements made by the Court.

Several new works have been published studying the Marshall Court. The most important are three volumes in the Oliver Wendell Holmes Devise History of the Supreme Court of the United States. Volume 2 is George L. Haskins' and Herbert A. Johnson's Foundations of Power: John Marshall, 1801-1815, New York, 1981. G. Edward White wrote a joint volume 3 and 4: The Marshall Court and Cultural Change, 1815-1835, New York, 1988. White earlier published two articles dealing with the subject: Edward White, "The Art of Revising History: Revisiting the Marshall Court," Suffolk University Law Review, XVI (1982), 659-685, and "The Working Life of the Marshall Court, 1815-1835," Virginia Law Review, LXX (1984), 1-52. Haskins also published additional material in "Law Versus Politics in the Early Years of the Marshall Court," University of Pennsylvania Law Review, CXXX (1981), 1-27. White's volume, which treats the Cohens case, shows a familiarity with this study, but his lack of a bibliography and his almost exclusive citation of original sources, without reference to the secondary studies, gives silence evidence that he has incorporated recent scholarship into the study (one of the series' goals), but does not facilitate reference to or acknowledgement of those secondary works.

Other studies of the Marshall Court include: Francis N. Stites, John Marshall: Defender of the Constitution, Boston,

1981, part of the Library of American Biography series, and two edited works dealing with Marshall: Thomas C. Shevory edited, John Marshall's Achievement; Law, Politics, and Constitutional Interpretations, New York, 1989, and The Constitution and Chief Justice Marshall, New York, 1978, edited by William F. Swindler. Additional works on the Court include: David Thelen, The Constitution and American Life, Ithica, 1988; William E. Nelson, "The Eighteenth-Century Background of John Marshall's Constitutional Jurisprudence." Michigan Law Review, 75 (1978), 893-960; J. P. Secola, "The Judicial Review of John Marshall and its subsequent development in American Jurisprudence," University of Bridgeport Law Review, 9 (1988), 11-57, and Lincoln Law Review, 18 (1988), 1-48; Robert Lowry Clinton, Marbury v. Madison and Judicial Review, Lawrence, Kansas, 1989; and Dwight Wiley Jessup, Reaction and Accommodation: The United States Supreme Court and Political Conflict, 1809-1835, New York, 1987.

A debate over sovereign immunity and the Eleventh Amendment is part of a larger controversy about how the Constitution should be construed. Most recently the question pitted Attorney General Edwin Meese against Supreme Court Justice William J. Brennan, Jr. They argued whether the original intention of the founders as recorded in the document should control the interpretation of the Constitution, or whether the general intent of the founders, in principles such as social justice, should prevail. Other issues which have been examined, as part of this larger debate, include judicial review and sovereign immunity. The discussion about sovereign immunity, and the related discussion about the Eleventh Amendment are closely related to the Cohens case. The debate stems from a difference in view about the role of the state governments, and to some extent the national government, in the protection of individual liberties. For those who see state governments as entities which limit personal rights, the doctrine that a state cannot be sued without its consent is viewed as a hindrance to the protection of those rights. Authors such as Tribe, Field, and Amar, cited below, have examined the historical record, and the Eleventh Amendment, to show that the framers held a limited view of sovereign immunity, and, by implication, that the doctrine should not limit a state's culpability. Other authors, including Easley and Jackson see greater evidence that sovereign immunity is a more fundamental doctrine in Constitutional history. A recent book on the Eleventh Amendment by John V. Orth pays particular attention to the interpretation of the amendment in later debt suits against states: The Judicial Power of the United States: The Eleventh Amendment in American History, New York, 1987. Articles which discuss sovereign immunity include: John E. Nowak, "The Scope of Congressional Power to create Causes of Action Against State Governments and the History of the Eleventh and Fourteenth Amendments," Columbia Law Review, 75 (1975), 1413-1469; Lawrence H. Tribe, "Intergovernmental Immunities in Litigation, Taxation, and Regulation: Separation of Powers Issues in Controversies About

Federalism," Harvard Law Review, 89 (1976), 682-713; Martha A. Field, "The Eleventh Amendment and Other Sovereign Immunity Doctrines: Part One," University of Pennsylvania Law Review, 126 (1977), 515-549; Martha A. Field, "The Eleventh Amendment and Other Sovereign Immunity Doctrines: Part Two," University of Pennsylvania Law Review, 126 (1978), 1203-1280; William A. Fletcher, "A Historical Interpretation of the Eleventh Amendment: A Narrow Construction of an Affirmative Grant of Jurisdiction Rather than a Prohibition Against Jurisdiction," Stanford Law Review 35 (1983), 1033-1131; John J. Gibbons, "The Eleventh Amendment and State Sovereign Immunity: A Reinterpretation," Columbia Law Review , 83 (1983), 1889-2005; Akil Reed Amar, "Of Sovereignty and Federalism," Yale Law Journal, 96 (1987), 1425-1520; Gerald Bobango, "Suits Against the Sovereignty: The Dubiety of the Eleventh Amendment," West Virginia Law Review, 90 (1987), 211-233; H. Stephen Harris, Jr. and Michael P. Kenny, "Eleventh Amendment Jurisprudence After Atascadero: The Coming Clash with Antitrust, Copyright, and other Causes of Action Over Which the Federal Courts Have Exclusive Jurisdiction," Emory Law Journal, 37 (1988), 645-720; Allen K. Easley, "The Supreme Court and the Eleventh Amendment: Mourning the Lost Opportunity to Synthesize Conflicting Precedents," Denver University Law Review, 64 (1988), 485-527; and Vicki C. Jackson, "The Supreme Court, The Eleventh Amendment, and State Sovereign Immunity," The Yale Law Journal, 98 (1988), 1-126.

The debate illustrates the need to include both legal and historical scholarship in such public policy debates. Many of these articles focus on the Eleventh Amendment, one of the major documents used to support state sovereign immunity, and Cohens v. Virginia which was a major case in the interpretation of the Eleventh Amendment. While several articles quote Cohens, and some, notably Jackson, examine the record of the case in some detail, the authors evidence far more familiarity with legal citations than the secondary historical literature, especially in thesis and dissertations, examining the subject. None of these studies, for example, discuss the arguments presented during the newspaper debate over the Cohens case presented on pages 216 to 224 in this study. That material provides the most extensive public, if partisan, review of the purpose of the Eleventh Amendment during the lifetime of the participants. Such information is vital for discussions of such issues which may influence public policy.

For a discussion on the more general topic of how the constitution should be construed see Part III, "The Constitution and the Court," in The U.S. Constitution and the Supreme Court, New York, 1988, edited by Steven Anzovin and Janet Podell. On judicial review see Jesse H. Choper, Judicial Review and the National Political Process: A Functional Reconsideration of the Role of the Supreme Court, Chicago, 1980; John Hart Ely, Democracy and Distrust: A Theory of Judicial Review, Cambridge, Massachusetts, 1980; P. Allen Dionisopoulos, and Paul Peterson,

"Rediscovering the American Origins of Judicial Review: A Rebuttal to the Views Stated by Currie and Other Scholars," John Marshall Law Review, 18 (1984), 49-76; Kermit L. Hall, The Supreme Court and Judicial Review in American History, Washington, D.C., 1985; and Albert P. Melone and George Mace, editors, Judicial Review and American Democracy, Ames, Iowa, 1988.

Additional studies have also been made of the Virginia background of the case and the individuals involved, including: Drew R. McCoy, The Elusive Republic, Political Economy in Jeffersonian America, Chapel Hill, North Carolina, 1980; Edward Dumbauld, Thomas Jefferson and the Law, Norman, Oklahoma, 1978; Robert E. Shalhope, John Taylor of Caroline: Pastoral Republican. Columbia, South Carolina: 1980; Lorraine E. Holland, "Rise and Fall of the Ante-Bellum Virginia Aristocracy: A Generational Analysis," (Unpublished Ph.D. Dissertation, University of California, Irvine, 1980); Charles T. Cullen, "St. George Tucker, John Marshall, and Constitutionalism in the Post-Revolutionary South," Vanderbilt Law Review, XXXII (1979), 341-345; Kermit L. Hall, and James W. Ely Jr., An Uncertain Tradition: Constitutionalism and the History of the South, Athens, Georgia, 1989; and Drew McCoy, The Last of the Fathers: James Madison and the Republican Legacy, New York, 1989. Much has been written during the past twelve years, much of which can provide a larger context for the Cohens case, and yet these studies require no major changes in this study of an important constitutional case.

INTRODUCTION

For a long time, lawyers and historians have examined United States Supreme Court decisions in an attempt to trace the development of the American legal system. These examinations have usually focused upon the Court itself and a case's importance based upon its impact on constitutional law. This approach, however, is too limited to understand the importance of some cases that raised not only constitutional questions but political, social, economic, and intellectual ones as well. Thorough studies of such individual cases can provide an understanding of the broad history of the Supreme Court and its impact upon such nonlegal areas as American intellectual and political development.

A prime candidate for such a study is Cohens v Virginia (1821), which set precedents defining the Supreme Court's power in relation to state courts and state legal systems, limited the meaning of the Eleventh Amendment, and helped interpret the nature of the federal system. For many persons, especially in Virginia, the case also became the symbol of the dangers of the federal government. Under the leadership of Spencer Roane, a member of the Virginia Court of Appeals, and with the tacit approval of Thomas Jefferson, Cohens became the vehicle these Virginians used in calling for limits on the federal judiciary and for a return to a more balanced political system in which the states provided a stronger check on central authority. Criticism of the Court and the _Cohens_ decision lasted more than a year and proved to be the most extensive opposition the Court received during John Marshall's tenure as Chief Justice. The conflict became so intense that Marshall feared for the future of the Supreme Court.

The case's important legal precedents and the resulting political opposition to the Court have made the _Cohens_ case a standard chapter in the constitutional history of the United States. Most accounts of the case, however, examine only these two national aspects. It is impossible to understand the case fully from such a national point of view. Local aspects of the case must be examined to understand the case's impact upon United States history and American legal development.

Economic and political forces in Virginia in 1820, for example, helped to make the _Cohens_ case a landmark decision. Economic distress from the nation's first depression, the Panic of 1819, and the resulting opposition to the Second Bank of the United States, which many Americans felt caused the panic--when combined with a significant loss of Virginia's economic and political power and an earlier series of unpopular Supreme Court decisions--caused many Virginians to re-examine their political beliefs and take a stand against the federal government and especially the Supreme Court.

The _Cohens_ case originated during this increasing state rights concern, and was thoroughly examined in Virginia newspapers and in the Virginia legislature before the case reached the Supreme Court. State rights Virginians hoped to provide political as well as constitutional arguments upholding the state's position. The campaign was partially successful, and their arguments limited John Marshall's options in the decision.

But Virginia leaders underestimated John Marshall. Marshall skillfully safeguarded the Court's powers and defused an explosive constitutional question while ruling for Virginia on the merits of the case. Marshall's decision contains some of his most nationalistic pronouncements while masterfully illustrating his skills as jurist and politician.

The decision enraged some Virginians and was hotly debated for over a year in newspapers across the country. A close examination of these debates, however, reveals that the reaction to the case was not a simple assault upon the Supreme Court by powerful state rights forces in Virginia led by Spencer Roane. The debate was sparked by Court supporters defending the decision and continued to be a debate between supporters and opponents of the Cohens ruling answering one another's arguments. The debate was not, as it has generally been viewed, a one sided attack upon the Court.

The newspaper debate over the decision provides a significant view of constitutional thought thirty years after ratification. Many, if not most, of the participants debating the nature of the federal government had participated in ratifying the Constitution and this is the last major debate on the Constitution by the generation that wrote and ratified it. Both defenders of the Court and opponents of the *Cohens* decision stressed their acceptance of the Constitution but argued that the other side endangered it. For many writers and politicians engaged in the debate, it became a conflict to determine the fate of the Union.

Virginia leaders failed to rally sufficient popular support to modify Marshall's decision by constitutional amendment or legislative enactment. That failure had an important impact on the future of state rights thought. Encouraged by their earlier successful opposition to the Alien and Sedition Acts resulting, as they saw it, in the election of Thomas Jefferson as President, state rights Virginians felt that they could use popular opinion to counter any future expansion of federal power. The earlier model, however, proved unsuccessful against the *Cohens* decision. Opponents of the decision became disillusioned with national appeals and searched for other methods to protect state rights. Their failure became an important element in the evolution of state rights thought from a national defense of freedom and local control to a defense of sectional interests.

CHAPTER I

LOTTERIES AND STATE REGULATION IN 1820: COMPETING FORCES AT AN HISTORIC MOMENT

The _Cohens_ case began in August 1820 when a Norfolk, Virginia borough court fined Philip I. and Mendez I. Cohen $100 for selling tickets in a Maryland lottery despite a recent Virginia statute prohibiting such sales. At first glance, the small sum involved ($100) and the merchandise being regulated (lottery tickets) would indicate that the later notoriety the case received must have come from the constitutional principles involved--the litigants being secondary at best. A closer look, however, reveals two important economic interests meeting at an historic moment, fully as important to the development of the _Cohens_ case as the constitutional questions it raised.

By 1820, lotteries in the United States were far more than a harmless pastime or a gambling nuisance. Lottery offices were among the most important financial institutions in the nation. Much of the nation's capital accumulation came from lotteries, and most lottery offices performed a variety of financial and banking services. The new Virginia statute threatened both the existence of a branch of Jacob I. Cohen Jr. and Brothers Lottery Office, one of the nation's most powerful lottery firms, and the future of many lotteries sold by most lottery offices, including the Grand National Lottery involved in this case. Lottery firms like the Cohens brothers were opposed in the case by the state of Virginia. The state government had tried to limit lottery abuses almost from the arrival of the first colonists in Jamestown. The 1819 statute was only the latest in a series of laws attempting to curb the detrimental side effects of lotteries. This law was inspired by more than a desire to prevent fraud. The law was an attempt to stop speculation by lottery firms during the Panic of 1819, which threatened the ability of Virginia banks to redeem their notes with specie. The protection of the state's financial stability, especially when combined with a defense of the state's right to legislate in matters relating to morality, made the protection of the law a high state priority. Far from involving secondary characters, the _Cohens_ case pitted a powerful economic interest against the state of Virginia.

These two forces came into conflict in 1820 when a number of economic and political forces converged to reinforce state rights attitudes in the state. The Panic of 1819 brought hardships to most state citizens. A ready scapegoat was the Second Bank of the United States, which had precipitated, if not caused, the panic. State rights attitudes were also increased by a series of unpopular Supreme Court decisions, including _McCulloch v. Maryland_ upholding the bank. Other factors, such as a loss in Virginia's economic and political power, increased the search for a scapegoat such as the United States government and especially the United States Supreme Court.

I

The Norfolk Borough Court characterized the Cohen brothers as "evil disposed persons," yet in many ways the Cohen family represented the fulfillment of the American dream. When Judith Cohen, the young widow of a Bavarian Jewish immigrant, moved to Baltimore in 1803, few in Baltimore imagined that her seven children would become social and financial leaders.

Family members later served in the state legislature, as the first Jewish member of the city council, on local commissions, and as officers for the stock exchange, banking, insurance, and railroad companies. These accomplishments were largely due to the leadership of Jacob I. Cohen, the eldest son, and his early connection with lotteries.[1]

Jacob Cohen worked briefly as a merchant and grocer before taking a job at the Medical College of Maryland lottery office in 1812. Before the end of the year he had opened his own office. Cohen's financial and promotional skills helped the office prosper; company operations expanded, and soon five of his brothers joined the firm, which became Jacob I. Cohen, Jr., and Brothers Lottery Office. Branches opened in Norfolk, Richmond, Philadelphia, New York, and Charleston.

The office concentrated on selling lottery tickets, but it also engaged in an increasing range of other financial services.

---

[1]For a closer examination of the Cohens family and their business activities see: W. Ray Luce, "The Cohen Brothers of Baltimore: from Lotteries to Banking," Maryland Historical Magazine, vol. LXVIII (Fall, 1973), 288-308.

The brothers received a variety of bank notes for lottery tickets. They profitably exchanged such notes throughout the United States. They furthered their banker/broker operations by buying and selling gold and by offering stocks and bank drafts to the public. These banking activities, along with decreasing lottery profits, eventually caused the brothers to stop selling lottery tickets in 1821 and open a banking firm. But in 1820 when the Cohens case began, the firm was dependent upon the sale of lottery tickets, especially Maryland lottery tickets.

How a lottery worked can be illustrated by a Baltimore lottery designed to finance the city monument to George Washington. Proponents gained necessary legislative approval in January 1810, and searched for the best method to raise the large sum.[2] One lottery alone could not raise the $100,000 needed, so the Washington Monument Lottery organized several "classes," or separate lotteries, with each class designed to raise part of the total. The process took longer than expected, continuing until 1824.

The fourth class of the monument lottery, which the Cohen office widely advertised in 1820, is typical of most lotteries during the period, although differences existed in the number and price of tickets, and in the number and size of the prizes as promoters designed ingenious lottery schemes to attract the public. Prizes in this class of the monument lottery ranged from

[2]John Samuel Ezell, Fortune's Merry Wheel. The Lottery in America (Cambridge, Massachusetts, 1960), 119, and Baltimore American, July 17, 1811.

a $40,000 grand prize to a thousand prizes of $25. Five thousand $20 tickets were sold. Thus ticket sales would raise $100,000--the amount to be awarded in prizes. Funds for the monument and for lottery expenses came from a fifteen percent discount on all prizes, which would raise $15,000.[3] Profit might increase from a rise in ticket prices near the end of the lottery, which often occurred if the larger prizes had not been drawn. The remaining tickets, having a greater chance of winning such capital prizes, commanded higher prices. Ticket prices in another Maryland lottery, the Grand State Lottery, increased from $8.50 to $9 in September 1822, and finally reached $14 at the end of February 1823.[4]

A lottery drawing was an exciting event. Two large wheels were generally used: one wheel held all ticket stubs, and the other wheel contained slips of paper, some of which designated a prize. First, a lottery official drew a ticket stub, then drew a slip of paper to determine what prize, if any, the ticket had won. Drawing thousands of tickets in this manner took a great deal of time, and so only a limited number of tickets could be drawn each day. A week, or even a month, might elapse before the next drawing. Because of this elaborate procedure, the complete drawing of a lottery often took months. Public places were generally used for the drawings and a considerable crowd might

---

[3]Baltimore American, April 27, 1820.

[4]Cohen's Gazette and Lottery Register, August 29, 1822, February 27, 1823.

gather if it seemed that a particularly large prize might be awarded. Many elements in Henry Stockbridge's description of a later abbreviated Baltimore drawing apply to earlier lotteries as well.

> A high state official had supervision of the drawings of the lotteries which took place almost daily with open doors in an upper room of the Post Office building . . . a cylinder constructed of glass --so that its contents could be seen--with a length of perhaps a foot and a half and a diameter of probably three feet was placed in elevated position so that all could see it . . . The wheel was then rapidly revolved till its contents were most thoroughly mixed, when it was stopped, the door opened and a carefully blindfolded boy drew out one of the numbers, which was then announced to the assemblage, the wheel again whirled and another number drawn and announced.[5]

The Cohen office, like other lottery offices, purchased large blocks of tickets in these lotteries, then vied fiercely against each other for patronage. The fact that the Cohen office succeeded testifies to their highly sophisticated promotional methods. Broadsides, posters, and especially newspaper advertisements all played a vital role in the attempt to convince reluctant purchasers to buy.

Advertising had to persuade patrons that a specific lottery offered the best available plan and that tickets should be purchased from the advertising office. Promoters designed some lotteries with large capital prizes, others with numerous prizes, and still others with low ticket prices to attract different

---

[5]Henry Stockbridge, Sr., "Baltimore in 1846," Maryland Historical Magazine, VI (March 1911), 25-26.

patrons. The lottery ticket dealers would then emphasize the advantages or benefits of the current scheme.

The Cohen brothers were not content, as some promoters were, to concentrate only on ticket sales and leave designing attractive lottery plans to others. In at least some lotteries they played a substantial role designing the lotteries they promoted. Jacob I. Cohen patented two lottery schemes, one of which was widely used in official Maryland state lotteries.[6] The company also helped plan several classes of the Washington Monument Lottery.[7] Maryland lottery tickets constituted the bulk of ticket sales in all company offices. This dependency insured that the Cohen brothers would ultimately have to challenge the Virginia law that threatened their right to sell Maryland tickets in their two Virginia offices.

The second requirement of lottery advertisements--to convince patrons to purchase from a particular office--demanded creativity and ingenuity to show that the office's tickets were particularly lucky and that the office provided helpful financial services, like accepting out-of-state banknotes. Offices such as Allen's Truly Lucky Office and Waite's Truly Fortunate Lottery

---

[6]M. D. Leggett, Subject Matter Index of Patents for Inventions, 2 vols. (Washington, 1874), II, 889, Cohen's Gazette, July 28, 1825; September 4, 1828.

[7]Baltimore American, January 12, 1814, and "Committee Minutes," Papers Relating to the Washington Monument, Book V., March 23, 1820; September 26, 1821, Maryland Historical Society (MHS)

office hoped their names would help generate such confidence.[8] All offices loudly proclaimed the latest success enjoyed by a ticket sold by their office and identified their past winners in current ads. Most Cohen ads, for example, listed all prizes over $5,000 won by company tickets. The list, which finally included over $1,500,000 in prizes, certainly inspired confidence.[9] Cohen's ads soon carried the impressive, if hard to prove, notation that "MORE CAPITAL PRIZES have been obtained at COHEN'S than in any other office in America."[10]

Perhaps the Cohen brothers' most effective tool was Cohen's Gazette and Lottery Register. Published from 1814 until 1830, the newspaper was distributed free to the firm's regular customers. The newspaper permitted a personal appeal to patrons. The distant lottery enthusiast gained access to the information available to those attending the drawings. Through a weekly report on current lotteries, a patron learned of the demand for tickets, prizes drawn during the week, and those remaining in the wheel. The Gazette also published complete lists of tickets drawn in a lottery. This service was especially important before the introduction of abbreviated methods of drawing. With such lists, distant ticket owners could learn the fate of any ticket--

---

[8]Baltimore American, January 31; September 1, 1820.

[9]Cohen's Gazette, September 1, 1830.

[10]Ibid., April 17, 1818.

no small satisfaction to isolated lottery patrons in an era of slow communications.

The Gazette also explained the office's advantages in more detail. The office's prompt payment of prizes was noted in most advertisements. Most lotteries agreed to pay winners sixty days after the lottery finished drawing. The holder of a winning number drawn during the first days of a large lottery might wait several months before receiving his prize money; winning Cohen's tickets could be redeemed for cash immediately. The company took obvious pleasure when the joint owners of ticket number 7616 in the Washington Monument Lottery collected $1,000 cash ten minutes after the prize was drawn.[11] Such prompt payments here made in case after case, including three prizes of $100,000 and several of $50,000.[12]

The Gazette often included short biographies of Cohen winners, hoping prospective buyers would identify with such winners even if the standard lottery ads did not convince them. Gazette readers in 1823 learned that Mrs. Williams of Fell's Point, Baltimore, won part of a $5,000 prize from a ticket her husband purchased for her before sailing to South America.[13] Mrs. Hannah Proctor, an "industrious widow," from Milton, Albemarle County, Virginia, the Gazette reported, could use her

---

[11] Ibid., October 4, 1822.

[12] Ibid., September 1, 1830.

[13] Ibid., February 27, 1823.

$1,000 prize to help support her family.[14] Such examples often included character sketches that said much between the lines. Mr. Elisha Tarver, from Crawford County, Georgia, who won $50,000 in 1824, had borne misfortunes that brought him to poverty "without a murmur." He possessed "those desirable qualifications which make him a firm friend, good neighbor, and estimable citizen."[15]

The Gazette often included similar stories about those who might have won. The Cohen's office sold ticket number 1191, the $50,000 winner in the Surgical Lottery, to Bostonian Ralph Huntington in 1818. Huntington resold the ticket, with others, to a local farmer. The farmer, upon finding that one of his tickets had won a $50 prize, sold them all back to Huntington for a small profit. Huntington then sold the ticket a second time to Benjamin Eaton, who won $50,000.[16] How many others were like Ralph Huntington, who had twice owned a $50,000 ticket? How many prizes were within the reader's easy grasp? The Cohen's publication used the theme of lost opportunity in their advertisements. Surgical Institution Lottery tickets sold out in December 1817.[17] Later advertisements reminded readers of the sell out and encouraged them to avoid disappointment by quickly

---

[14]Ibid., March 11, 1825.

[15]Ibid., August 12, 1824.

[16]Ibid., January 9, 1818.

[17]Ibid., December 12, 1817.

purchasing tickets in current lotteries.[18] When unsold tickets drew large prizes, the paper noted the lost opportunity. Several individuals, for example, told the Cohens that they had intended to buy a ticket in the Cathedral Lottery in 1820. In this particular case, the Gazette said so few tickets remained that if a fraction of those people thinking of purchasing a ticket had done so, one of them would have been $20,000 richer. [19]

The Gazette made particular use of two promotional methods used to some degree by most other lottery offices: the renewal of lottery tickets and the selling of fractions or shares of a ticket. Small prize winners were urged to use their good fortune to gain another chance at the larger prizes undrawn. Many lotteries were designed to encourage the "renewal of tickets." Ways were found to award smaller prizes during the first few days' drawings. For example, the Masonic Hall Lottery in 1818 awarded a twenty-five dollar prize to the first three thousand tickets drawn, even if they drew blank stubs.[20] This renewal not only encouraged early ticket sales, but allowed winning ticket owners to "renew" a ticket before the lottery finished drawing. Such small prizes could run as high as ninety dollars, but ticket costs were in the same price range. Average buyers could not afford such sums and so most offices sold shares or fractions of

---

[18] Ibid., December 12, 1817; February 27, 1818.

[19] Ibid., November 30, 1820.

[20] Ibid., May 1, 1818.

a ticket. The Cohen brothers used this variation to great benefit. Their ads usually indicated the prices of various shares of a ticket and the highest amount each could win. On paper, the breakdown looked impressive. For example, a one-eighth interest in a ticket in the Grand State Lottery cost only $1.50, but could win $12,500.[21] The Cohen's office sold many prize-winning tickets in shares, including capital prizes of $100,000 and $40,000.[22] Tickets were often highly fragmented and ticket parts might be owned by individuals in several states. Ticket number 5859, a $500 winner in the Cathedral Lottery in 1820, was divided into seven shares: one-fifth in Marietta, Pennsylvania; one-fifth on the Eastern Shore of Maryland; one-tenth in Harrisburg, Pennsylvania; one-tenth in Lexington, Kentucky; one-tenth in Emmitsburg, Maryland; and the final three-tenths in Baltimore.[23] Winning tickets sold in shares always received special notice in the Gazette.

Unlike many offices, the Cohen's Baltimore office specialized in mail order sales. Customers throughout the nation received the Gazette and Lottery Register, and the office placed ads in a number of newspapers to attract "Distant Adventurers." The scope of such advertisements can be seen in the list of newspapers the Cohen brothers used to publish an 1819 Maryland

---

[21]Ibid., May 22, 1823.

[22]Ibid., July 22, 1824; April 17, 1818; Baltimore American, June 11, 1814.

[23]Cohen's Gazette, September 11, 1820.

Lottery prize list. The list was published in: The Philadelphia Aurora and Freeman's Journal; York (Pennsylvania) Gazette; Harrisburg Republican; Easton (Maryland) Gazette; National Intelligencer; Georgetown Herald; Richmond Enquirer; Norfolk Herald and Beacon; Petersburg Intelligencer; Raleigh Star; Charleston City Gazette and Courier; Savannah Republican; Augusta Chronicle; and Pittsburgh Gazette.[24] Almost every Cohen's ad carried a footnote assuring the reader that mail orders from any part of the nation would be promptly filled.

Judged by either the number of prize tickets sold, or the distribution of those prizes, the success of the Cohen's office was impressive. In almost every lottery advertised in the Gazette, the office sold at least one-half of the prize tickets. During the Grand State Lottery number two in 1824, for example, tickets purchased from the office won the $100,000 prize, the $20,000 prize, one of two $10,000 prizes, one of two $5,000 prizes and an undisclosed number of smaller prizes. All of these winning tickets had been sold in shares and illustrate the large customer area the office served in 1824. Winners came from Crawford County, Georgia; Fauquier County, Virginia; Savannah, Georgia; Northampten County, North Carolina; Norfolk, Virginia; Lisbon, Ohio; Kingston, New Jersey; Shelbyville, Tennessee; Warrenton, North Carolina; Northampten, Massachusetts; Richland District, South Carolina; Louisville, Kentucky; Rensselaer County, New York; and Baltimore, Maryland. It is ironic that of

---

[24] Ibid., January 15, 1819.

all the major winners only one, one-fifth of the $5,000 prize, was owned in Baltimore.[25]

Such success took place amidst increasing local and national competition. Six lottery offices large enough to advertise in the Baltimore American and Commercial Daily Advertiser in 1820 had more than doubled to thirteen five years later.[26] Three of the offices, Yates and McIntyre, Allen's Lottery and Exchange, and Waite's Lottery and Exchange Office, were branches of national firms.[27] Competition was intense. All offices advertised the same lotteries and twelve of them were located on Market Street in Baltimore.[28]

The Panic of 1819 and the economic dislocation it produced brought hard times for lottery venders. While lottery tickets offered some individuals a way to regain lost fortunes, money for such purchases was drastically reduced. The University of Maryland Lottery with a grandiose first prize of $250,000

---

[25]Ibid., July 22, 1824.

[26]Baltimore American, January 1820; and January 1825.

[27]Ibid., January 3; March 5, 1825; Hugh G. J. Aitken, "Yates and McIntyre: Lottery Managers," The Journal of Economic History, XIII (Winter, 1953), 36-58; Baltimore American, January 4, 1825, Henrietta Larsen, "S & M Allen, Lottery, Exchange, and Stock Brokerage," Journal of Economic and Business History, III (1930-1931), 424-445.

[28]Baltimore American, January 1, 3, 4, 10, 14, 1825.

collapsed, and Cohen's Gazette and Lottery Examiner suspended publication for over a year.[29]

In the midst of the panic, Philip I. and Mendez I. Cohen moved to Norfolk, Virginia, and opened the firm's first branch office. Why they did this is unclear. The expansion probably represents company planning done before it felt the panic's full impact. It is possible, however, that the panic itself prompted the new branch office. Perhaps the opening was an attempt to disperse company resources when it became evident that the Baltimore office could no longer support all those working there. The expansion may also have been an attempt to tap the potential new market of Norfolk's large sailor population or those persons hurt by the panic who might see a lottery prize as the solution to their economic problems. Whatever the exact reasons for its establishment, it is clear that the Norfolk office opened during difficult economic times and that its survival was by no means assured.

II

Lotteries were important sources of funds in Virginia beginning with the English lotteries which helped finance Virginia colonization. By means of lotteries, private individuals as well as associations and governments collected funds to finance a wide variety of needed projects from roads to churches. As lotteries became increasingly popular and sophisticated, the

---

[29]Cohen's Gazette stopped with the June 9, 1819, issue and resumed publication September 11, 1820.

temptation for fraud also increased. States and localities passed regulations to prevent misrepresentation and underhanded activities. The Virginia statute of 1819 was one in a series of Virginia laws attempting to allow lotteries while limiting their harmful effects.[30]

An examination of some Virginia colonial and state lotteries illustrates the variety of projects funded. The Virginia Company, the colony's sponsor, used a lottery to bolster sagging company coffers. The lottery, like many later ones, became embroiled in controversy and yielded only limited benefits.[31] Later colony lotteries benefitted both private and public purposes. William Byrd III and Richard Graves organized private lotteries to pay their debts.[32] More commonly, citizens joined to finance local projects; a group in Fairfax County sought money in 1750 for a market and a church; £900 was raised to construct a road over the mountains in Augusta County; and the colony itself

---

[30]Virginia, The Revised Code of the Laws of Virginia 2 vols. (Richmond, 1820), I, 570.

[31]See: Terrence H. O'Brien, "The London Livery Companies and the Virginia Company," The Virginia Magazine of History and Biography (VMHB), LXVIII (April 1960), 137-155; Robert C. Johnson, "The Running Lotteries of the Virginia Company," Ibid., 156-165; and Robert G. Johnson, "The Lotteries of the Virginia Company, 1612-1621," Ibid., LXXIV (July 1966), 259-292.

[32] Mary Newton Slandard, Colonial Virginia, Its people and Customs (Philadelphia, 1917), 152; "Letters of Thomas Adams, 1768-1775," (VMHB), VIII (January 1915), 52.

used a lottery to help finance the French and Indian War.[33] Following the Revolution, lotteries continued to benefit similar projects, although all schemes required legislative approval. The General Assembly approved a 1782 lottery to help Richmond finance a stone bridge over Shockoe Creek.[34] Two years later the Mayor and Council of Williamsburg were given authority to raise $2,000 to repair the war damaged capitol for use as a school.[35] Masons in Richmond, Williamsburg and Cabin Point used authorized lotteries to build meeting halls.[36] A 1785 bill carefully matched an authorization of five hundred pounds to the Elizabeth River Parish to rebuild their church with a like grant for the German Lutheran Church in Winchester.[37] The most liberal grant given during the period, passed in 1811, allowed the literary fund, which was the central Virginia education fund, to raise $30,000 a year for the next seven years. The General Assembly said fund managers could conduct the lottery themselves,

---

[33] "Virginia Gazette Extracts," William and Mary College Quarterly History Magazine (W&MQ), XI (October 1903), 74-75; Carl Bridenbaugh, "Baths and Watering Places of Colonial America," W&MQ, III (3d Ser) (April 1945), 164; W&MQ William Waller Hening The Statutes' at Large: . . . 13 vols., (Richmond, 1819), VI, 453-461.

[34] Hening, XI, 157.

[35] "James City Petitions," Tyler's Quarterly Historical and Geneological Magazine, II (January 1921), 183-184; Hening, XI, 407.

[36] Hening, XII, 364; "Williamsburg Lodge of Masons," W&MQ, I (July 1892), 30.

[37] Hening, XII, 228.

or hire a manager to run it with profits shared "as to them appear reasonable."[38] The War of 1812 limited lottery activity, but following the War the General Assembly resumed approving three or four lotteries a year. Internal improvements received the greatest percentage of the increasingly large authorizations, although education continued to claim strong support.

Although there was in Virginia moral opposition to lotteries--especially among Quakers, and Virginia Baptists who considered them a specie of gambling "not sufferable in members of churches"[39] most citizens held them in high esteem. Not only did many churches employ lotteries to finance new buildings but many community leaders acted as directors or promoters for local schemes. Such respectable Virginians as Colonel George William Fairfax, George Mason, Major Lawrence Washington, Colonel William Fitzhugh, and Major Augustine Washington acted as directors in the 1750 Fairfax County lottery for a market and church.[40] William and Thomas Nelson, William Byrd, John Page, Peyton Randolph, Robert Carter Nicholas, Richard Bland, Benjamin Harrison of Berkeley, Benjamin Waller, Charles Carter of Shirley, Archibald Cary, George Wythe, John Blair, and Patrick Henry

---

[38]Virginia, Acts Passed at a General Assembly of the Commonwealth of Virginia . . . (1819-1811), 9.

[39]George William Beale, A History of the Rise and Progress of the Baptists in Virginia (Richmond, 1894), 125.

[40]"Virginia Gazette Extracts," W&MQ, XII (October 1903), 74-75.

performed similar duties for a 1772 lottery to raise funds to improve navigation on the "Potowmack."[41]

Despite general public acceptance, most promoters adopted self-regulations to maintain public confidence. The Fairfax lottery already mentioned advertised that the lottery would be managed as nearly as possible by English methods, and at least five managers would attend the public drawings.[42]

Such self-regulation, however, did not insure lottery practices which were above reproach. Economic difficulties often led lotteries, especially private lotteries, to institute questionable practices. William Byrd III encountered many such problems in his 1768 lottery. Byrd's heavy debts required the sale of part of his extensive land holdings. Yet large land sales would probably drive land prices far below market value. Byrd's solution was to organize a lottery awarding land as prizes-hoping to raise the required liquid assets while maintaining the land's market value. Ten thousand five pound tickets were printed, each giving the purchaser a chance to win part of the £56,000 in prize land.[43] Despite ticket sales in England and large purchases by George Washington and others, the

---

[41] Hening, XIII, 577-579.

[42]"Virginia Gazette Extracts," W&MQ 74-75.

[43]Letters of Thomas Adams, 1768-1775," VMHB, VIII (January 1915), 52.

£50,000 proved hard to raise.[44] Unsold or retained tickets won £18,000 worth of land, nearly one-third of the total, when the lottery was drawn.[45] It is unclear how many tickets Byrd retained, whether he kept them through design or lack of demand, or if his tickets drew prizes in proportion to their number. Whatever the case, Byrd's winning of large prizes in his own lottery undoubtedly aroused suspicion. Byrd had additional problems with the lottery. Many debts for tickets sold on credit were not settled and six years later, in 1774, Byrd's will directed his executors to sue those holders of unpaid lottery tickets.[46] George Washington did not receive any profit from the two hundred acre lot he and nine associates won. Washington finally concluded that one of his associates had sold the land and kept the profits.[47] Land titles from the lottery became so tangled that in 1781--thirteen years after the lottery--the Virginia legislature passed a special law allowing Byrd's lottery managers to give title to the prize land in fee simple.[48]

---

[44]Ibid., 364; John C. Fitzpatrick (ed.), Writings of George Washington 39 vols. (Washington, 1931), XXVII, 442-445.

[45]"Letters and Other Papers, 1705-1829," VMHB, XXIII (October 1915) 364.

[46]"Will of Colonel William Byrd 3d," VMHB, IX (July 1901), 86.

[47]Fitzpatrick (ed.), XXX, 397-398; XXXV, 107-108.

[48]"Will of Colonel William Byrd 3d," p. 86.

Such abuses prompted a colony law requiring General Assembly approval for all state lotteries drawn after May 1, 1769.[49] Following the Revolution the newly organized state government reinstituted the law in 1779.[50] The law required legislative review of the lottery plan and its directors, and other public safeguards as well. The legislature provided elaborate safeguards for one public lottery before 1769, a lottery to help finance the French and Indian War. Ticket boxes were to be secured with seven locks and each manager received only one key. Lottery wheels must turn fifteen minutes before the first drawing and one-half minute between subsequent drawings.[51] A 1772 lottery to aid navigation on the Potomac, one of the first approved after the 1769 law, not only listed unusually distinguished managers, including Patrick Henry, Peyton Randolph, Benjamin Harrison, George Wythe, Charles Carter, Richard Bland, and others, but provided that if the lottery was not drawn by November 1, 1773, all money would be returned. The managers were given the option of organizing a new, smaller lottery scheme, if £10,000 was raised by that time.[52] Stronger state controls requiring lottery trustees to post bond that they would faithfully discharge their duties began as early as a 1786

---

[49]Hening, VIII, 353-354.

[50]Ibid., X, 206-207.

[51]Ibid., VI, 453-461.

[52]Ibid., VIII, 571-572, 77-79.

bill.[53] That provision later became standard, especially for professional lottery managers.

The Virginia legislature next attempted to regulate the sale of out-of-state lottery tickets. These lotteries drained large amounts of cash from the state. They were also objectionable on moral grounds because, while local lotteries might be defended as a painless way to donate to a worthy cause, distant lotteries could hardly be viewed as anything but gambling.

The legislature enacted a law in 1813 requiring a $50 license from each agent or business establishment selling out-of-state lottery tickets. Violators faced a $500 fine.[54] A year later, the legislature raised the license to $75 and made the $500 fine applicable to each offense.[55] These laws attempted, unsuccessfully, to stem the cash flow resulting from out-of-state ticket sales.

The license fee did make the sale of such tickets more professional. Local businesses stopped selling out-of-state tickets because they could not afford the $75 fee. Specialized lottery offices proliferated and could easily afford the fee. The increasing volume of these offices prompted the 1818

---

[53]_Ibid._, XII, 406.

[54]Virginia, _Acts Passed at a General Assembly, . . ._ 1812-1813 5, 8, 9.

[55]_Ibid._, 1813-1814 , 15.

legislature to raise the license cost for selling out-of-state tickets to $300.[56]

The new fees were in effect only a year when an 1819 general Virginia code revision completely prohibited the sale of all lottery tickets not authorized by the Virginia Assembly. The legislators justified the law as necessary to stop a cash outflow that paid for other states' internal improvements when similar Virginia projects faced financial difficulties. State officials also wished to stop the drain of specie from state banks caused by the lottery offices' exchange of state bank notes. Most lottery offices profited not only from the sale of lottery tickets but also from the exchange of banknotes they received. Lottery offices received banknotes issued by banks that varied widely in their ability to redeem their notes with specie. This led to an intricate exchange system with each banknote being discounted or given a premium according to distance or current faith in the bank. Such discount rates were often standardized weekly in larger cities. The Cohen office prepared weekly lists of Baltimore discount rates for the _Gazette_ and for the _Baltimore American and Daily Commercial Advertiser_.[57] Lottery offices profited by accepting distant banknotes at a discount and then trading them for local notes redeemable at face value or demanding specie from the issuing bank. The 1818 Virginia Legislature complained that lottery companies were using the

---

[56]_Ibid._, 1817-1818, 4.

[57]_Baltimore American_, September 7, 1819 to October 30, 1820.

large amounts of cash they held in undrawn lotteries to buy discounted Virginia banknotes in other parts of the country and then presenting the notes to Virginia banks for specie.[58] The Virginia concern with specie flow came as Virginia banks were trying desperately to continue specie payments despite the Panic of 1819 and the Second Bank of the United States' demand for specie payments.

By regulating lotteries, state leaders were defending what they viewed as a basic right to regulate establishments threatening state finances, and to police morally questionable activities. Clearly the lottery law involved a right the state would defend.

III

The intense reaction to the *Cohens* case, however, cannot be completely understood simply by examining the protagonists' strong economic interests or the legal principles the case decided. Much more is involved. Forces within the state ranging from the panic of 1819 to changing political alignments corresponded with the *Cohens* prosecution. It is as much these forces coinciding in 1820, as the litigation itself, which made the case a symbol and a battleground.

The importance of the case's timing can readily be seen by comparing *Cohens v. Virginia* with another Supreme Court decision,

---

[58] *Richmond Enquirer*, February 9, 1826.

Martin v. Hunter's Lessee decided five years earlier.[59] The Martin case, at least in the early stages, involved ownership of large land tracts in Virginia's Northern Neck--economic interests as important as the regulation of lottery tickets. This earlier Virginia decision examined constitutional principles similar to those of the Cohens case, including whether the United States Supreme Court could review the decision of a state court. This early Supreme Court decision prompted an official review of the decision by the Virginia Court of Appeals and an anonymous series of newspaper articles written by Judge Spencer Roane, but little else. Reaction to the Martin case is almost conspicuous by its absence.

Undoubtedly more than opposing economic forces and important legal principles were involved in the year-long controversy over the Cohens case. Many new forces arose during the five years between the two court cases, including economic dislocation stemming from the Panic of 1819, the nation's first depression. No previous experience prepared Virginians or other Americans for the Panic's intensity or its duration. The Panic severely hurt Virginia. Flour prices in Alexandria stood at a twenty year low.[60] Tobacco prices dropped from $12 to $5 per hogs head,

---

[59] For a discussion of the Martin case see John A. Treon, "Martin v. Hunter's Lessee: A Case History" (Unpublished Ph.D. dissertation, University of Virginia, 1970).

[60] Richmond Enquirer, December 1, 1820.

while wheat lost half its value, going from $2 to $1 per bushel.[61] In June 1821 James Mercer Garnett complained to John Randolph of Roanoake that his corn and wheat crops did not bring one-third the price they had commanded four or five years before.[62] But it was not just commodity prices that fell. Richmond land prices dropped twenty-five to fifty percent almost immediately, and many planters were like Peachy Gilmer, who said, "my land and negros are unsold and neither will now command money at any price."[63]

The apparently prosperous were often hardest hit. The allure of large profits and a continuing Virginia reverence for land caused many planters to over extend themselves. When the bubble broke, they could pay for their land neither by the sale of crops, nor--because of depressed land prices--by selling the land itself. Wilson Cary Nicholas, for example, owned vast land holdings and had served in many responsible positions. Not only had he been Governor of Virginia, but a United States Senator, and president of the Richmond Branch of the Bank of the United States. No one doubted that he was a wealthy and prosperous man. On paper, his assets more than covered his obligations, but the

---

[61]<u>Ibid.</u>, February 1, 1820

[62]James Mercer Garnett to John Randolph of Roanoake, June 12, 1821, Garnett-Randolph Papers, University of Virginia Library (U.Va.)

[63]P. R. Gilmer to John Hartwell Cocke, July 4, 1819, Cock Deposit, U.Va.

depressed land market left him unable to pay his debts. The resulting litigation not only brought ruin to his family, but severe financial problems to many other prominent Virginians, including Thomas Jefferson, who had co-signed one of his notes.[64] John Preston, state treasurer, who had served earlier as Governor, had shortages of $138,992 in state funds.[65] The money, he explained, had been used to help friends in need. Peggy Nicholas vividly described the suffering in Richmond in a letter to Jane Randolph.

> There never was anything equal to the gloom of these times. Many men in this place, who thought themselves last year in affluence, are now thousands worse than nothing. Every day, we hear of some one breaking and these failures, the whole community are affected by in one way or another.[66]

Contemporary letters reveal the Panic's almost universal effect on Virginians. W. T. Nivison wrote that in Richmond "almost all the high-flyers have been struck to the earth by the hardness of the times."[67] Francis Corbin enlarged the picture to include rural areas: "but the times! the times. . . . We are

---

64Joseph C. Cabell to John Hartwell Cock, September 7, 1820, October 23, 1823, Cabell Papers, U.Va.; Isaac Coles to Joseph C. Cabell, August 28, 1819, Cabell Papers, U.Va.

65Richmond Enquirer, December 12, 1821; C. W. Gooch to David Campbell, Campbell Papers, Duke University Library (DU); David Campbell to John Campbell, January 8, 1821, Campbell Papers, DU; Bernard Peyton to Wilson Cary Nicholas, January 17, 1820, Nicholas Papers, U.Va.; and Joseph C. Cabell to John Hartwell Cocke, January 19, 1820, Cabell Papers, U.Va.

66Peggy Nicholas to Jane Randolph, May 20, 1819, Edgehill-Randolph Papers, U.Va.

67W. T. Nivison to Sarah Nivison, October 2, 1819, Tazewell Papers, Virginia State Library (VSL).

all broke, I believe, in the country, as well as in the Towns."[68] James Carr made an even gloomier report: "We have no news in this part of the country but what is known and felt in every part of the world almost; --hard: very hard times, and no very near prospect of better."[69]

Those writers who spoke of reasons for the hard times generally treated two themes that later appeared in arguments over the Cohens case. Many writers felt that loss of Republican simplicity and moral principle was at least part of the cause of the present difficulties; others looked to the unconstitutional use of power by the central government, especially the creation of the second Bank of the United States, as causing the crash. Robert Saunders wrote that the panic was a result of extravagant living, "a reproach to the industry and plain habits of Republicans!"[70] M. M. Robinson said he never expected to see such suffering, "but it is neither more or less, than the melancholy of a set of debauchers recovering from their intemperance...In returning to temperate habits, debauchers always suffer much."[71] Dr. Phillip Barraud of Norfolk reiterated the point in a highly mixed metaphor: "The loss of

---

[68]Francis Corbin to F. W. Tazewell, April 12, 1820, Tazewell Papers, VSL.

[69]James Carr to Dabney S. Carr, July 24, 1819, Carr-Cary Papers, U.Va.

[70]Robert Saunders to Joseph Prentis, May 11, 1819, Webb-Prentis Papers, U. Va.

[71]M. M. Robinson to John Hartwell Cocke, September 16, 1819, Cocke Papers, Shield Deposit, U.Va.

Fortune is secondary in the evil consequences growing out of this mischief. The prostration of our Nation's morals appears to be frightfully reduced to a disgraceful height."[72]

While many writers saw the loss of Republican virtues, presumably in others, as the reason for the widespread economic problems, others looked to banks, and especially to the second Bank of the United States. It proved to be an easy target. The bank helped finance widespread land speculation before new leadership curtailed credit and called in loans. That move triggered the Panic of 1819 and the bank became its most visible cause. Francis Corbin wrote: "No prudence, no foresight could guard against the unexampled wickedness of those who have had the management of our money in the Banks."[73] Dr Barraud agreed: "Curse on these Banks they transfere universal Ruin to the whole community--not merely to the commercial world but even to the followers of the plough."[74]

Illustrating the strength of such anti-banking sentiments in the state was the support given to three sets of anti-bank resolutions introduced in the Virginia House of Delegates following John Marshall's decision in McCulloch v. Maryland (1819) which upheld the constitutionality of the Bank of the

---

[72]P. Barraud to John Hartwell Cocke, May 31, 1819, Cocke Deposit, U.Va.

[73]Francis Corbin to F. W. Tazewell, April 12, 1820, Tazewell Papers, VSL.

[74]Dr. P. Barraud to St. George Tucker, January 4, 1819, Tucker-Coleman Papers, William and Mary Library (W&M).

United States. The House voted 117 to 38 in favor of a resolution that "the general government have no rightful authority, under the constitution, to grant a charter of incorporation to a bank of the United States."[75] The three resolutions, including a proposed constitutional amendment limiting federal banks to the District of Columbia, were defeated in the Senate but their overwhelming support in the House illustrated the depth of feeling in Virginia against the Bank of the United States.

The decline of Virginia alarmed many state citizens only slightly less than the Panic of 1819. John Randolph of Roanoake complained loudly about the state's falling position in a letter to his friend James Garnett:

> When I look back upon the history of our Country for the last forty years & think what she might have been, to see what she is, I am filled with grief & indignation. When the Revolution began we were rich and powerful. The northern states were poor. Our influence never was destroyed until by the operation of the federal Constitution.[76]

Randolph emphasized the role of the federal government in the state's decline more than other writers did, yet all observers sensed that, whether viewed by population, economics, or political power, Virginia was losing power in the Union. This decline affected Virginians in a personal way hard to understand today. Coming out of the comparatively recent colonial and revolutionary experience, state loyalties were still paramount

---

[75]Richmond Enquirer, February 10, 1820.

[76]John Randolph of Roanoake to James M. Garnett, November 1, 1823, Randolph-Garnett Papers, U.Va.

for many citizens. The federal system created new loyalties, but they did not necessarily supersede earlier ones.

Virginians were proud of their leadership as the oldest and largest state. A Virginia legislative resolution helped to bring about the Declaration of Independence, written by a Virginian. The state provided George Washington, the Revolutionary commander-in-chief and took the lead in calling the Constitutional Convention. James Madison, another son of Virginia, was "Father" of the resulting document, the Constitution of the United States, which was patterned in part on the "Virginia plan." Every United States President except one had been drawn from her ranks, and that one, John Adams, had been limited to one term partially through her opposition. A Virginian even headed the Supreme Court.

But such dominance was under attack. The growth of the nation itself threatened Virginia's position. By 1810 New York overtook Virginia in population and the size of its congressional delegation. Ten years later, the 1820 census showed Virginia falling further behind New York, and because of the Constitution's three-fifths clause, Virginia's congressional delegation fell behind both New York and Pennsylvania.[77] Virginia's population problems stemmed from more than a low rate of population growth. Soil exhaustion and poor economic conditions in the state led to a large emigration from Virginia

---

[77]<u>Richmond Enquirer</u>, November 23, 1821.

to newer, more productive western lands.[78] This migration often affected the state's most energetic groups. Office holders like General Court Judge Peter Randolph and John Campbell of the Governor's council resigned to start life in newer and presumably more hospitable areas.[79] David Watson wrote his son James, who was away at school, that he need not worry about finding a wife when he returned because, "so many of our young men run off to the new countries & leave the girls behind, that there will be a great choice for you all when you need wives.[80]

Virginia stood on the verge of losing not just its earlier numerical superiority, but also the state's position in national leadership. The "Virginia Dynasty" was ending. Virginia's leadership created jealousy and mistrust in other states, which would not allow Virginia to continue to monopolize the nation's top elective offices.[81] The election of 1824, maneuvering for which commenced with James Monroe's second election as President

---

[78]See Avery O. Craven, Soil Exhaustion as a Factor in the Agricultural History of Virginia and Maryland. 1606-1860 (Gloucester, Massachusetts, 1965), and Lewis C. Gray, History of Agriculture in the Southern United States to 1860 (Washington, D. C., 1933).

[79]Anthony F. Upton, "The Road to Power in Virginia in the Early Nineteenth Century, VMHB, Vol. LXIII (July 1954), p. 277; Richmond Enquirer, December 11, 1821; and Thomas Watkins Leigh to F. W. Gilmer, February 21, 1821, Gilmer Papers. U.Va.

[80]David Watson to James Watson, Jr., July 7, 1819, Watson Papers, U.Va.

[81]On opposition to Virginia see Central Gazette, August 17, 1821; Richmond Enquirer, June 9, 1820; August 31, 1821; National Intelligencer, September 12, 1821; and Allan Nevins (ed.). The Diary of John Quincy Adams, (New York, 1928), 226.

in 1820, emphasized the point. None of the candidates mentioned came from Virginia even though two, William H. Crawford and Henry Clay, had been born in the state. Changing population patterns and the nation's growth left little hope that future elections would be different. Virginia, it appeared certain, had lost much of its earlier leadership role. The heading on an article in the Richmond Enquirer expressed a longing for former times. "JOIN OR DIE, was the motto when our confederacy was represented by the disjointed members of a serpent of which Virginia was the head."[82]

Virginia's loss of power loomed larger when joined with the sectional nature of the debates over the admission of Missouri. The debates, lasting more than two years and at times extremely bitter, divided the country into slave and free sections.[83] Virginia, an article in the Richmond Enquirer complained, gave up large tracts of land North and West of the Ohio for friendship. Such gifts were now not sufficient. "The more we yield, the more is demanded of us. The time has now come when the best interests of the southern states demand that we should make a firm and inflexible stand, against the encroachments attempted upon the

---

[82]Richmond Enquirer, March 10, 1820.

[83]For a discussion of the change in state rights thought to a defense of sectional interests see: Norman Risjord, The Old Republicans (New York, 1965), 9-10; Jesse T. Carpenter, The South as a Conscious Minority, 1789-1861 (New York, 1930), 5; For Virginia and the Missouri Compromise see: Glover Moore, The Missouri Compromise (Lexington, 1953).

constitution and upon our rights."[84] Virginians and others saw sectional interests influence the election of John W. Taylor of New York as Speaker of the United States House of Representatives in 1820. James Pleasants expressed his fear that "in spite of all things to the contrary, a Geographical division of parties is in future to be that of our country."[85] The prospects seemed particularly dim to the editors of the Richmond Enquirer, who feared political parties based on geography rather than principles.

> Parties that are formed upon the best modes of administering a constitution, may be frequently reached through the medium of argument. Reason may address; and reason may convert them. Besides, . Your next door neighbor may be of a different party from yourself. You know him to be a kind and honorable man, and this social feeling contributes to produce a greater tone of toleration and restraint than where men of the same views and interests associate together and are separated from others by a degree of latitude, a river or a mountain.[86]

Such observations in 1820-1821 are important not because they show the nation on an unalterable course toward the Civil War, but because they provide contemporary views of Virginia's future, which seemed clouded by economic, political, social, and sectional problems. Many felt that these problems could be blamed in some degree upon unconstitutional operations of the national government and might be cured, in part at least, by a firm state rights stand in the Cohen case.

---

[84]Richmond Enquirer, February 24, 1820.

[85]James Pleasants to Joseph C. Cabell, February 4, 1821, Cabell Papers, U.Va.

[86]Richmond Enquirer, May 19, 1820.

Joining economic depression and a concern for the decline of Virginia was a strong intellectual tradition of state rights construction. The combination of this state rights tradition with the newer forces helps explain the reaction to the Cohens case. Virginia's ratification of the Constitution came only after long and at times bitter debate over whether the state would give up too many rights if she joined the new federal government. George Mason and Edmund Randolph, two Virginia delegates to the Constitutional Convention, refused to sign the finished document and former Governor Patrick Henry led the forces opposing ratification. The Virginia ratifying convention finally approved the Constitution 89 to 79 but still sought amendments to guarantee that it was a federal and not a national government they were creating. Those amendments did not quiet fears of national power. A decade after the ratification, Thomas Jefferson and James Madison used this apprehension of national power together with support for state rights as major parts of their opposition to the Alien and Sedition Acts. The result became the "Revolution of 1800" which placed Thomas Jefferson in the Presidency. Virginians in 1821 still took great pride in their part in these activities--the Virginia Resolutions opposing the Alien and Sedition Acts and their support for the "principles of '98," and the "Revolution of 1800." Even during the relatively calm period following 1800 under the "Virginia dynasty," John Randolph of Roanoake and a group of "Old Republicans" who broke with Jefferson when they felt he used federal power too carelessly, kept the particularist tradition alive in the state. The "Old Republicans" in the state represented a faction more vocal than numerous, but a strong tradition of state rights support existed in the group and in the state.

Latent support for state rights in Virginia increased in the years just before the _Cohens_ case because of a series of decisions of the United States Supreme Court upholding several national powers. _Martin v. Hunter's Lessee_ (1816) has already been discussed. Public reaction to the decision was not great, although the decision was reviewed in Virginia when the Virginia Court of Appeals formally met, heard arguments, and reversed the Supreme Court's decision. Neither side pushed the case, thus avoiding a direct confrontation, but both sides felt victorious. The case not only alerted many Virginia lawyers to the Supreme Court's claim of a power to review decisions of state courts, a claim which would be argued again in the _Cohens_ case, but provided a precedent, however shaky, of a state's right to review decisions of the Supreme Court.

Three economics decisions in 1819, a year beset with economic problems, heightened disillusionment with the Supreme Court. In _Dartmouth College v. Woodward,_ the Court upheld a colonial charter in the face of a conflicting law enacted by a later state legislature. Many state supporters viewed the severe limiting of a state legislature by a contract enacted before the state existed as an arbitrary limitation on the legislature. _Sturges v. Crowninshield_ seemed to further limit state legislatures, especially in what they could do to mitigate the Panic of 1819. The decision found a recent New York state bankruptcy law unconstitutional, and many observers thought it declared all state bankruptcy laws unconstitutional. The ruling, limiting as it did a state's ability to mitigate economic distress, was controversial and unpopular, especially because it came during the Panic of 1819.

Far more unpopular than either of these, however, was the third opinion handed down in 1819--McCulloch v. Maryland. The case which started as a test of Maryland's right to tax the Baltimore branch of the Bank of the United States soon took on national implications. The Court examined not only the state's right to regulate federal corporations operating within her borders, but also the constitutionality of the Bank itself, a question which had been hotly debated for years. The pronouncement that Maryland could not tax the bank aroused many, but the rest of the decision was worse. In upholding the bank, Marshall approved a broad construction of the Constitution. In words highly reminiscent of Hamilton's justification for the first Bank of the United States, the Court approved the use of any power felt to be "necessary and proper" to implement powers delegated to the federal government. Such an interpretation, many feared, would lead to a consolidated national government exercising broad powers, many of which had been reserved for the states or citizens of the United States. Cries of protest were heard in several states, including Virginia. The Virginia House of Delegates resolutions have already been discussed. Spencer Roane wrote a series of articles for the Richmond Enquirer criticizing the decision. Roane concluded that the Supreme Court had "erroneously decided" the case so

> as to give Congress an unbounded authority, and enable them to shake off the limits imposed on them by the Constitution. I have also endeavored to show that the Supreme Court has, . . . created itself the exclusive judge in this controversy. I have shown that these measures may work an entire change in the Constitution, and destroy entirely the state authorities.[87]

These cases, and especially the McCulloch case, helped unite those individuals opposing the Bank of the United States as the cause of their economic problems with those who had long been suspicious of national power, directing both against national power in general and the Supreme Court in particular.

---

[87]Ibid., June 22, 1819.

CHAPTER II

THE RICHMOND JUNTO?

VIRGINIA POLITICS IN 1820

Historians have traditionally viewed the *Cohens* case as a political struggle pitting a united, state rights Virginia directed by Spencer Roane and the Richmond Junto against John Marshall and the United States Supreme Court. The *Cohens* case was a political struggle fought in part for political goals, but it was a struggle involving several state political factions as well as John Marshall and the Richmond Junto. An overestimation of the Richmond Junto's power has obscured the fact that Virginia was not the stable, Junto dominated state that some historians have described, but was in a transition between the first and second American party systems --between the family and deference politics of the eighteenth century and the two-party politics of the Jacksonian period. Virginia political alignments in 1820-1821, therefore, are as important to an understanding of the *Cohens* case as the economic and social background already examined.

Votes in the Virginia House of Delegates on several key issues between the end of the War of 1812 and the *Cohens* case show a number of political parties, interest groups, and family alliances exercising political power. Economic and social factors growing out of the Panic of 1819 made opposition to the Supreme Court a popular political issue. An issue so popular, in fact, that it might allow the Junto to unite several state political groups into a strong political party, just as Jefferson and Madison had done on a national level in 1798-1800. This does not mean that the Richmond Junto's opposition to the Supreme Court was primarily motivated by political rather than ideological concerns. It does mean, however, that both supporters and opponents of the Supreme Court saw the <u>Cohens</u> case as a political issue which might change state political alignments and could not, therefore, be ignored.

I

If a Virginian in 1820 had been asked to identify the major political forces in the state, he or she might logically have first identified the Republican and Federalist parties. Although the <u>Cohens</u> case came during the "Era of Good Feelings," ostensibly the nadir of party politics, strong feelings remained from the earlier Republican-Federalist contests. A majority of state politicians followed Thomas Jefferson and James Madison into the Republican fold and continued to feel loyalty to the party.[1] Charles Cooke carefully couched his appeal to Albemarle County voters in 1821 to take advantage of such sentiment. "As we have among us no divisions, and subdivisions of party, it

---

[1]Harry Ammon, "The Republican Party in Virginia, 1789-1824" (Unpublished Ph.D. dissertation, University of Virginia, 1948).

cannot be necessary for me to descent to particulars as to my political creed; it will be sufficient to say that I am a Republican--in that sense of the word, which uniformly bears, and in which it is clearly understood among us."[2]

Although a majority of Virginians who identified themselves with a political party in 1820 were Republicans, that identification meant widely different things to different Republicans. Political parties were distrusted by many, if not most, Americans in 1820, and even many of the most active partisans considered parties as only temporary necessities. In 1820 political alliances in Virginia were not political parties in the modern sense. Little internal unity was demanded or expected, and the Republican Party contained an amalgam of interests. Faced with the lack of contested presidential elections to sharpen the party's platform and ideology, and faced with the realities of national administration, Republicans became increasingly diffuse.

Federalists in Virginia faced even greater obstacles maintaining their identity. Tainted with disloyalty by the party's opposition to the War of 1812, the party was fast becoming the first casualty in America's continuing party battles. Many Virginia Federalists, however, thought the party's unpopularity following the War of 1812 was temporary and waited for the party's revival. Until 1821, for example, the party

---

[2]Central Gazette, March 16, 1821.

published a political newspaper in Richmond, The Richmond Daily Mercantile Advertiser, which urged Federalists to have patience until they regained power, arguing that Federalists were "real republicans."[3] In the Virginia elections in 1820, Federalists still won election as Federalists. Two Federalists were elected in Fauquier County to replace the two Republican delegates to the House of Delegates.[4] Two Federalists lost in Morgan County and one won in Loudon County at the same time.[5] Both candidates for the United States House of Representatives from the Northern Neck a year later were Federalists.[6] David Hackett Fischer lists a number of Virginia Federalists active into the 1820's.[7] More importantly, however, votes in the Virginia House of Delegates show a lingering influence of Federalism--regardless whether the delegates were elected as Federalists--in such traditional Federalist areas as the Northern Neck, Eastern Shore, south central area, Richmond, and the Shenandoah Valley.

Votes in the House of Delegates on the Second Bank of the United States and a proposed stay law illustrate both lingering party loyalties and underlying divisions within existing political alignments. During the 1819-1820 session, the House of

---

[3]Richmond Daily Mercantile Advertiser, March 23, 1821.

[4]Richmond Enquirer, April 28, 1820.

[5]Ibid., April 17, 18; May 2, 1820.

[6]Alexandria Gazette, March 16, 1821.

[7]David Hackett Fischer, The Revolution of American Conservatism (New York, 1965), 370-387.

Delegates passed lengthy instructions to Virginia's congressmen against the Supreme Court's McCulloch v Maryland decision upholding the Second Bank of the United States. The instructions are carefully written to censure the bank, support state sovereignty, oppose the Supreme Court's authority to decide cases involving state sovereignty, and provide an explicit reaffirmation of Virginia's major state rights document, James Madison's report to the Virginia legislature in 1800 on the answers to the Virginia Resolutions. A series of House votes on the resolutions against the bank divided along nationalist/state rights lines highly reminiscent of earlier Federalist/Republican splits. A look at Map I shows nationalist support for the Supreme Court in several traditional Federalist areas, the Valley of Virginia, Eastern Shore, and western Virginia, with scattered support from the Northern Neck and several counties in south central and east central Virginia, while state rights support was concentrated along the James River, in tidewater and piedmont areas, and in southwest Virginia.

Map II illustrates the distribution of an 1819-1820 House of Delegates vote on a proposed stay law drafted to provide debtor relief. As expected, the law found greatest support in the piedmont and western areas of the state while major opposition to the law existed in the counties bordering the James River and in southwest Virginia.

Combining the stay law and bank votes (see Map III) graphically illustrates geographical divisions in both

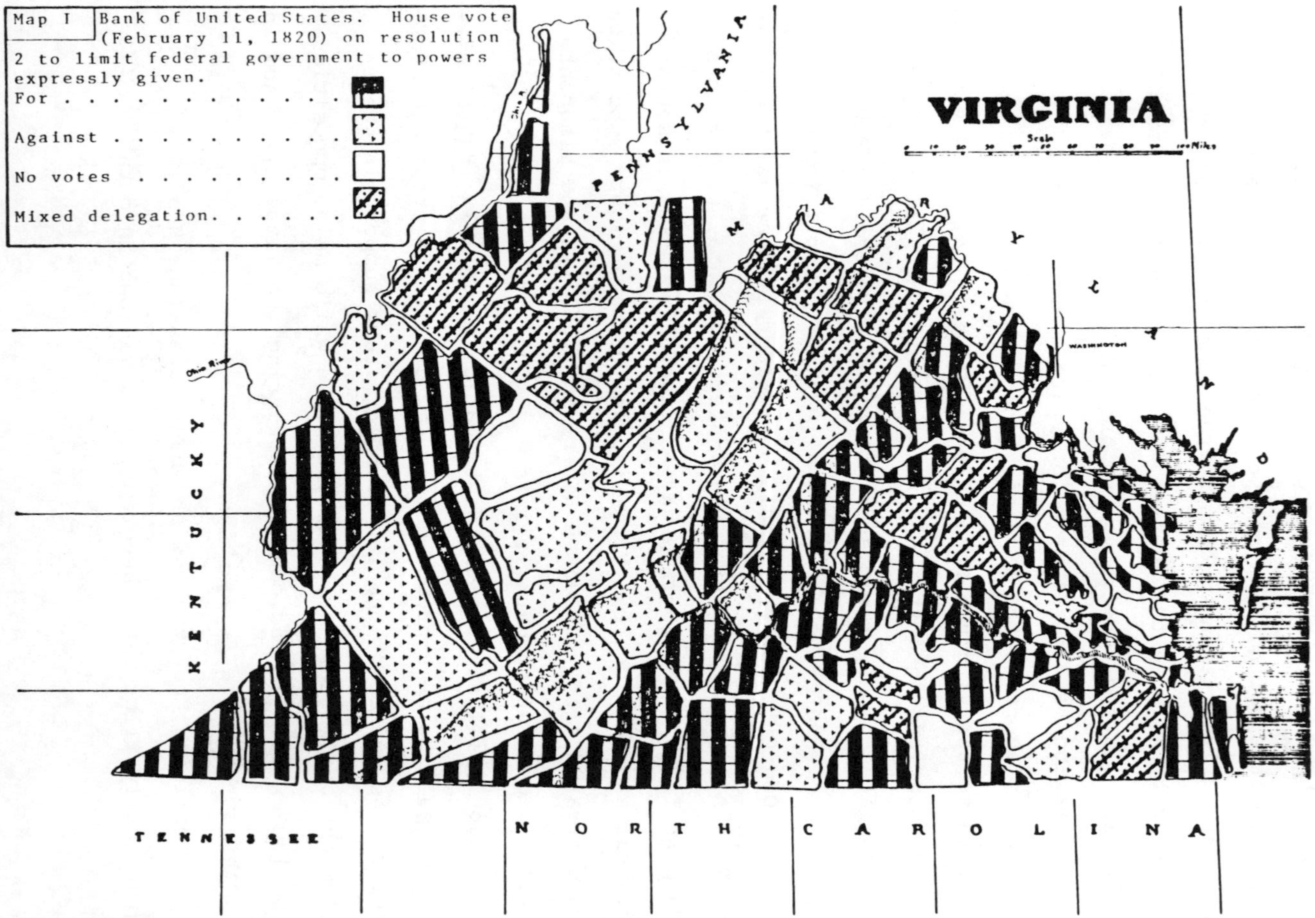

Map I Bank of United States. House vote (February 11, 1820) on resolution 2 to limit federal government to powers expressly given.

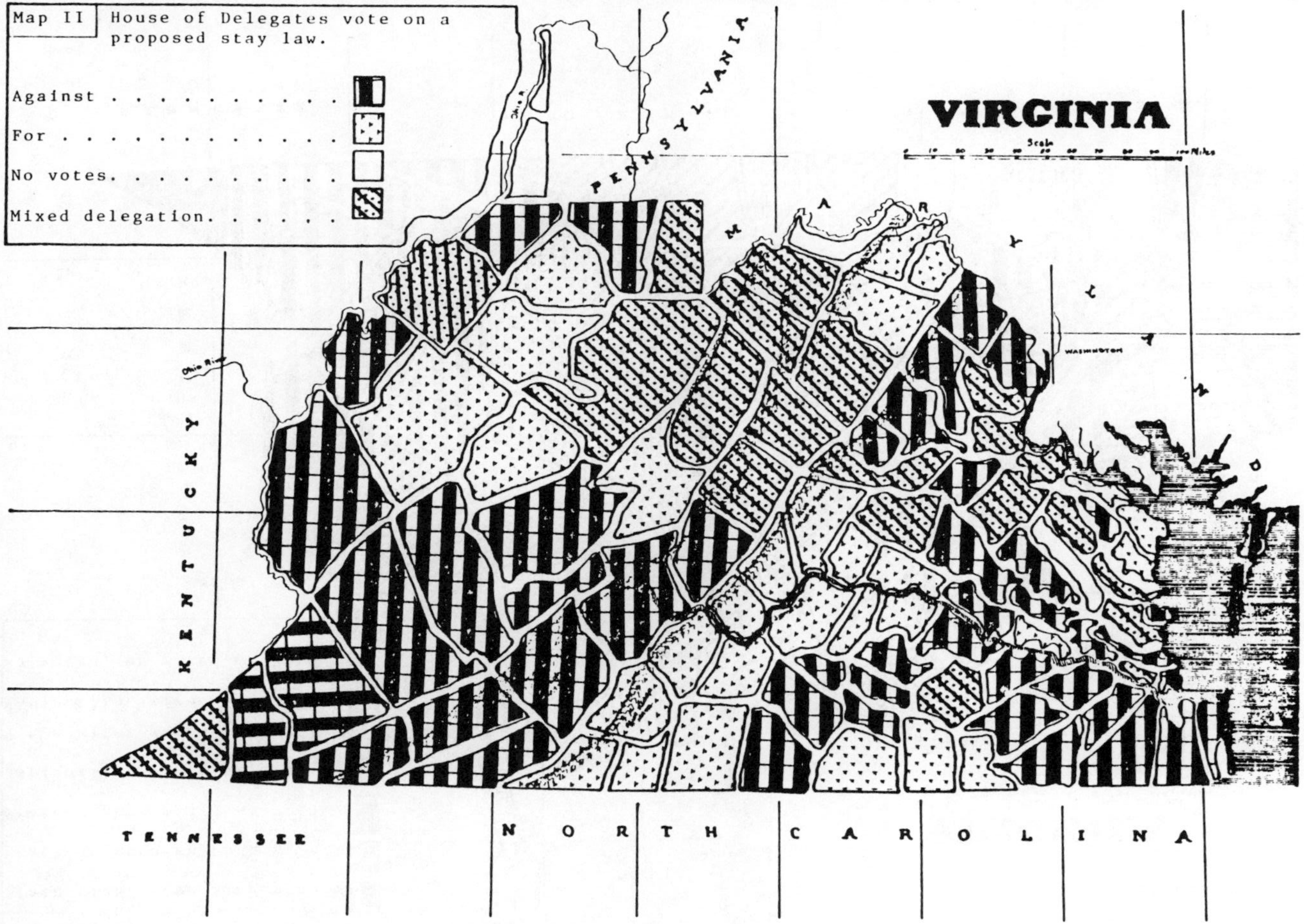

Map II House of Delegates vote on a proposed stay law.

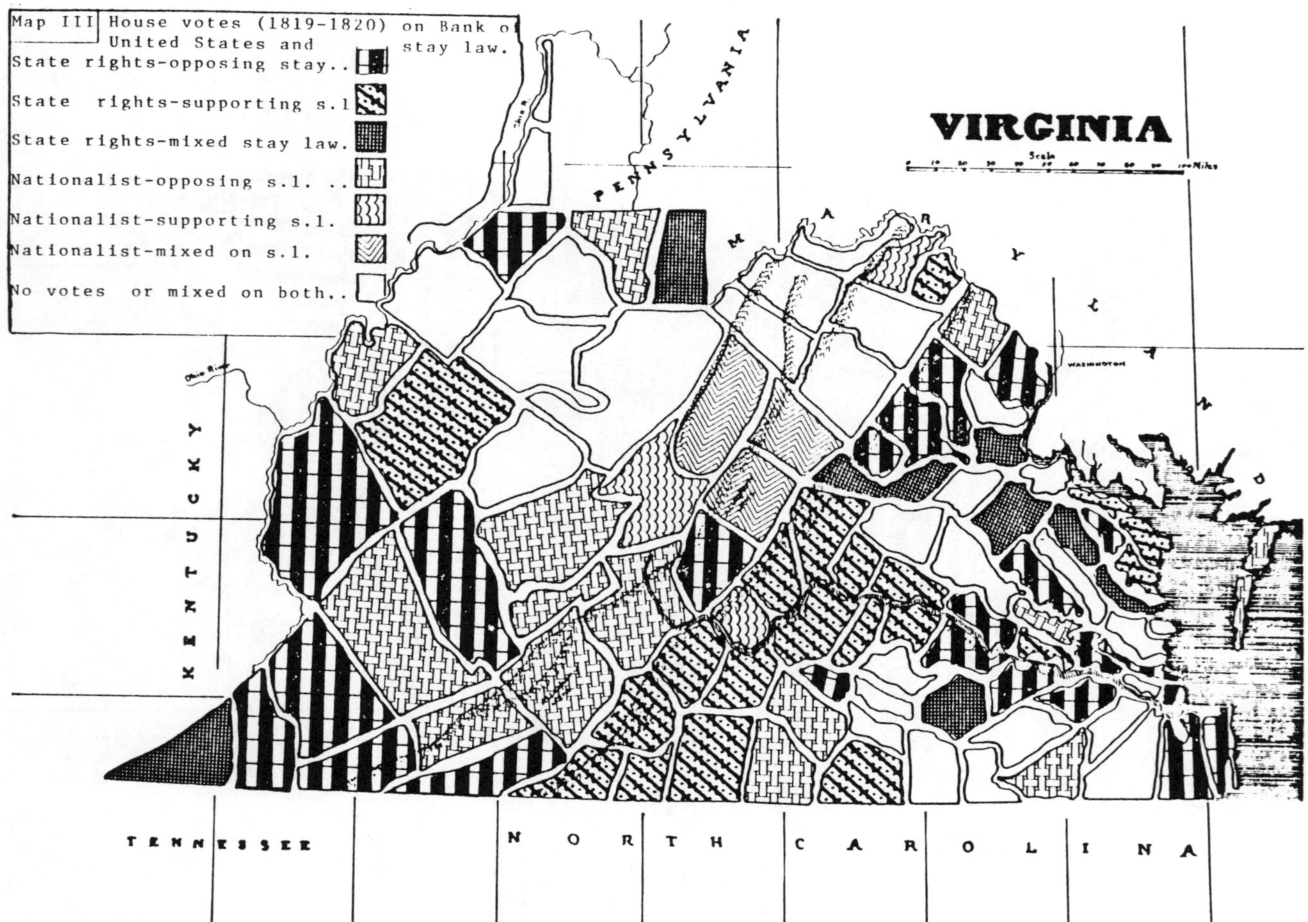
Map III House votes (1819-1820) on Bank of United States and stay law.
State rights-opposing stay..
State rights-supporting s.l
State rights-mixed stay law.
Nationalist-opposing s.l. ..
Nationalist-supporting s.l.
Nationalist-mixed on s.l.
No votes or mixed on both..
VIRGINIA
Scale
100 Miles
PENNSYLVANIA
MARYLAND
WASHINGTON
KENTUCKY
TENNESSEE
NORTH CAROLINA
Ohio R.

nationalist and state rights support. Because of their belief in the sanctity of contracts, Federalist delegates from all parts of the state would be expected to oppose the stay law. Fourteen of the twenty nationalist counties did so; while only three counties gave undivided support to both the Supreme Court and the stay law.

The House of Delegates votes on these two issues also show a deep split among state rights supporters. The resolutions against the Supreme Court passed with majorities ranging from a low of 114 to 44 to a high of 136 to 16.[8] Strong sentiment against the bank was in evidence throughout the state, but was concentrated east of the Blue Ridge Mountains in south-west Virginia. The votes might be cited to show the strength of the Republican party in the state. The facade of Republican unity quickly disappeared, however, when the vote on the stay law is combined with the bank vote. Two distinct groups of state rights supporters emerge. Support for state rights and the stay law was highly concentrated in a tier of counties two or three wide from Albemarle County south to North Carolina, with scattered support elsewhere. Surprisingly, only two counties west of the Blue Ridge, Kanawha and Jefferson, gave full support to both state rights and the stay law.

State rights counties opposing the stay law were clustered along the lower James River from Richmond to the Atlantic; in the

---

[8]Virginia, House of Delegates Journal (1819-1820) (Richmond, 1820), 56-65, 175-179.

extreme southwestern corner of the state--counties such as Grayson, Washington, Scott, Russell, Giles, and Cabell; and in scattered areas such as four northern piedmont counties, Madison, Culpepper, Fauquier, and Fairfax, The Richmond Junto opposed the stay law, which was narrowly defeated. It is not clear whether the defeat owed more to geography or Junto strength in the House, It is clear, however, that despite impressive Republican strength in the state, the party was highly divided geographically on some issues like the stay law.

The votes also illustrate the growing impact of western political interests on both parties. Western interests grew and diversified as western Virginia's population increased. Western politicians generally supported the creation of new counties, reapportionment to increase western representation, the creation of western banks, and a movement of the state capital to a more central location. They were often antislavery and inclined toward more radical economic policies. Western interests won some legislative victories in 1817, when the House of Delegates agreed to call a state constitutional convention to deal with many of these problems. The state senate defeated the measure, although the senate was reapportioned giving western areas nine of the twenty-four senate seats rather than the four they previously held.[9] The legislature also created two new western banks to aid western economic development. Such concessions,

---

[9]Carol Minor Tanner, "Joseph C. Cabell, 1778-1856" (Unpublished Ph.D. dissertation, University of Virginia, 1948), 223-224.

however, were made only to placate repeated western demands. William Wickham wrote Littleton W. Tazewell: "I hope enough was done at the last session to quiet the western counties and to prevent any mischief at the next."[10] Wickham 's hope proved premature. Western demands continued, leading to the Constitutional Convention of 1829-30, and ultimately to the creation of West Virginia from many of those western counties. Much of this state sectionalism surfaced in 1821, in an unsuccessful bill to move the state capital to a more central location. David Campbell, a westerner, downplayed the importance of the issue to western delegates, while reaffirming their growing power:

> If we were very anxious about it in the Counties above the mountain it would produce very great warmth. The people here become alarmed whenever you name the subject. They have observed, that we mountain folks whenever we take it into our heads are very apt to carry any measure we wish.[11]

The preceding examination of major political interest groups should not obscure the fact that many, perhaps most, issues in the General Assembly were decided by groups formed and disbanded according to the issue involved. Creation and funding of the University of Virginia, for example, aroused numerous opponents ranging from friends of existing colleges to westerners who wanted the school located on the other side of the Blue Ridge Mountains. Joseph C. Cabell, a state senator and university

---

[10]Wm. F. Wickham to L. W. Tazewell, May 2, 1817, VSL.

[11]David Campbell to Arthur Campbell, January 15, 1822, Campbell Papers DU.

trustee, noted the school's opponents in a letter to fellow trustee, James Madison. Western delegates wanted the university located in Lexington or Staunton, fearing that if the capital followed the university, as they hoped it would, it would remain east of the Blue Ridge in Charlottesville. Presbyterian clergy, Cabell continued, opposed the school both because it would limit monies available for church schools and because they feared that without religious guidance it would be deistic. Federalists joined with other opponents of Thomas Jefferson to oppose the school because of his role in its founding. Lastly, Cabell said, friends of William and Mary and Washington College saw the new institution as a threat to continuing support for their institutions.[12] A varied group of opponents and supporters were, no doubt, as diverse. The decision of such groups to support or oppose the University, however, was not determined by the stance of larger political groups. The Federalist/Republican split, western interests and family connections all played a part in the contest, but most support or opposition was determined by the issue involved and had little carryover into other debates.

Geographic forces did play a dominant role in the 1819 vote on the James River and Kanawha Canal. Despite the standard characterization of Federalist support for internal improvements and Republican opposition to them, the Virginia vote followed geographical rather than political lines. A look at, voting map

---

[12]Joseph C. Cabell to James Madison February 16, 1818, Madison Papers, LC.

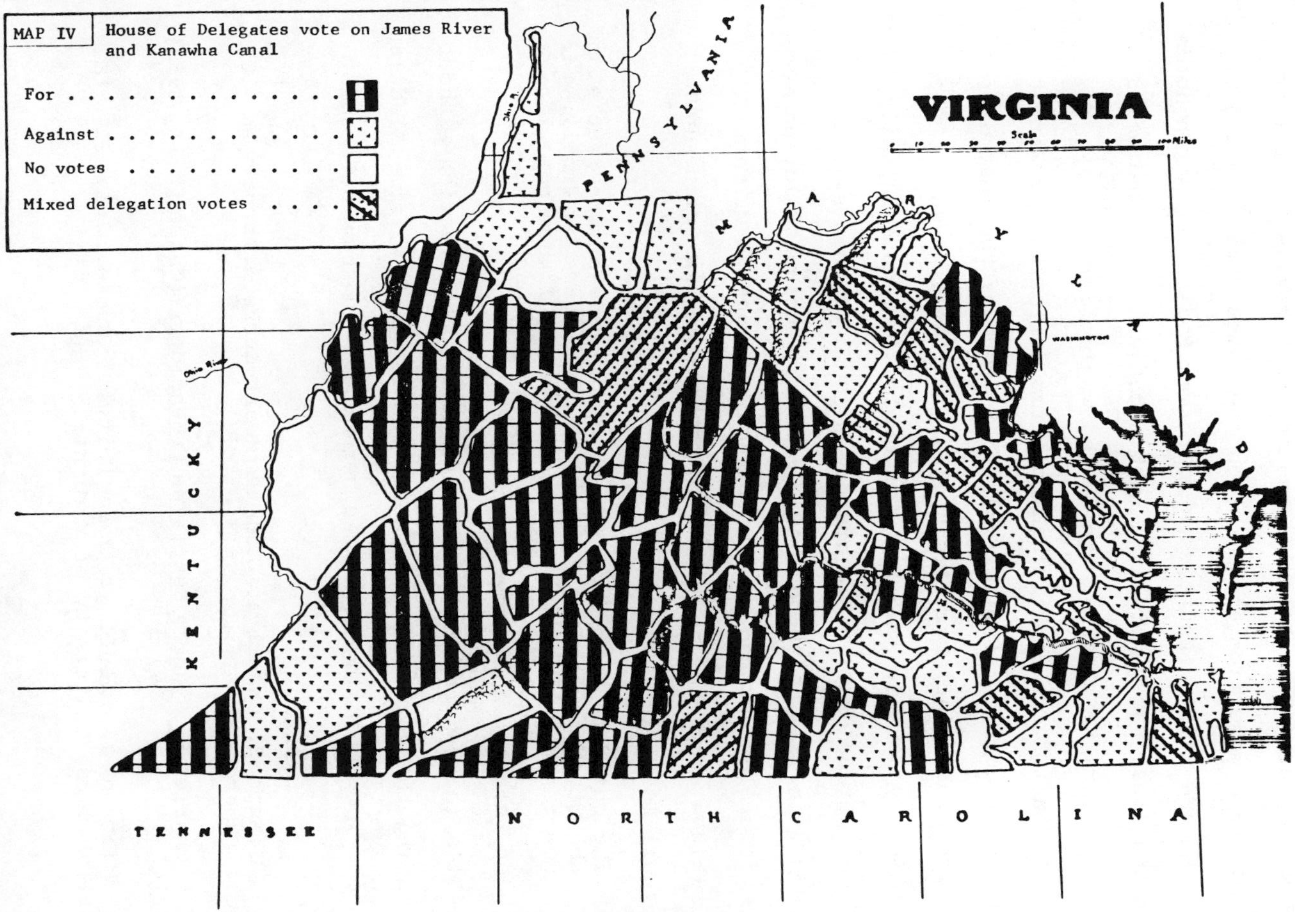

MAP IV House of Delegates vote on James River and Kanawha Canal

IV confirms Joseph C. Cabell's statement that the opposition to the canal came from those located on other rivers.[13] Scattered support did come from areas not on the James River, including Loudoun and Fairfax Counties, two former Federalist strongholds, but the issue was generally a battle between those who would benefit from the canal and those who would not.

A final force in Virginia politics following the War of 1812, deference and family loyalty, is perhaps the most difficult to assess. In *Gentlemen Freeholders*, Charles S. Sydnor graphically portrays the importance of deference and family in an earlier period of Virginia history.[14] Much of this system remained in 1821, although new election techniques alarmed some politicians accustomed to older practices. Joseph C. Cabell complained about the new election methods to his friend John Hartwell Cocke in 1819:

> The opposite party are aiming at the mass of the people, by the utmost exertions. They know their game perfectly. . . How to meet them with the people there, I know not; I have ever visited only the first men of the county and depended on them for a recommendation.[15]

Cabell's fears were unnecessary and he won the election without embracing the new methods. Cabell was right, however. Election methods were changing from an older order, based on deference,

---

[13]Joseph C. Cabell to John Hartwell Cocke, February 4, 1819, Cabell Papers, University of Virginia.

[14]Charles S. Sydnor, *Gentlemen Freeholders* (Chapel Hill, 1952), *passim*.

[15]Joseph C. Cabell to John Hartwell Cocke, July 22, 1819, Cabell Papers, University of Virginia.

toward the popular appeal associated with Jacksonian politics. This change was an additional source of apprehension to some Virginia politicians, both Republican and Federalist, who saw their world changing in ways they did not understand. Despite changes in the system, however, family connections and deference remained an important part of the political system in 1821.

A closer look at two Virginia families will help illustrate the importance of such family groups. The Tucker family excelled in law and politics. St. George Tucker, an emigrant from Bermuda, attended the Annapolis convention leading to the Constitutional Convention, trained others for the law at William and Mary, sat on the Virginia General Court, the Virginia Court of Appeals, and in 1821 served as a United States District Judge. Henry St. George, a son, had in 1821 just resigned from the United States House of Representatives to serve in the Virginia Senate. Later he would teach law at the University of Virginia and serve as President of the Virginia Court of Appeals. Another son, Nathaniel Beverley, a Missouri judge, would also teach law at William and Mary. Tucker's sons-in-law included John Coalter, a judge on the Virginia Court of Appeals, and Joseph C. Cabell, a state senator and colleague of Jefferson in the establishment of the University of Virginia. Lastly, Tucker's stepson was John Randolph of Roanoake.[16]

---

[16]See the appropriate sketches in the Dictionary of American Biography, and Beverly Randolph Tucker, Tales of the Tuckers ... (Richmond 1942).

The Preston family also provided numerous political officials, except they specialized more in governors and United States Congressmen.[17] The three Preston brothers, John, Francis, and James all held important state positions. John served as General of the Militia, State Treasurer, and a member of the state senate. Francis was also a General of the Militia and served as a United States Congressman. James was elected Governor of Virginia and served in Congress. The family's best known member, however, was brother-in-law John Floyd, a Member of Congress, General of the Militia, Governor of Virginia, and Secretary of War. A nephew, John McDowell, represented Virginia in Congress and continued family tradition as Governor. First cousins John Breckenridge, United States Senator and Attorney General; James Breckenridge, Member of Congress; John Brown, United States Senator; and James Brown, Member of Congress and Minister to France, also belonged to this amazing family.

Members of such families might differ on politics, as James Barbour, Secretary of War under John Quincy Adams, did with his brother Philip P. Barbour, who was appointed to the Supreme Court by Andrew Jackson. They might live in different geographic areas of Virginia, as happened in most families, but when issues directly involving the family occurred, family interests had to be considered, although they did not necessarily dictate policy. A broadening of interests and an underlying agreement despite

---

[17]See "The Preston Papers," The Virginia Magazine of History and Biography, XXVI (October 1918), 363-365, and the appropriate sketches in the Dictionary of American Biography.

political differences resulted. Rather than wage complete political warfare, most families realized they could not monopolize political positions in the state, but must share them with other important families.

The best known of these family groups was the Richmond Junto. Since the Junto played a major, perhaps dominant, role in the opposition to the Cohens decision, it is necessary to examine the group in some detail.

Most information about the Richmond Junto comes from a series of letters in the Washington Republican and Congressional Examiner in 1823.[18] The anonymous author claimed that the state was controlled by a cabal formed by the merger of two powerful state groups: the "old party," including members of the Nicholas and Smith families, and a family group centered in Spencer Roane and Thomas Ritchie.

The "old party," the letters continued, formed "a phalanx, more formidable . . . . than any other political corps which could be organized by any family connection in our whole country."[19] The group centered around the four Nicholas brothers, Wilson Cary, Philip, George, and John. All served as congressmen, one was Governor of Virginia, and two served as Attorneys General,

---

[18]Henry Lee , "Letters on the Richmond Party," Washington Republican and Congressional Examiner, November 11, 13, 15, 18, 20, 22, 1823. The letters were quickly published as a pamphlet: Henry Lee , Letters on the Richmond Party, By a Virginian, Originally Published in the Washington Republican (Washington 1823). They will hereafter be referred to as Washington Letters, and page numbers will be from the pamphlet.

[19]Ibid., 8.

one in Virginia and one in Kentucky. Their brother-in-law, Edmund Randolph, topped an illustrious career with positions as United States Attorney General and Secretary of State. The Nicholas brothers were closely related by marriage to General Samuel Smith, United States Senator from Maryland, and his brother Robert Smith, Secretary of State under James Madison. The letters claim that this group, with branches in Virginia, Maryland, Kentucky, and New York tried to groom Edmund Randolph for the presidency of the United States, and when that attempt failed, supported Robert Smith for the office. The group pressured James Madison into appointing Smith as Secretary of State, but his hopes for the presidency ended when he resigned following a disagreement with President Madison. Thus, thwarted in their drive for the presidency, the group moved from national to state politics. In Virginia, they joined with the powerful family group centering in Spencer Roane and his cousin, Thomas Ritchie, to form the Richmond Junto. In addition to Roane and Ritchie, the article named a host of related Virginia politicians as part of the Roane group: John and William Brockenbrough, Andrew Stevenson, Dr. William Foushee, Richard Morris, Peter V. Daniel, Francis T. Brooke, William Roane, Robert G. Scott, William Selden, and Richard E. Parker.

Later studies of the Junto follow most elements found in the 1823 letters and conclude that a small group of men, centered in Richmond, controlled the state for their own aims and advancement.[20] Rex Beach, in his study of the Junto, concluded that "under the guidance of Roane, the Richmond party became increasingly dominant in Virginia politics, and at his death in 1822 it was in almost absolute control of the judicial, financial, and legislative branches of the state government."[21]

The political power of the Junto, however, should not be overestimated. Junto members held important state positions, but did not exert in the various state governmental departments the power to control the state. Even in those areas where they held greatest power, the Governor's Council, the Virginia Court of Appeals, and Virginia banks, their power was limited, and in 1821 often under attack.

The governor's Council was an important body in Virginia. Colonial fear of a strong executive led to limits on the Governor's powers and the use of the council to check his prerogatives. The resulting executive became, in fact, a committee executive. The Governor could not overrule the other

---

[20]Rex Beach, "Judge Spencer Roane: A Champion of State Rights" (Unpublished Master's thesis, University of Virginia, 1941); Harry Ammon, "The Republican Party in Virginia, 1789:1824" (Unpublished Ph.D. dissertation, University of Virginia, 1948); John Treon, "_Martin v. Hunter's Lessee:_ A Case History" (Unpublished Ph.D. dissertation, University of Virginia, 1970); Rex Beach, "Spencer Roane and the Richmond Junto," _William and Mary Quarterly_, 2nd. ser. XXII (January 1942), 1-17; Harry Ammon, "The Richmond Junto, 1800-1824," _The Virginia Magazine of History and Biography_, 64 (October 1953) 395-418; Joseph H. Harrison, Jr., "Oligarchs and Democrats; The Richmond Junto," _The Virginia Magazine of History and Biography_, 78 (April 1970) 184-198.

[21]Beach, _W&MQ_, 16.

council members, and could not even vote, except to break a tie.[22] Three, possibly four, of the eight member Governor's Council in 1821 can be counted as Junto members.[23] The council was led by senior council member, and thus Lt. Governor, Peter V. Daniel. Daniel was Edmund Randolph's son-in-law and served a number of important state and national offices culminating in his appointment in 1841 to the United States Supreme Court.[24] William Roane, son of Spencer Roane, and his brother-in-law, William Selden also served on the council in 1821 as did William Scott who may have been a Junto member.

The governor's council was not, however, a vehicle through which the Junto controlled the state. The council's powers were limited because they shared the Governor's purposefully limited powers. The council and the governor did exercise important functions, including the appointment of new judges when an incumbent died, but these appointments required General Assembly

---

[22]Virginia Revised Code of 1819, I, 36. See also William H. Gaines, Jr., Thomas Mann Randolph: Jefferson's Son-in-law (Kingsport, Tenn.; 1966), 117, Tanner, Cabell.

[23]Peter V. Daniel, William H. Roane, and William Selden are those identified as Junto members with William Scott as a possible member. John Campbell who has been identified by at least one author as a Junto member and served on the council from 1811-1817 and 1821-1829 shows the problems of identifying membership in the Junto. He greatly admired Spencer Roane and married his daughter after the Judge's death, but he continued to think of himself as a Westerner and had conflicts with Robert Scott and the Prestons who have also been identified as Junto members. See John Campbell to David Campbell April 11, 1822, Campbell Papers, Duke University.

[24]John P. Frank, Justice Daniel Dissenting . . . (Cambridge, 1964).

approval. The council's major independent powers were negative and designed to check the governor.

The council could not fully exercise its limited powers in 1821 because of a public dispute with Governor Thomas Mann Randolph and attacks on Junto member Peter V. Daniel in the House of Delegates. The governor and the council disagreed as to whether the governor must follow the council's advice in civil matters, who should determine the order of business at their meetings, and if meetings should be held when the governor was out of town. Much of the effectiveness of the executive was lost when the dispute became public in December 1821, when both sides published public letters in the *Richmond Enquirer*.[25] Peter V. Daniel was almost removed from the council in 1821.

Members of the governor's, council held office during good behavior but every three years the legislature removed two members and elected two new members. The "scratch," as it was called, occurred in 1821 after news of Junto member John Preston's default as treasurer of Virginia. An Assembly group, led by David S. Garland and Charles Yancy, felt Daniel as Lieutenant Governor should have checked Preston's books more closely and wanted Daniel removed. Daniel remained on the council but only after two other members volunteered to have

---

[25]David Campbell to Mrs. Mary Campbell, January 1, 1822, Campbell Papers, DU; Gaines, 127, 130, 133-134; *Richmond Enquirer*, December 15, 18, 1821. See also John Campbell to David Campbell June 20, 1821, Campbell Papers, Duke University. For later conflicts see same to same, April 11, 1822, *Ibid.*, and Bernard Peyton to John H. Cocke, November 30, 1821, Cocke Papers, University of Virginia.

their names removed. Even so, Daniel was second in the voting each time a vote was taken to see who would be removed.[26]

The Virginia Court of Appeals has been viewed as the greatest center of Junto power. The court's justices were men of great reputation, at the pinnacle of the legal system, in a state where the practice of law often served as the road to economic and political recognition. The judge's salaries, for example, were second only to the governor's.[27] The court, obviously a powerful body, oversaw the entire state legal system, but its powers were passive and it had few appointive offices at its disposal. It could review appealed cases, but could not initiate such proceedings.

A look at the membership of the court in 1821 raises questions about the supposed Junto dominance of the court. The Court of Appeals had five members until 1809, when the number was reduced to three with the death of one justice and the resignation of another. Spencer Roane was the only Junto member on the court, which also included William Fleming, court

---

[26]Virginia Patriot and Daily Mercantile Advertiser, January 9, 1821. See also David Campbell to John Campbell, January 8, 1821, Campbell Papers, DU. Daniel's prestige was not greatly higher in 1824. During the scratch of that year he was again the second highest in both votes to remove a member. Richmond Enquirer, January 10, 1824. The two other definite Junto members on the council served much shorter terms. William Roane, son of Spencer Roane served seven years while his brother-in-law, William Selden, served only until 1824 and the next "scratch."

[27]Cf. Anthony F. Upton, "The Road to Power in Virginia in the Early Nineteenth Century," The Virginia Magazine of History and Biography, 62, (July 1954), 271; and Robert Saunders to Joseph prentis, November 18, 1818, Webb-Prentis Papers, University of Virginia.

president, and St. George Tucker. Conflicts among the judges flared and Tucker and Roane were, at times, barely on speaking terms.[28] Some authors view this personality clash as the cause of Tucker's resignation from the court.[29] Whatever the cause, Tucker resigned in 1811, and the court was enlarged to its traditional five members. The three appointments made at that time are crucial to an understanding of the court--not only because all remained on the court until Roane's death in 1822, but also because most authors feel their appointment led to Junto control of the court. Francis T. Brooke, one of the three new members of the court, clearly fits the Junto label. He married Thomas Ritchie's sister and although later, as Henry Clay's Virginia spokesman, Brooks often opposed the Junto, he may have been a Junto member in 1821. The author of the Washington letters opposed his appointment, seeing it as the result of Roane's power on the court.[30] Most writers on the Junto have quickly concluded that the other two new judges, William H. Cabell and John Coalter, were also Junto members.[31] A misreading of the Washington letters leads to this view. The author of those letters asserts that Roane was stacking the court

---

[28]Beach, W&MQ, pp. 10-15; Henry St. George Tucker to St. George Tucker, January [-] , 1818, Tucker-Coleman Papers, William and Mary; St George Tucker to John Coalter, March 22, 1817, typescript Grinnan Papers, University of Virginia.

[29]Treon, 135-136.

[30]Washington Letters, 34.

[31]Treon, 137; Beach, W&MQ, 15.

with members of his family. The letters cite Brooke's appointment and assert that Brooke, Cabell, and Coalter are related. No claim, however, was made that Cabell and Coalter were Junto members or closely related to Roane.[32] In a state where most prominent families intermarried, it is important to determine not only who were related but what were their closest ties. Using this guide, both Coalter and Cabell fit more closely into Tucker's camp than into Roane's. William Cabell studied law under Tucker and his brother, Joseph C. Cabell, married Tucker's step-daughter. Moreover, he was a frequent correspondent and companion to the elder Tucker. John Coalter had even closer ties. He served as a tutor in the Tucker family and married another of Tucker's daughters. His correspondence and visits were even more frequent than Cabell's.[33]

If Cabell and Coalter were not Junto members, why did the author of the Washington letters fear Junto dominance of the court? He claimed that if a vacancy occurred in the Court of Appeals, Roane hoped to have his cousin, General Court Judge William Brockenbrough, appointed.[34] "Had he lived, it is confidently believed that he never would have rested content until at least a majority of the court should have been formed of judges taken from his party or from his family connection."[35]

---

[32]Washington Letters, 34.

[33]Tucker-Coleman correspondence, William and Mary.

[34]Washington Letters, 34.

[35]Ibid.

It is important to note no intimation is made that such a condition already existed. Spencer Roane, however, did have great power on the court. He often served as court spokesman, and as the second senior judge, presided at the court after 1817, when court president William Fleming did not attend because of illness. If Roane appears to dominate the court, however, he did not necessarily do so by secret, undemocratic methods, relying on close family ties, any more than such an accusation would fit John Marshall's dominance of the national tribunal. Even the author of the Washington letters admits that Roane "was distinguished for intellectual vigor, [and] profound legal knowledge."[36] It is even more tenuous to equate control of the court--if he did dominate it--with control of state politics. The powers of the court did not reach that far.

The Junto's lack of power in relation to the Court of Appeals, and the importance of family connections, were graphically illustrated, in 1822, in behind-the-scenes movements to select Spencer Roane's successor on the Court of Appeals. According to the Washington letters, the Junto sought to advance Junto member Judge Brockenbrough from the General Court to the Court of Appeals, but desisted because public opinion supported state Chancery Court Chancellor John W. Green.[37] That view is partially correct, but far too simple. Suggested nominees not only included Brockenbrough, but Philip P. Barbour, another Junto

---

[36]Ibid., 27-28.

[37]Ibid., 38.

member, and others as well.[38] The Tuckers wanted Henry St. George Tucker placed on the court while United States Attorney General William Wirt and Francis W. Gilmer pressed Green's cause.[39] Whether through public opinion or Wirt and Gilmer's activities, Green gained the nod. Interestingly, the next two court appointments went to Dabney S. Carr, Thomas Jefferson's grandson with close ties to Wirt and Gilmer, and Henry St. George Tucker, a member of the Tucker family. Judge Brockenbrough had to wait until 1834 for an appointment to the Court of Appeals, and Barbour never was appointed to the appeals court, but served on the Virginia General Court and the United States Supreme Court.[40]

The last center of Junto power mentioned in the Washington letters--control of state banking--is more difficult to assess.

---

[38]William Wirt to Francis W. Gilmer, October 27, 1822, Gilmer Papers, University of Virginia.

[39]Ibid., and John Coalter to St. George Tucker, October 27, 1822, Tucker-Coleman Papers, W&M. For an earlier attempt to have Henry St. George Tucker appointed to the General Court see St. George Tucker to Joseph C. Cabell February 28, 1819, Bryan Family Papers, University of Virginia.

[40]The Junto's inability to determine the replacement for Spencer Roane at a time when they supposedly controlled the state raises serious questions about how much power they really had. Historians have noted the lack of state offices held by Junto members but attributed it to a willingness to share power or a preference for working behind the scenes. Harry Ammon wrote that "no effort was made to create a substantial patronage as an inducement to party service . . ." Notably the members of the Junto made no effort to monopolize the state offices, and only infrequently their names appear as state officers." Ammon, VMHB, 417-418. Joseph H. Harrison notes the same lack of offices when he mentions the offices of Governor and United States Senator. "To these honors the Junto was more successful in preferring its allies than its members." Harrison, 192.

Two Junto members, Philip Norborne Nicholas and Dr. John Brockenbrough, served as president of the Farmer's Bank of Virginia and the Bank of Virginia, respectively. Another Junto member, Wilson Cary Nicholas, was president of the Richmond branch of the second Bank of the United States. Andrew Stevenson was a bank director for the Bank of Virginia. It is not clear, however, what this Junto involvement in banking meant in terms of political or financial control within the state. A thorough study of Virginia banking is needed before we can answer basic questions about the banks' internal workings, their relationship to the state government, and the role of the Junto in state banking.

What we do know of state banking raises a number of questions. Each of the four state banks had several branches. Directors of both the parent bank and the branches were selected at general meetings and then they elected the bank's president. We do not, however, know the working relationship between a bank's president and its directors or between the parent institution and the branches, although more local freedom seems to have existed than some authors have suggested.[41]

---

[41]Richmond Enquirer, April 18, 1820, and January 4, 1821. The best study of banking in the state is George T. Starne's Sixty Years of Branch Banking in Virginia (New York, 1931). Directors for the branches were often local investors and at times conflicts occurred between the branches and the parent banks. Following the Panic of 1819 both the Bank of Virginia and the Farmers Bank of Virginia refused to accept notes from their branches except in payment of debts. Starnes, 65-66. In 1821 a group of stockholders in the Farmer's Bank in Winchester passed a resolution censuring the mother board of directors for not giving a dividend and paying high salaries. Niles Weekly Register August 21, 1821. For

The relationship between the Virginia government and state banks is also hazy. The state owned stock in the state banks and the state treasurer voted for bank directors.[42] What pressures were placed upon the state treasurer when he cast the state's votes for bank directors? If he was a Junto member, were his major loyalties to the Junto, other groups, or to the General Assembly? How did these groups influence or control him? We can only Surmise that if the treasurer ignored the General Assembly's wishes he would have been reminded of his duty to the state. It is not possible to know, with certainty, how much influence the Junto had over state banks, what differences occurred in a bank's policies when the president was a Junto member, or how a bank's operations were affected when a Junto member served as one of the bank's board of directors as Andrew Stevenson did for the Bank of Virginia's Richmond branch in 1820 and 1821. Junto members were never a majority on any boards, but their role in Virginia banking will remain unclear until a more complete study of Virginia banking is finished. We do know that, in some instances, Junto members had less power than they desired. Wilson Cary Nicholas, for example, had little say about selecting his replacement at the Richmond branch of the Bank of the United States.[43]

---

conflicts in the Lynchburg branch see Richmond Enquirer, February 22, 1821.

[42]Starne, 30.

[43]Philip Norborne Nicholas to Wilson Cary Nicholas, September 9, 1819, Nicholas Papers, University of Virginia.

Banking control brought enemies, as well as power and prestige.[44] Eastern domination of the state's banking facilities helped divide the state politically for many years. The creation of western banks, the Northwestern Bank of Virginia, and the Bank of the Valley of Virginia, in 1817, helped placate western interests, but the resentment remained. After the panic of 1819 anti-banking sentiment was common at all levels of society and in all geographical areas. Such resentment increased with worsening economic conditions, and it is possible that the Junto gained more opponents than influence by any control of state banking during the period.

Such banking control did not benefit all men identified as Junto members. Neither Wilson Cary Nicholas' close association with the Bank of the United States nor his brother's presidency of the Farmer's Bank of Virginia saved him from financial ruin after the panic of 1819.[45] Dr. William Foushee, Thomas Ritchie's father-in-law and postmaster of Richmond, was so hard pressed he could not send his sons out-of-town to school and had

---

[44]Robert Saunders to Joseph Prentis, January 28, 1820, Webb-Prentis Papers, University of Virginia.

[45]Joseph C. Cabell to John Hartwell Cocke September 7, 1820, Cabell Papers, University of Virginia. Cf Same to same October 23, 1823, and Isaac Coles to Joseph C. Cabell, August 28, 1819, Cabell Papers, University of Virginia. Several Junto members did assist Nicholas with his legal problems. Andrew Stevenson served as a lawyer for Wilson Cary Nicholas and Dr. John Brockenbrough gave legal advice even though he decided not to act as a trustee. Philip Norborne Nicholas advised his brother to retain Philip P. Barbour, who has often been identified as a Junto member, so that his opponents would not hire him. Philip N. Nicholas to W. C. Nicholas, September 11, 1819, and January 20, 1820, Nicholas Papers, University of Virginia.

to ask Clairborne W. Gooch for a loan because two lawsuits threatened him.[46]

Personal actions of Junto members regarding banks and banking were also ambiguous. Members of the group directed some banks, while others strongly opposed banking. For example, while Wilson Cary Nicholas was president of the Richmond branch of the Bank of the Bank of the United States; Andrew Stevenson and Philip Norborne Nicholas directors and Spencer Roane himself a stockholder, the Junto worked hard to pass Virginia resolutions opposing the bank, and Roane penned a long series of critical articles against Marshall's pro-bank decision in McCulloch v Maryland.[47] Such activities raise doubts whether Junto members held united or consistent views concerning banks and banking. If banks were in fact the basis of the Junto's power, it seems unlikely that Junto members would have used such strong measures and public statements against the basis of that power.

Thomas Ritchie's association with Virginia's Republican newspaper, the Richmond Enquirer, also provided the Junto with political advantages. Read by most state leaders, the Enquirer was Virginia's most influential paper. It took strong political positions and no doubt influenced state opinion. The Enquirer also published opposing views. Thomas Ritchie, the paper's

---

[46]William Foushee to John Hartwell Cocke, April 11, 1821, Cocke deposit, University of Virginia; and William Foushee to Clairborne W. Gooch Papers, University of Virginia.

[47]Richmond Enquirer, March 30; April 2; and June 11, 15, 18, 22, 1819. They are reprinted in John Branch Historical Papers of Randolph-Macon College, II (1905), 51-122.

editor, professed respect for freedom of the press. An appeal to that principle often led to insertions of pieces opposing the Enquirer's stand. As state printer, Ritchie was also vulnerable to criticism if the Enquirer printed only one side of a question. Ritchie did print divergent opinions in the Enquirer, but often controlled such statements.[48]

Regardless of the Junto's success in getting their viewpoints published, the major difficulty in viewing Ritchie and the Junto as manipulating public opinion through Enquirer articles is the assumption that they had a carefully considered philosophy they wished to implement. Aside from some general interests in ensuring eastern supremacy in the state and support for state rights--two goals most Virginians living east of the piedmont could accept--it is hard to be too specific. In fact, Joseph Harrison, the latest Junto investigator, identifies the lack of a clearly defined program as one of the group's fatal

---

[48]Ritchie refused to print a speech on resolutions about the Cohens case given by Samuel Blackburn in the state senate because he considered the speech slanderous, but reprinted a speech on the same side by Chapman Johnson when the first printed version was not approved by the legislator. Richmond Enquirer, February 22; March 1, 1821. For other comments about the openness of the Enquirer see R. S Garnett to William C. River, January 27, 1818; February 14, 1818, Rives Papers, Library of Congress. Even Wilson Cary Nicholas veiled his authorship from Ritchie at times. See Wilson Cary Nicholas to Joseph C. Cabell, February , 1820, Cabell Papers, University of Virginia; see also John Marshall to Joseph Story June 15, 1821, Proceedings of the Massachusetts Historical Society, XIV (1900-1901), 327-328, John C. Calhoun to Henry Wheaton, July 15, 1821, Wheaton Papers, Pierpont Morgan Library, and Washington Letters, 41.

flaws.[49] The Enquirer's editors were also being threatened in 1821. The Panic of 1819 caused many state legislators to look closely at state expenditures. Retrenchment laws were introduced to cut government costs. The legislature slightly reduced their own pay and enacted minor cuts for most state officers. Thomas Ritchie managed to limit the cuts in his position as state printer, but was unable to stop a two-thirds pay cut for his partner, Adjutant General Clairborne W. Gooch. Gooch resigned the position rather than accept the reduction from $1,500 to $500 a year.[50]

Most accounts of the Richmond Junto's control of state politics are based on nineteenth century newspaper articles. A closer look at those articles raises questions about their reliability. The Norfolk Gazette and Public Ledger, a Federalist paper, printed the first such article in 1804.[51] Twelve years later, The Albany Advertiser printed three articles about the Junto in August and September 1816. The Advertiser, a Federalist

---

[49]Harrison, 197. This lack of unity also existed before, but became especially noticeable after Spencer Roane's death. Roane, for example, felt Ritchie held back too much during the Cohens controversy. The Junto's lack of unity on banking has already been mentioned. Later a disagreement between Thomas Ritchie and his partner in the Richmond Enquirer, Clairborne W. Gooch, over the calling of the 1829 state constitutional convention led to a split in the partnership. Gooch was more opposed to granting concessions to the West than Ritchie was and finally sold his interest in the paper rather than continue the partnership in disagreement.

[50]Richmond Compiler, January 17, 1821.

[51]Norfolk Gazette and Public Ledger, November 16, 1804.

paper, wrote to oppose Virginia influence in national affairs.[52] Two major articles on the Junto appeared seven years later in 1823. The Lynchburg Virginian claimed a group of men in Richmond would unduly influence the selection of a presidential candidate because men of lesser experience in the assembly would defer to them.[53] The final 1823 series, the six letters published by the Washington Republican and Congressional Examiner about the Junto, is the longest series and has been used as the basis for most later studies of the Junto.[54]

When examined as a group, these articles tell much about the motivation of their authors. All of the articles appeared just prior to a national election and warned of the influence of Richmond politicians in national politics. All articles were printed by papers supporting opposing candidates. The Norfolk Gazette and The Albany Advertiser were Federalist papers, while the Virginian supported John Quincy Adams, and the Washington Republican was John C. Calhoun's organ in the nation's capital. Each article, in fact, emphasized national politics. Even the Washington letters spend more time on the old party's attempts to have their members elected President than on the Junto's control of Virginia.[55]

---

[52]Albany Advertiser, August 28, 29; September 17, 1816.

[53]Lynchburg Virginian, April 29, 1823.

[54]Washington Republican and Congressional Examiner, November 11, 13, 15, 18, 20, 22, 1823.

[55]Washington Letters, 4, 30.

The political content of the Lynchburg Virginian articles, for example, is apparent when the 1823 article is compared with statements published by the paper two years earlier. Following Monroe's election in 1820 several newspapers speculated about who would be the next president. John Hampden Pleasants, editor of the Virginian, said that although it was too soon to talk of such things, he supported John Quincy Adams, but admitted that his real choice was Spencer Roane who, he felt, "would keep a steady helm, amid the conflicts of opposing interests, the increasing turbulence of faction and the growing propensity to intrigue."[56] Pleasants toasted Roane during an 1820 Lynchburg Fourth of July celebration: "Spencer Roane--The pillar of the Judiciary, the palladium of republicanism, the prop of the sinking cause of '96."[57] Clearly much changed during the two years between these articles and the one denouncing the Junto, but the change dealt more with presidential politics than with greater Junto control of the state.

The Washington letters are equally political. The Washington Republican and Congressional Examiner was John C. Calhoun's principal paper. Calhoun saw "radicals" in New York and Virginia as major obstacles to his presidential ambitions. To counter their influence, he opposed the Virginia stand in the

---

[56]Lynchburg Press, January 18, 1822. The Lynchburg Press, edited by Pleasants, was consolidated with the Lynchburg Gazette in August 1822 to form the Lynchburg Virginian.

[57]Lynchburg Press, July 7, 1820, and Richmond Enquirer, July 21, 1820.

Cohens case and helped get a series of articles opposing the Virginians reprinted in the National Intelligencer, hoping thereby to limit the influence of Virginians supporting William E. Crawford, another potential presidential candidate.[58]

The Washington letters, directed against these same Virginians, have traditionally been identified as the work of Alexander McRae, who supposedly penned the articles as revenge for his removal from the governor's council by fellow Junto members in 1808, when he refused to support James Madison.[59] It now appears that Henry Lee, and not McRae, submitted the series. Lee, sometimes referred to as "darkhorse Harry Lee," is a tragic figure in Virginia history. A half-brother of Robert E. Lee, he appeared to be headed toward a prominent role in Virginia society; however, following the death of his child and the morphine addiction of his wife, he found solace with his sister-in-law. Virginia Society ostracized him when it was discovered he had lost most of his sister-in-law's fortune and seduced her while serving as her guardian. Stratford, the family seat, was sold to restore her fortune, but he never could reenter his old

---

[58]John C. Calhoun to Henry Wheaton July 15; September 2, 1821; and May 8, 1823, Wheaton Papers, Pierpont Morgan Library.

[59]Hugh Blair Grigsby, The History of the Virginia Federal Convention . . . (Richmond, 1890), II, 348-349; Harrison, 186. McRae is an interesting, shadowy figure in Virginia history. Often involved in controversy, including an investigation of the Mutual Assurance Society leadership during which he opposed several Junto members, he may have written the letters, but it is doubtful his resentment stemmed from his council removal. See: American Beacon, August 14, 1821; Lynchburg Press, August 17, 1821; Richmond Enquirer, July 3, 6, 10, 17, 1821; Alexandria Gazette, August 14, 1821.

circles. His talents were, however, employed as a political writer for John C. Calhoun and Andrew Jackson.[60] Benjamin Watkins Leigh indicated Lee's authorship in a letter to Lee in 1824:

> You were mistaken, when you supposed there was a 'Richmond Party'--if, indeed, what you published last summer on that subject, were not (as I more than half suspected) a mere banter--but there is a Virginia Party, which has inevitable sway at home.[61]

The letters could serve Lee's social as well as political goals--a way of getting back at men who would not let him participate fully in Virginia society.

> Why else has it happened that so many of the connections have risen to places of distinction and power, whilst other men of equal worth, and superior talents, not connected with the party, have been passed neglected by, and what is yet worse, been denounced, as meriting no preferment whatsoever.[62]

The letters themselves raise doubts about the extent of Junto political control. Some Junto members, the author admits, do not know they are part of this political machine.

---

[60]Burton J. Hendrick, The Lees of Virginia: Biography of a Family (New York, 1935), 380-383, 400-403; Ethel Armes, Stratford Hall, The Great House of Lees (Richmond, 1936), 366-410; For contemporary opinion, see Dabney Carr to F. W. Gilmer, March 12, 1822, Gilmer Papers, University of Virginia.

[61]Benjamin Watkins Leigh to Henry Lee, November 29, 1824, Virginia Historical Society. Is Leigh referring to the Washington Letters? The time element is disturbing. Leigh discusses material published last summer whereas the Washington Letters were published almost a year previously, but all other facts fit. Lee was employed by John C. Calhoun in whose paper the letters appear. There are no other similar series in the paper during the previous summer Leigh mentions, and Lee was very familiar with Virginia politics. See: Charles M. Wiltse, John C. Calhoun Nationalist, 1782-1828 (Indianapolis, 1944), 319; and Armes, 380.

[62]Washington Letters, 33.

> I have ever believed, that some few of the gentlemen even in Richmond, who co-operate with the Party, are not aware of their true character, nor of the dangerous extent to which they carry their views. And I have long believed, nay, I am convinced, that by great dexterity, the "falconis' of the party have managed So to deceive and mislead many patriotic and honourable men, as to render them perfectly subservient to their views, whilst firmly persuaded that they were promoting the public welfare.[63]

When the political nature of articles about the Junto is added to the social motives of the author of the Washington letters, and his admission that at least some participants did not know of the Junto, Junto control of Virginia becomes problematic at best.

Virginia politics in 1820-1821 are important to an understanding of the Cohens case in much the same way as the economic and social forces already examined. Economic issues such as the stay law, retrenchment, and resolutions against the Supreme Court's decision on the second Bank of the United States revealed new political diversity which had been dormant during the War of 1812 and partially hidden by the success of Republicans on a state and national level. The new forces, such as the growth of western political power and new elections techniques, assured basic changes in Virginia's political alignments, at the same time economic and political forces reinforced the popularity of state rights. Spencer Roane and other Junto members who had doggedly supported state rights against the Supreme Court, undoubtedly saw an opportunity in the Cohens case: perhaps popular support could finally be rallied to confirm, by legislation or amendment, the constitutional theories

---

[63]Ibid.

they had so long espoused. Changing political alignments could also be dangerous to state rights Republicans--a combination of western interests with lingering Federalist strength, for example, might leave the Republican party a minority. Virginia nationalists felt similar concerns. The popularity of state rights represented a threat which might lead to unwelcome changes in the American constitutional system or the state's political alignments. Clearly the Cohens case happened during a period of political transition, which insured that Virginia politicians could not ignore the case.

CHAPTER III

GENESIS AND STATE DEBATES

A test case pitting the Grand National Lottery against the new Virginia lottery law was almost inevitable. The District of Columbia needed funds to build civic improvements, such as the city hall and prison, benefitted by the Grand National Lottery. Limited population and a small tax base made it necessary to tap non-district revenue sources to meet the costs. A lottery seemed an ideal solution, collecting part of the funds from nearby states. State laws, like the Virginia law restricting the sale of tickets in out of state lotteries, threatened the Grand National Lottery by limiting ticket sales. The Grand National Lottery was unusual because it had been authorized by Congress, and as early as 1819 its backers argued that it was therefore exempt from state regulation.[1] Clearly it was only a matter of time until the question was settled in the courts, and the _Cohens_ case thus became a test of the Virginia law and the meaning of the lottery's congressional authorization.

The _Cohens_ case began in June 1820 when William Jennings testified to a local grand jury that he had purchased tickets in

---

[1] _Norfolk and Portsmouth Herald_, July 7, 1819. Hezekiah Niles, in an article published the same day the decision of the borough court was delivered, said he had frequently heard "The question whether tickets in the national lottery could be sold in states having laws prohibiting the sale of foreign tickets." _Niles Registry_, September 2, 1820.

the Grand National Lottery from the Cohens' Norfolk office despite the new Virginia law prohibiting such sales.[2] The next eight months--until February 1821 when the Supreme Court heard the case--were important ones for the case. During that period the case was thoroughly examined in newspapers, the Governor's address to the legislature, and in the Virginia General Assembly. The debates refined state rights arguments to a point that most of the arguments delivered before the Supreme Court had already been used in the state discussions. While it is impossible to determine the effects of these state debates on the Supreme Court's decision, at least two major results can be identified. First, the discussions surfaced so much opposition to the lottery vendor's contention that congressional laws for the District of Columbia were immune to state restraints that it would have been hard for John Marshall and the Supreme Court to uphold the power unless expressly given by Congress in the legislation. Secondly, a major point of contention in the state debates became the right of the Supreme Court to hear the case. The controversy over the Court's jurisdiction became more important than the case's merits, and many of the case's most important precedents came in the Court's decision on jurisdiction.

The importance of the discussion before the Court met can, perhaps, best be seen by speculating on what might have happened

---

[2]6 Wheaton, 265. Manuscript copies of the borough court proceedings are available at the Norfolk courthouse, and in the *Cohens* case file, National Archives. For convenience references will be made to the printed report in 6 Wheaton, 264-290.

if the case had not taken place in Virginia, and a similar New York case involving the Grand National Lottery had reached the Supreme Court before the Cohens case. The New York case began before the Cohens case, but difficulties in getting an indictment delayed the case until the Virginia case had been appealed to the Supreme Court.[3] It is, of course, impossible to know what differences might have occurred in a Supreme Court case involving the New York case, but it is possible that with less opposition to the power claimed for the District law, the Court might have upheld the lottery and thus opened a new avenue to federal power. Marshall's decision makes clear that he would like to have upheld the lottery. The major difference, however, one can speculate, was the Virginia decision to object to the Court's jurisdiction. It is not clear that New York would have objected.[4] Without a formal argument on the Court's jurisdiction the major precedents of the decision--involving the Eleventh Amendment and the right to appeal state criminal cases--would not have been given. The timing of the case and its location in Virginia are important not only because Virginia was anxious to oppose the Court's jurisdiction, but because that opposition provided John Marshall and the Court an opportunity to reply to the Virginia view of the

---

[3]Richmond Enquirer, December 1, 7, 1820; Richmond Compiler and Commercial Advertiser, November 30, 1820; and Virginia Herald (Fredericksburg), November 29, 1820. Alexander Smyth to Governor Thomas Mann Randolph, February 27, 1821, Executive papers, Virginia State Library (VSL).

[4]The official reaction in New York seems to have been more directed at the merits of the case than the Court's jurisdiction.

Court's power. The result was one of Marshall's most nationalistic decisions.

There are several indications that the Cohens case, like several other landmark Supreme Court cases, was an arranged case: the use of the Grand National Lottery rather than a Maryland state lottery, the decision to limit the case to the federal question, the speed with which the case was appealed to the Supreme Court, and the rapid dissemination of legal opinions supporting the lottery.[5] The Cohens company was closely associated with Maryland State lotteries, and judged by either lotteries advertised or prizes won, these Maryland lotteries provided the major share of the company's business. It was not a Maryland lottery ticket, however, that was used to test the Virginia law, but a Grand National Lottery ticket. The likelihood that the lottery was carefully selected is increased because tickets in the Grand National Lottery were used to test cases involving both the Virginia and New York laws banning the sale of out of state lottery tickets. When the case reached the Norfolk Borough Court in late August 1820, both sides agreed to limit the case to the conflict between the federal lottery and the state's lottery law.[6]

Perhaps the most telling evidence that the case began as a test case comes from the speed with which it was appealed. The

---

[5]Albert J. Beveridge. The Life of John Marshall 4 vols. (Boston, 1919), IV, 343: C. Peter Magrath. Yazoo (Providence, 1966) 50-60; Niles Weekly Register, Supplement to vol. XV, 70-72.

[6]6 Wheaton, 268-9.

appeal happened so fast that the Supreme Court agreed to hear the case before it came to trial in the borough court. The form sent to the borough court requesting a record of the case for the February Supreme Court session is dated the first Monday in August--August 1, 1820--the day of the Supreme Court's summer session.[7] By that time the Grand Jury had met, but the borough court would not meet until August 29, 1820. The Supreme Court's request form clearly indicates that it thought the case had been decided and all possible appeals rejected. The state itself did not receive the request to appear before the Supreme Court as defendant in error until October 17, 1820, well after the case had in fact been decided by the state court; but the Supreme Court's request for a copy of the court's record before the final local decision is, to say the least, irregular.[8]

The publication of a statement by five of the country's top constitutional lawyers is the final indication that the appeal of the case to the Supreme Court was prearranged. The lawyers' opinion, written before the decision of the borough court, was not used in the local deliberation, but was published four days after the Norfolk decision.[9] The opinion was written by William Pinkney and signed by David B. Ogden, Thomas Addis Emmet, John

---

[7]Appellate form dated the first Monday of August 1820, signed by E. B. Caldwell, Clerk of the Supreme Court, Norfolk Court House. See also minutes of the Supreme Court, Volume C, 132-146, National Archives.

[8]Richmond Enquirer, October 27, 1820.

[9]Ibid., September 29, 1820.

Wells, and Walter Jones. The opinion published immediately after the decision seems clearly designed to rally support for an appeal to the Supreme Court.

The opinion of the five eminent jurists did not, however, solidify opinion in favor of the lottery. In fact, the opposite proved true. The opinion of the five lawyers became a rallying point for state rights opponents of the powers claimed for the District of Columbia. The _Enquirer_ published only one small notice about the case saying it "touched incidentally . . . the great question of _state rights and duties_," until a rumor of Pinkney's opinion brought a lead editorial examining the case just before the Norfolk decision.[10] The editorial discussed the state and national implications of the case, ending with a general appeal for vigilance.

> Too little attention is paid to State Rights; for it is fashionable with many even to scont them--we are not disposed to chime in with these doctrines, but on the contrary to 'snuff the approach of violation in every tainted breeze.' To think of raising the lever on the disfranchised 10 mile square to batter down the rights of the states, is out of the question.[11]

No one was surprised when Norfolk's major and alderman, sitting as the borough court, found the Cohen brothers guilty and fined them the maximum $100 fine plus expenses. The _Richmond Enquirer_, for example, did not even report the borough court's decision, but eight days after it was given the Richmond paper

---

[10] _Richmond Enquirer_, August 8, 1820.

[11] _Ibid._, August 25, 1820, reprinted in _Norfolk and Portsmouth Herald_, August 26, 1820.

reprinted the opinion of the five lawyers upholding the lottery as a national institution.[12] The lawyers claimed that congressional approval made the lottery a national lottery. Congressional power over the District is usually local, but since the lottery benefits a national project, the power authorizing it, like all others Congress possesses, must be binding upon the entire country.

> This is a lottery authorized by Congress for the purpose of making important improvements in the city which may be styled the national city, in the improvements of which the nation is concerned. It is, therefore, a national lottery and authorized by a national legislature, and it would be monstrous if any state legislature could impede the execution of a law made for national purposes, relative to a district over which the national legislature have the exclusive right of legislation.[13]

No doubt exists, they continued, of Congress' right to establish a lottery and since Congress can establish a lottery they can also delegate that power to the District government. State regulations would not only lessen the lottery's value but also impair a citizen's right to buy a ticket. No state rights are violated by the lottery. Congress must approve all such lotteries and state representatives can work to defeat or repeal any law they oppose. Any state opposition to such laws after enactment would thus fight their own sovereignty.[14]

---

[12]<u>6 Wheaton</u>, 266-290, <u>Richmond Enquirer</u>, September 5, 1820, <u>Niles Register</u>, September 2, 1820, reprinted in <u>Norfolk and Portsmouth Herald</u>, September 15, 1820, <u>Virginia Herald</u> (Fredericksburg), September 27, 1820, and <u>Lynchburg Press</u>, September 29, 1820.

[13]<u>Richmond Enquirer</u>, October 27, 1820.

[14]<u>Ibid.</u>

Publication of the opinion of the five lawyers marked the effective start of newspaper debate about the Cohens case. Within the next three months, four long articles by "Senex", "Pelopidas", "Publicola", and Henry Brackenridge and several short Enquirer introductions examining the jurists' statement were printed in Virginia and Maryland newspapers.[15] These articles focused on congressional power for the District of Columbia and the relationship between District and state laws. Most examined the background of the creation of the District and then vehemently disagreed with the five lawyers. "Publicola" attempted to place the debate in a larger constitutional framework and suggest general remedies if the Court upheld the lottery, but most authors concentrated on the "flimsy grounds" the lawyers presented to justify the superiority of District laws to state regulation.

Richmond Enquirer editors claimed that the lawyers attempted to justify the power with a word--national. No one could object to a "national legislature" operating in a "national capital" for a "national object." The Enquirer's editors, however did object. Congress, they said, cannot define their power and determine what objects are national ones. The Constitution was written to determine what are national objects.[16] "Senex" and "Publicola"

---

[15]Norfolk and Portsmouth Herald, September 5, 1820 (Senex); Richmond Enquirer, September 19, 1820 (Pelopidas); and Ibid. September 29, 1820 (Publicola); Ibid., November 28, 1820.

[16]Richmond Enquirer, September 19, 1820, reprinted in Norfolk and Portsmouth Herald, November 1, 1820.

denied that the lottery projects were, in fact, national projects, while Henry Brackenridge took exception to the lawyers' view of Washington as a national city. Congress is interested in the growth of Washington, he agreed, but no more so than in the growth of Baltimore.[17]

The authors agreed that the District of Columbia was not created to be a "national city" or to enlarge congressional power, but to protect the national government from state interference after problems in Philadelphia threatened that independence. Congress thus became a municipal council, or at most, a state legislature directing District affairs and like other such bodies their power is limited to definite territorial boundaries and has no effect beyond that area. The author appealed to history. Members of the Virginia ratifying convention had been concerned about the extent of congressional power over the District when examining the Constitution prior to ratification. Edmund Pendleton attempted to calm those fears:

> What then is the power? It is that Congress shall exclusively legislate _there_, in order to preserve the police of the place, and their personal independence; that they may not be overawed or insulted; . . . Suppose they were . . . to grant exclusive privileges to citizens residing _within_ that place, &c. It would have no operation _without the limits of that district_ . . . _For their exclusive power is confined to that district_.[18]

If District laws were national laws, as the lawyers now claimed, then not only were District lotteries national lotteries

---

[17]_Richmond Enquirer_, November 28, 1820.

[18]_Ibid._, September 19, 1820.

beyond state regulation, but other District institutions were also national institutions. "Pelopidas" warned of a District bank, a university, and even a congressionally chartered District East India Company. "Senex" noted that similar results would come from grants to federal forts and arsenals, which were mentioned in the same section of the Constitution.[19] The lawyers' views, if extended, Brackenridge wrote, would make Michigan's territorial laws superior to state regulation since that territory also receives its ultimate authority from Congress.

> It could never have been supposed that not only all the higher attributes of sovereignty were resigned to the general government, but that even the remaining powers of the state were liable to be rendered null at pleasure by the right of Congress to exclusive legislation over the District of Columbia.[20]

"Publicola" wrote that the effect was to give the city of Washington power to legislate for the nation, while the *Enquirer's* editors feared the ultimate consequences of such power:

> Congress may do anything in the District; and having done it, their power 'knows no locality within the boundaries of the Union!!' 'The states have no existence relatively to the effect of such power.' They are as if they were not.--But we cannot bend our minds to such a usurpation that fixes its lever upon this little point, to move, as it pleases, the state governments.[21]

---

[19] *Ibid.*

[20] *Ibid.*, November 28, 1820.

[21] *Ibid.*, September 5, 1820.

"Pelopidas" expanded the *Enquirer's* analogy fearing that the claimed power would "become the lever of Archimedes, and the District the spot from which the whole power of the states is to be subverted."[22]

These articles were designed to counter what appeared to be a major power grab. The power claimed for the District laws was not granted by the Constitution, involved the transfers of basic congressional powers to another governmental body, and would interfere with a state's internal legislation. "Pelopidas" claimed the new construction of the Constitution, which offered potential for a significant expansion of federal power, was "a construction of the Constitution the most alarming that has ever been attempted to be propagated."[23] A few, like the *Enquirer's* editors and "Publicola," looked to what might be the ultimate results. "Publicola" hoped the election of men faithful to state rights might remedy the approaching conflict, but cautioned that if the choice became limited "between submission and resistance," it is "reasonable to believe that the people of the '*old dominion*' would not 'long debate which of the two to choose.'"[24] Most of the articles, however, were designed as a rebuttal to the,five lawyers rather than a call to action.

---

[22]*Ibid.*, September 19, 1820.

[23]*Ibid.*

[24]*Ibid.*, September 29, 1820.

II

Governor Thomas Mann Randolph received an official summons in mid October 1820, directing the state to appear at the Supreme Court's next session to show cause why the judgment against the Cohen brothers should not be reversed.[25] The governor in council quickly selected two Virginia Congressmen, Philip P. Barbour and Alexander Smyth, to represent the state and waited for further developments.[26] The summons marked several changes in the discussion of the case as any uncertainties about whether the case would be appealed were eliminated. During the next three months new issues were introduced, state options were debated, and the thrust of state newspaper articles changed from a limited examination of the case's issues to a more general discussion of constitutional theory.

A Richmond Enquirer article about the case in late October 1820 illustrates some of the new issues raised by the summons. The editors listed three reasons why they felt the case would fail. First, the Norfolk Borough Court was not the highest court of appeal within the state. Second, that a state was a party to the case, and lastly, the "absurd principle" on which the case

---

[25]Ibid., October 10, 27, 1820.

[26]Virginia, Council, Minute Book, October 25, 1820, Virginia State Library. Virginia, Executive Letterbook, October 25, 1820, VSL. Both Smyth and Barbour quickly agreed to represent the state. Council minutebook, December 2, 1820, VSL. Barbour was especially enthusiastic saying that in "the discharge of my duty as counsel, I should be advocating what as a man, I conscientiously believe to be a sound construction of the Federal Constitution." P. P. Barbour to Thomas Mann Randolph, (undated) Executive papers, VSL.

was based, that District of Columbia laws extend beyond District boundaries. Making the state a party to the case they found most objectionable. Virginia had long opposed federal suits involving states. As early as 1793, during the discussions leading to the Eleventh Amendment, the state legislature expressed that concern in a resolution which the Enquirer reprinted.

> Resolved that a state cannot under the constitution of the United States, be made a defendant at the suit of any individual or individuals, and that the decision of the Supreme Federal Court, that a state may be placed in that situation, is incompatible with, and dangerous to the sovereignty and independence of the individual states, as the same tends to a general consolidation of those confederated republics.[27]

Congress approved the Eleventh Amendment the next year: "The judicial power of the United States shall not be construed to extend to any suit in law or equity, commenced or prosecuted against one of the United States by citizens of another state, or by citizens or subjects of any foreign state." After state ratification, Virginians assumed this amendment would prohibit cases against the state. Now that assumption was in doubt.

Newspaper debates about the reach of District of Columbia laws led to the introduction of the issue into the United States House of Representatives. During arguments about a bill incorporating a national vaccine institute, located in Washington, to help eradicate smallpox, Representative Livermore of New Hampshire proposed that the charter be limited to the District of Columbia so that no question could arise about the

---

[27]Richmond Enquirer, October 10, 1820.

extent of the institution's powers. William Burwell of Virginia opposed the restriction, fearing such action might imply that without restrictions the institute superseded state regulation. Burwell called the construction put on congressional powers in the Cohens case "too absurd to be entertained by many men of sense in this country," calling it "the most dangerous and absurd construction ever given to the Constitution." Charles F. Mercer of Virginia

> said he concurred with his colleague in his view of the recent opinion of some gentlemen learned in the law, on the subject of the powers of Congress. He did not see, however, how, by possibility, the passage of this bill could countenance that opinion.[28]

The House deleted Livermore's amendment and then passed the vaccine bill, apparently agreeing with the Virginia delegation that the limited nature of congressional power made an amendment unnecessary.[29]

When the Virginia legislature assembled in December 1820, Governor Thomas Mann Randolph initiated two measures designed to define state policy. First, he included a lengthy report about the case in his annual address to the legislature December 4, 1820. After summarizing the case, he focused on the evils of lotteries and of using constitutional power over the District of Columbia to protect them. Lotteries are "the only kind of gambling in which all classes and ages, and both sexes, can generally engage, and is . . . the most extensive mode ever

---

[28]Ibid., December 7, 1820.

[29]Ibid., December 5, 7, 1820.

exhibited in society.[30] Protecting such gambling by Congressional power, if upheld, would allow virtually any other form of gambling to be introduced from the same source, since most forms of gambling had been used to raise money. The great "national" city mentioned by the five lawyers evoked Randolph's fear, not his pride. Historical precedents, he felt, showed that freedoms were often lost because of the "baneful influence of metropolitan usurpation and tyranny." Inhabitants of great capital cities quickly learn to influence popular governments. Closing on a slightly brighter note, he hoped that the summons would be all the state would have to bear and that the "strange opinion" would not be upheld.[31]

Three days later Governor Randolph asked the council what instructions Barbour and Smyth should be given. Council member Robert Smith suggested instructions directing the two congressmen to "enter a formal and solemn protest against the jurisdiction of that court."[32] The congressmen would be free to determine the best method of protest, but, after protesting, they were directed not to argue the case's merits. The council discussed the

---

[30]Virginia, House of Delegates Journal (1820-1821) (Richmond 1821), 12.

[31]Ibid., See: Richmond Compiler, December 5, 1820; Norfolk and Portsmouth Herald, December 8, 1820; American Beacon (Norfolk), Virginia Herald (Fredericksburg), December 9, 13, 1820; and Farmer's Repository (Charleston), December 20, 1820. Another section of the Governor's speech also received a great deal of attention. He proposed a gradual emancipation of all slaves within the state.

[32]Council Minutes, December 7, 1820, VSL.

instructions but took no action. The next day, December 8, 1820, William Roane, Spencer Roane's son, offered resolutions which mirrored his father's state rights concerns and may have benefitted from the older Roane's help. The resolutions mark the transition from arguments based on specifics of the case to a general discussion of constitutional theory. The resolutions center on the "vital question"--"the continued encroachments, which the general government are making on the rights of the states." The resolutions are designed as propaganda rather than as a law brief. There is, the resolutions thunder, no "shadow of implication" to support the five lawyers' claims and "nothing but a love of power, to which men in offices are too prone, and a calculation (perhaps too well founded) on the tacit acquiescence and non-resistance of the states could ever have given ground to the present cause." The district's lottery power, now claimed for the first time, amounts to a blanket right to tax the states, "in all cases whatever." If the Supreme Court upholds the case "every trace and vestige of state independence will be obliterated."

> In this case the dearest rights, the very sovereignty, of this Commonwealth is assailed. The State of Virginia does not recognize a power in any tribunal under heaven to arraign, and adjudge away her sovereignty and her right to self government and self preservation.[33]

The resolutions appear to have been too radical. At least the council chose not to approve them.

The legislature was no more decisive in dealing with the Cohens case than the Governor's Council had been. The special

---

[33]Ibid., December 8, 1820.

House of Delegates committee, which was selected to make recommendations on the section of the Governor's speech dealing with the case, waited nearly a month before reporting back to the House. During that month a series of six letters by "State Rights" appeared in the Richmond Enquirer. The letters, which were printed from December 14, 1820, to the first week in January 1821, were written, the author claimed, to "neutralize the influence" of the five eminent lawyers.[34] It is clear, however, from the content of the letters and their timing, that their main purpose was to influence the legislature. The letters completed the change in arguments from examining specifics of the case to an examination of constitutional theory which had been started by William Roane's proposed instructions. The letters quickly examine the five lawyers' arguments, repeating many of the topics found in earlier rebuttals to the lawyers. The authors discuss the reasons for the creation of the District of Columbia; the limited nature of congressional power over the District; the lack of constitutional justification for the lottery either by constitutional delegation or necessity; the inability of Congress to delegate their powers; and the ramifications of the claimed powers on federal forts and arsenals.

"State Rights" spends more of his essay, however, developing his view of the government established by the United States Constitution. That government, he claimed, is a federation--two

---

[34]Richmond Enquirer, December 14, 19, 21, 28, 30, 1820, January 2, 1821.

equal powers joined to govern--not a national consolidated government. The United States has not even assumed a name, he contends, "because they never constituted themselves into a consolidated nation."[35] He emphatically denied that Congress is a national legislature writing laws for national purposes.

> Congress is not a national legislature to superintend national objects, but a federal legislature limited to federal objects, defined by a compact between independent nations or states, beyond which limitations it cannot escape.[36]

Congressional representatives do not have the same power as the people they represent. The people are sovereign and can do as they wish. Their representatives are not. The lawyers are mistaken to claim that by opposing this law the states oppose their own sovereignty because Congress does not have sovereignty.

The six articles oppose the creation of a great national city-a London or a Rome--and trace the corruption of money upon a federal government. The author lists a lottery which taxes all to benefit a single city in his list of corruptive influences and worried about the precedent which might free federal taxation. Experience in all civilized nations, he wrote, shows "That the tendency towards the corruption of free governments, is concentrated in pecuniary interest; and that a nation blind to its arts, must inevitably become its prey."[37] In his anxiousness to oppose the five lawyers, the author stooped to

---

[35]Ibid., December 21, 1820.

[36]Ibid.

[37]Ibid., December 14, 1820.

prejudice and ridicule, comparing, at one point, the lottery tickets to Papal indulgences, and later asking why armies of prostitutes could not be sent into the states to raise money for the federal government.[38]

If the articles sought to influence the legislature as well as instruct the public, they succeeded. Six days after the series ended a special committee of the House of Delegates investigating the lottery question issued a report and a series of resolutions, written by Junto member William Selden, which followed a state pattern used often since the Virginia Resolutions in 1798. Following a mixed reaction from other states to the Virginia and Kentucky Resolutions, James Madison penned a long report explaining the resolutions and outlining in detail the constitutional relationship between the state and federal governments. The report and resolutions were quickly passed and became, for all intents and purposes, official state policy. During the next twenty years they acquired additional veneration as Madison's authorship became known. The report's importance to many Republicans is seen in a resolution passed by the Ohio legislature in 1820.

> The resolutions of Kentucky and Virginia, and of Massachusetts, Rhode Island, the Senate of New York, New Hampshire, and Vermont, in reply, and the answer to these replies by the Legislature of Virginia, were a direct and constitutional appeal to the states and to the people upon the great question at issue. The appeal was decided by the presidential and other elections of 1800. The states and the people recognised [_sic_] and affirmed the doctrines of

---

[38]_Ibid._

> Kentucky and Virginia, by affecting a total change in the administration of the Federal Government.[39]

Madison's report declared that since the states were the "sovereign parties to their constitutional compact," they became the rightful judges as to whether the compact has been violated.[40]

> In case of a deliberate, palpable and dangerous exercise of other powers, not granted by the said compact, the states who are parties thereto have the right, and are in duty bound, to interpose for arresting the progress of the evil, and for maintaining within their respective limits, the authorities, rights and liberties appertaining to them.[41]

Madison's report established both the duty of a state to intervene to oppose an unconstitutional act, and, by its example, the method of protest. The House of Delegates passed two such reports during their 1819-1820 session--in response to the Supreme Court's decision in *Marbury v Madison*, and in response to the debates over the admission of Missouri.[42] Both reports were, however, later defeated by the state senate.

The committee report on the *Cohens* case, or Selden report, like Madison's pattern, examined broad political philosophy as well as the *Cohens* case itself. The report closely examined the federal system beginning with the British colonial system, which, it claimed, was a federal system with England exercising power

---

39 *American State Papers*, 646.

40 *The Virginia Report of 1799-1800* . . . (Richmond, 1850), 192.

41 *Ibid.*, 190. cf. 190-196.

42 *Richmond Enquirer*, December 23, 29, 1819; January 4, 6, 7; February 22, 25, 1820. *House of Delegates Journal* (1819-1820) (Richmond, 1820), 57-65, 76-77.

over external powers such as war and commerce and the American colonists exercising "absolute control" over internal matters. British discontent with sharing power led to their attempt to subvert that federal system by seizing the power to regulate the colonists' internal affairs, which, in turn, precipitated the revolution. Governmental powers continued to be divided according to national or local purposes under the Articles of Confederation and the Constitution. The states possessed all sovereignty but agreed to give up limited parts of it to the general government, retaining, however, all powers not expressly delegated. Neither government is the final arbiter of the compact's provisions. Areas of conflict between the governments may arise, but:

> If this occasional conflict of authority in the different governments of the Union may be justly regarded as a dangerous consequence of our federative system, the wise framers of the constitution have prescribed no antidote against its possible and foreseen occurrence. It is highly probable they greatly preferred it to that fearful and absolute supremacy which could alone invest one government with power to abrogate the rightful laws of another and the exercise of which by the General Government would directly affect the existence of the state governments, the balance of the constitution and the integrity of the Union.[43]

The Constitution does not, the report declared, provide justification for the claimed supremacy of District of Columbia laws. The states retained all powers not delegated, including taxing powers and powers to legislate for moral issues, which the powers now claimed for District laws would violate. After a lengthy examination of the Federal court system, the report

---

[43] House Journal (1820-1821), 102-106.

concluded that state officials are not "controllable by the authorities of the general government." Federal courts are not supreme over state courts any more than the national legislature is supreme over the state legislatures. The acts of the state legislatures cannot be reviewed by the national Congress and neither can the decisions of state courts be reviewed by the national tribunal.

The report includes an impressive mustering of evidence, including quotes from Madison's address to the Virginia ratifying convention, The Federalist Papers, the Virginia and Kentucky Resolutions, the Virginia Report, and John Taylor's new book, Construction Construed and Constitutions Vindicated.

The committee's report ends with two resolutions. The first denied the right of the Court to examine the case.

> Resolved, therefore, That the Supreme Court of the United States have no rightful authority under the constitution, to examine and correct the judgment for which the commonwealth of Virginia have been 'cited and admonished. . .' and that the General Assembly do hereby enter their most solemn protest against the jurisdiction of that court over the matter.[44]

The second, more mundane resolution, directed the executive to send a copy of the report and resolutions to the state's counsels and to state senators and representatives.

The House of Delegates examined the report January 9, 1821, ordered the seven page report printed, and referred it to the committee of the whole for debate on January 22, 1821.[45] The

---

[44]Ibid.

[45]Richmond Enquirer, January 11, 1821.

Richmond Enquirer quickly published the report, saying it was "entitled to the most serious perusal."[46] The Enquirer's editors noted that they hoped the state would debate the Court's jurisdiction and ignore the lottery's legality.[47]

The report and resolutions were hotly debated by the House of Delegates as opponents first tried to delay the resolutions. When the report came before the entire House on January 22, 1821, several amendments were introduced modifying the report. In order to avoid basic changes in the document, George Loyall, a Norfolk delegate in whose district the case occurred, moved to send the report back to the special House committee that wrote it.[48] Despise opposition from Samuel Blackburn, an old Federalist from Bath County who would become the report's most vocal opponent, and others, the report was sent back to the special committee.

The committee quickly made some unspecified changes in the report, and five days later, Saturday, January 27, 1821, reported

---

[46]The report was reprinted in full in the Richmond Enquirer, January 11, 1821; Virginia Patriot and Daily Mercantile Advertiser (Richmond), January 12, 1821; The Virginia Patriot (Richmond), January 12, 1821; and American Beacon (Norfolk), January 17, 18, 1821. Excerpts were printed in The Richmond Compiler, January 10, 1821; Norfolk and Portsmouth Herald, January 15, 19, 1821; Genius of Liberty (Leesburg), January 16, 23, 1821; Alexandria Gazette and Daily Advertiser, January 19, 1821; Central Gazette (Charlottesville), January 19, 1821; and Petersburg Republican, January 16, 1821.

[47]Richmond Enquirer, January 11, 1821.

[48]Richmond Enquirer, January 23, 1821; Richmond Compiler, January 23, 1821; and Virginia Patriot and Daily Mercantile Advertiser, February 3, 1821.

out a slightly amended report and resolutions. The House accepted the amendments and scheduled full debate. Debate on the amended report was delayed, however, when on January 31, 1821, Thomas Miller, Powhatan delegate, introduced a completely new report. The shorter, more moderate Miller report concentrated more on the Cohens case than on abstract political philosophy. The report traced the history of the case and then discussed two basic objections to the case. First, that the Supreme Court must show that cases can be appealed from a state court to a federal court and that a state may be made a party to such a case against its will. The report cited the Virginia Court of Appeals decision in Martin v. Hunter's Lessee to show that appeals cannot be made from a state court to the Supreme Court. There is even less justification, it continued, for compelling a state to be a party to a case against its will. "Between independent and sovereign states, there can be no common umpire, but by consent."[49] The Constitution allows the general government to work upon the people themselves and if a state enforces an unconstitutional law, the offended party can sue the officer enforcing the law to gain freedom or justice. Secondly, the report objected to the subject matter of the case--that a District of Columbia law could overrule a state law. If the interpretation given by the five lawyers on the extent of District of Columbia laws is "established the District of

---

[49]House Journal (1820-1821), 154-157; Richmond Enquirer, February 1, 3, 1821.

Columbia becomes the law giver of the whole confederacy." Virginia did not realize that in giving up territory for the creation of the new national capital "she was laying the corner stone of an empire from which she was one day to receive her laws."[50] Both the Selden and Miller reports were laid on the table for almost a week until February 6, 1821, when supporters of the Selden report, including William Selden, George Loyall, and Andrew Stevenson, finally brought the reports to the floor of the House.[51]

The nearly two week delay in examining the reports, between January 22 and February 6, 1821, brought three new letters about the case in the Richmond Enquirer.[52] All the letters were addressed to the legislature and exhorted the Republican legislators. "Last of the Republicans" asked the successors of 1776 and 1799 to prove themselves and promised to die in the last ditch, if necessary, to save the state's liberty.[53] All three articles objected to the Supreme Court's jurisdiction in the case, and the two letters by "Rights of the States" attacked the Court directly. The Supreme Court, the author erroneously

---

[50]Ibid.

[51]Virginia Patriot, January 29, 1821; Richmond Compiler, January 29, 30, 1821; Central Gazette, February 2, 1821; Richmond Enquirer, January 30, 1821; February 1, 3, 6, 8, 1821; Alexandria Gazette, February 6, 1821.

[52]"The Last of the Republicans," Richmond Enquirer, January 25, 1821; "The Rights of the States," Ibid., January 30, 1821; February 1, 1821.

[53]Richmond Enquirer, January 25, 1821.

claimed, has never declared a national law unconstitutional,[54] and the Court's dependence upon Congress for funds and a definition of its jurisdiction leaves doubts that a ruling will ever be made against a congressional act. The Court, the author continued, exerts improper influences on new judges who change their principles as well as their jobs as they move from state to national posts.[55] History has shown, he asserted, that there is scarcely any congressional usurpation which the Supreme Court will not uphold. If the Supreme Court is the final judge in all conflicting cases, then the states and individual citizens lose the ability to protect their interests. Great danger therefore comes from small constitutional violations which are not challenged and in time become accepted by the public. Now is the time to tell the Court it shall go no further.[56] The letters mark a new emphasis in discussions of the case. The Supreme Court itself became the focal point of the articles, rather than specifics in the Cohens case or general constitutional theory.

The articles helped supporters of the resolutions finally bring the two reports to the committee of the whole on February 6, 1821, and in a skillfully handled maneuver by supporters of the Selden report, both reports were sent back to the special

---

[54]The author was mistaken. The court had declared Section 13 of the Judiciary Act of 1789 unconstitutional in Marbury v. Madison, 1 Cranch 137. In light of later debates over judicial review it is interesting to note that by 1821 the case had made little impression--at least on the author of this article.

[55]Richmond Enquirer, January 30, 1821.

[56]Ibid., February 1, 1821.

committee which authored the Selden report. Few were surprised the next day when that committee reported out only the Selden report. The committee's action, on February 7, 1821, started a furious four-day debate on the report. John S. Barbour from Culpepper started debate with a motion to indefinitely postpone the report--a motion he reintroduced at the beginning of debate the next two days. Barbour, a cousin of Philip P. and James Barbour, who would later serve in the United States House of Representatives and as chairman of the 1852 Democratic convention, argued that the Supreme Court was an impartial arbiter and the *Cohens* case was "not of that *palpable* and *alarming* usurpation, which according to the Report of '98-'99 would justify the interposition of the state legislatures."[57]

The debates were long and intense, especially between a handful of supporters and the most vocal opponents of the report who spoke each day. John Barbour's motion to indefinitely postpone the report and resolutions finally came to a vote on Friday, February 9, 1821, the third time it was presented, and lost 51 to 127. Additional attempts to delay the measure were also defeated, and near the close of the Friday session a vote was taken on the Selden resolutions. The first resolution opposing the Supreme Court's right to hear the case and protesting the Court's jurisdiction won overwhelming support,

---

[57]*Ibid.*, February 8, 1821. For details of the House debates see footnotes 57 to 65 and *Richmond Compiler*, February 8, 1821; *Petersburg Republican*, February 13, 1821; *Virginia Patriot*, February 9, 1821; *Alexandria Gazette*, February 12, 1821.

passing 138 to 18. Andrew Stevenson then introduced a new resolution instructing the state's counsels to argue only the Supreme Court's jurisdiction, which passed without a division, as did the second original resolution instructing the Governor to send a copy of the report and resolutions to the lawyers representing the state and to all Virginia congressmen.

The committee report, however, encountered difficulties when Richard Morris from Hanover County attempted to revive the Miller report and substitute it for Selden's report. Despite a concerted effort by supporters of the Selden report to continue debate, the House adjourned without voting on either report. The final day of debate, Saturday, February 10, 1821, quickly became a showdown between supporters and opponents of the committee report. The basic decision whether the Selden or Miller report would accompany the resolutions which had already been passed was complicated when Burwell Bassett, a delegate from James City County, objected to the section of Miller's report approving suits against state officers rather than against a state itself. Burwell refused to accept the point, which he said was an important part of <u>Osborn v. The Bank of the United States,</u> then in litigation. Bassett succeeded in removing that section of Miller's report, after which the amended Miller report was defeated by the House 59 to 91. Opponents of the Selden report tried a bold counter move. They introduced a motion to remove the entire report and replace it with a short synopsis of the case. Andrew Stevenson, a supporter of the Selden report, quickly countered with a motion separating deleting the original report from substituting a new synopsis. The motion to strike out the Selden report lost 56 to 82, and since no amendments could now be made in the report, the House finally voted on the report, passing it without a division. The Report and the resolutions then went to the Senate for what appeared to be an even tougher examination.[58]

The debates in the House of Delegates on the Cohens report and resolutions provide a view of Virginia constitutional and political thoughts as the Supreme Court prepared to examine the case. The discussions illustrate an almost unanimous opposition to the claim that congressional authorization of the Grand National Lottery invalidated the Virginia law against out of state lotteries. Some legislators questioned whether the case came up to the standards demanded by Madison's report before the legislature should intervene, and a few, notably Samuel Blackburn, even opposed Madison's report, but not even the most vocal opponents of the resolutions had much to say in support of the District of Columbia law.

The House also showed great concern about the state's sovereignty, and the Supreme Court's lack of jurisdiction in the case. The resolution protesting the Court's jurisdiction was approved almost unanimously--138 to 18. Some legislators continued to argue that no appeal was possible from a state court to the Supreme Court, but most were content to skip lightly over

---

[58]Central Gazette, February 16, 1821.

the subject, referring the skeptic to the report of the Virginia Court of Appeals in Martin v. Hunter's Lessee, and then concentrate on the problems caused by making Virginia a party to the case without its consent. Few supporters of the state's sovereignty were as vocal as Andrew Stevenson, who on the second day of major debates, claimed "The people were originally seduced into an adoption of the Constitution; by being persuaded that there was a tribunal to watch over their state rights and that this body was the state legislature." Samuel Blackburn was as outspoken in opposition when he ridiculed the idea that the state legislature was acting in a sovereign capacity. He wondered aloud if he saw the "Emperor of Augusta," "the King of Rockingham," and the "Dukes of Richmond, Westmoreland, and Norfolk." Despite Blackburn's skepticism, most delegates, as evidenced by the House votes, believed that the state's sovereignty was involved and felt the state should officially oppose the Supreme Court's jurisdiction in the case.

Despite such general agreement, the General Assembly evidenced an uneasiness about the extreme state rights position taken by the report. Many delegates were concerned that the Selden report was too bellicose. Richard Morris felt the report was "calculated to excite irritation."[59] Samuel Blackburn wanted the report rejected if it was intended to intimidate the Court. It cannot seriously be intended to instruct or enlighten the justices of the Court, and its real objective, which is to

---

[59]Richmond Enquirer, February 13, 1821.

declare war against the United States, should not be sanctioned by the Virginia Legislature.[60]

The House of Delegates debate on the Selden report quickly surfaced lingering Republican-Federalist party loyalties. William Selden, Junto member and author of the report, and Samuel Blackburn, an old Federalist delegate from Bath County, made little effort to conceal their feelings as they spoke at length several times during the four days of debate. Blackburn ridiculed the report's style, saying it might do as a Fourth of July speech, a stump oratory, or an election speech, but it fell far short of the dignity needed for a state paper.[61] Selden later charged Blackburn with giving a speech against Thomas Jefferson during John Adams' administration which prompted John Adams' statement that there was a party in Virginia that should be ground into the dust. Blackburn admitted his part in the episode and counter-attacked by intimating that Selden wished to dismember the union, and suggested an eleventh commandment dealing with political relations: "Thou Shalt not, . . . dare in any wise mention or hint at a dissolution of the Union."[62] One newspaper account reported that "There was much wit as well as warmth in the manner of Messrs. Blackburn and Selden toward each

[60] Blackburn's speech was reprinted in full in the Central Gazette, March 9, 16, 1821.

[61] Ibid.

[62] Alexandria Gazette, March 19, 1821.

other!"[63] The warmth of the exchange, however, seems to have gone beyond the accepted House code. David Patterson, an Augusta delegate, asked for a one day delay in the debates because no good could come from a discussion "which had been conducted with so much warmth." It is, he said, important "to the dignity of the house to arrest it."[64] The exchange was so spirited that Thomas Ritchie refused to publish one of Blackburn's speeches in the Enquirer unless Blackburn removed some personal references about Selden which the editor felt were slanderous. Blackburn refused and published the speech in Charlottesville's Central Gazette. Even John Barbour, who took the lead in attempting to postpone the report and resolutions, claimed that a cool deliberate decision had been endangered by the warmth shown by the two gentlemen toward each other.[65] The Selden-Blackburn confrontation alarmed several delegates because it emphasized party politics and threatened to revive the Republican/Federalist debates of the past. The debate proved to be an apex of partisan conflict about the case in Virginia.

House passage of the Selden report and resolutions occurred only after a lengthy, highly contested debate, and it appeared that Senate passage would be even harder. During the previous legislative session the Senate had tabled resolutions opposing the Supreme Court's decision in Marbury v. Madison

---

[63]Ibid.

[64]Richmond Enquirer, February 10, 1821.

[65]Ibid.; Virginia Patriot, February 10, 1821.

upholding the Bank of the United States which the House had passed 117 to 38. Senate debate on the Cohens resolutions, however, proved to be quicker and simpler than the House debate. Senate opponents of the report followed the House precedent and tried to postpone consideration of the report. Chapman Johnson from Augusta County moved to postpone the report because he felt the Supreme Court had a right to review state laws. Although Johnson opposed the report, he did not think that the District lottery law was a federal law. Henry St. George Tucker, St George Tucker's son, who would later serve as President of the Supreme Court of Appeals and then as Professor of Law at the University of Virginia, supported the postponement. Tucker declared that the resolutions were too early, but that he would vote for them if they were not postponed. The federal writ was not serious, he continued, but an adverse ruling by the Supreme Court would be. The motion to postpone the resolutions, held Saturday, February 17, 1821, lost by the narrowest of votes--12 to 12.[66]

The resolutions, however, were soon drastically changed. First the Senate removed the Selden report and replaced it with a short introduction explaining the case. George Hay, President Monroe's son-in-law, then introduced three new resolutions. The first denied Supreme Court appellate jurisdiction in any case decided by a state court. The second maintained that even if such appeals existed in cases between individuals, the

---

[66]Richmond Enquirer, February 20, 1821.

Constitution and the Eleventh Amendment prohibited such suits involving a state. The third new resolution declared that a congressional law for the District of Columbia was local in nature, not a law of the United States. The state senate narrowly passed the first two resolutions before unanimously passing the final one. The senate then passed, 22 to 2, the first House resolution declaring that the Supreme Court has no jurisdiction in this case and entered the legislature's protest against the case. The other two House resolutions were not passed because the Supreme Court's term had started four days earlier, making it too late to instruct Barbour and Smyth, and the Senate did not deem it appropriate to send copies to Virginia's congressmen. The amended resolutions then passed the Senate 14 to 10.[67]

The House was, no doubt, disappointed that the Senate had eliminated the Selden report and changed their resolutions so drastically. The Senate had, nevertheless, passed resolutions against the Supreme Court's jurisdiction in the _Cohens_ case. Rather than risk a confrontation and perhaps defeat by revising the Senate's introduction and resolutions, the House of Delegates quickly passed the Senate's version without division, February 19, 1821. The House action came on the first working day after the Senate's passage of the resolutions, and the only recorded

---

[67]_Ibid._; _Virginia Patriot_, February 19, 1821.

debate centered on another John S. Barbour motion to postpone debate, which lost 38 to 112.[68]

Voting patterns on the resolutions mirrored closely the ideological patterns revealed in earlier state rights issues. Nationalist support during the House vote to take up the resolutions (see Map V) centered in the western areas of the state, especially the Valley of Virginia and the western areas which would become West Virginia. Opposition to the resolutions also existed in the northern counties of the state, the piedmont region, the eastern shore, and a scattering of other areas. The final Senate vote on the resolutions (see Map VI) illustrated the geographical breakdown even more clearly. Opposition to the resolutions came from a block of counties in the Valley of Virginia, but enlarged at times to include counties on both sides of the valley. The additional centers, like those in the House, appear in northern Virginia, the Eastern Shore, extreme northwestern Virginia, and south central Virginia.

The Senate debates and votes reveal feelings about the Cohens case similar to those evidenced in the House debates. A virtually unanimous opposition existed against the claim that the District lottery law superseded any state regulation. Even those who thought Congress could approve a lottery immune from state regulation were unsure such power had been given to the District in this instance. The debates also evidence considerable support

---

[68] House Journal (1820-1821), 201-202; Richmond Enquirer, February 20, 22, 1821; Virginia Patriot, February 20, 23, 1821.

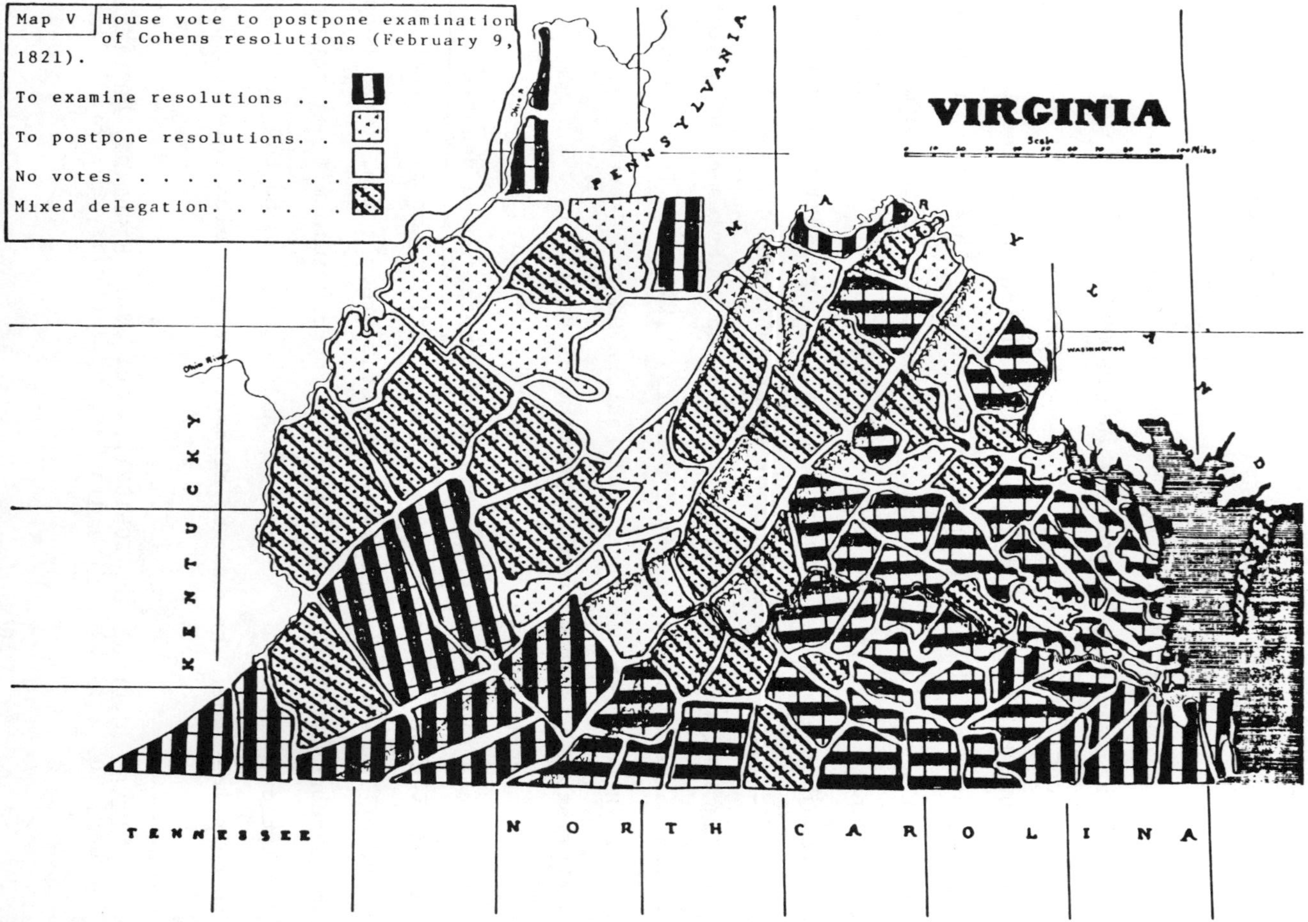
Map V
House vote to postpone examination of Cohens resolutions (February 9, 1821).
To examine resolutions . .
To postpone resolutions. .
No votes. . . . .
Mixed delegation. . . . . .
VIRGINIA
PENNSYLVANIA
MARYLAND
WASHINGTON
Ohio R.
Ohio River
KENTUCKY
TENNESSEE
NORTH CAROLINA

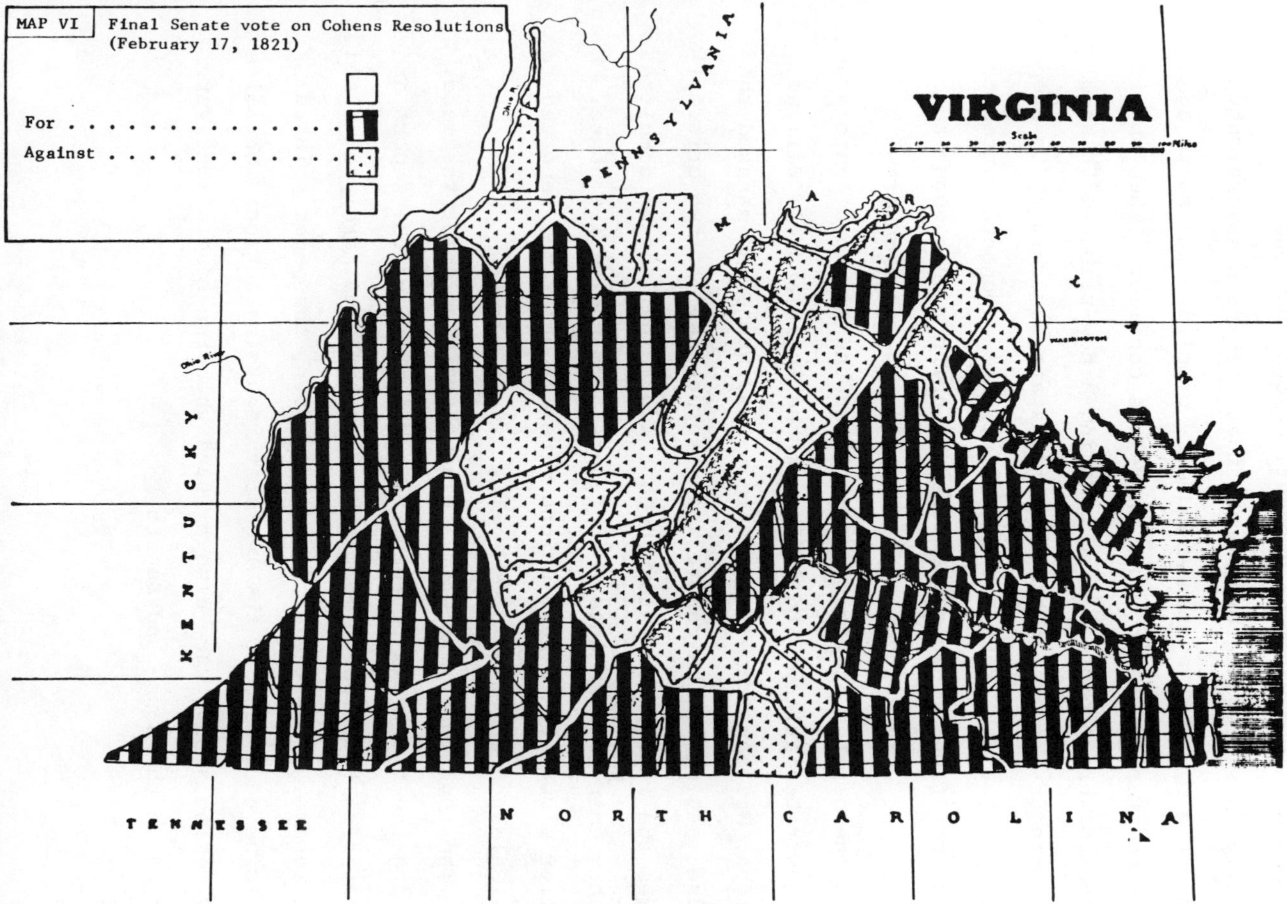
MAP VI
Final Senate vote on Cohens Resolutions
(February 17, 1821)
For
Against
VIRGINIA
Scale
100 Miles
PENNSYLVANIA
MARYLAND
WASHINGTON
Ohio R.
Ohio River
KENTUCKY
TENNESSEE
NORTH CAROLINA

for the basic principle of the Report of 1799 that a state could in some manner counter an unconstitutional national law. Finally, most legislators agreed that a state's sovereignty, supported by the Eleventh Amendment, precluded any suits against a state itself. Beyond that there was conflict. When specific remedies were proposed, from creating a new tribunal to handle state-federal conflicts to imposing state sovereignty to stop the case, objections arose. The resolutions' opponents wanted to be sure that federal decisions would be uniform throughout the nation and were reluctant to oppose the federal government.

The debates are instructive about the Richmond Junto's well-orchestrated attempts to influence the legislature. William Selden, William Roane's brother-in-law, wrote and managed the House battles on the report and resolutions. At two critical times the report was returned to the original Selden committee rather than face an uncertain future from the entire House. Even Miller's substitute resolutions were, at one time, reported to the Selden committee.

The Enquirer timed well its news articles about the case. During the two weeks between the publication of the report and debates on the report, most newspaper articles merely examined the report. When the debate slowed down, the paper printed articles addressed to the legislature urging action. Articles advocating action were also printed when the resolutions were passed in the House and Senate.

The prominence of Junto members in the *Cohens* debate does not necessarily mean that it was a Junto measure foisted upon the legislature by the undemocratic manipulations of the Richmond Junto. Support for the *Cohens* Resolutions, as has been shown, was much broader than the Junto. Opposition to the measures also included some who by family ties might have been expected to support them. One delegate often identified as a Junto member, Richard Morris, led the movement to substitute Miller's resolutions for the Selden report. Another delegate, John Barbour, cousin to Philip P. Barbour, who might have been expected to support the motion because of family ties, was actually the foremost advocate of an indefinite postponement.

The careful management evidenced in the House seems to have been absent in the Virginia Senate deliberations. The upper house of the legislature quickly changed the report to remove most House of Delegates objections. The resulting report and resolutions were almost entirely a Senate creation, but were quickly agreed to by the House, who, it appears, were more concerned that the legislature take a stand on the case than that the Selden report be approved as written.

The legislative results show the delegates' concern about the *Cohens* case, but a lack of agreement about how the state should oppose the case. Many legislators were reluctant to propose a specific remedy until the Court made its decision. The Virginia legislature did go on record supporting certain state rights political principles, and reports of their debates helped inform Virginians about the case. The legislature now waited for the Supreme Court, which had just begun hearing the case, to hand down its decision.

CHAPTER IV

THE SUPREME COURT

Legal scholars and historians have analyzed the arguments in Cohens v. Virginia, and especially John Marshall's decision. Earlier studies, however, have failed to fully appreciate the political climate in which the case was appealed, nor have they explored the status of District of Columbia laws as a factor in shaping the highly political decision.

The Constitution granted Congress the authority "to exercise exclusive legislation in all cases whatsoever" over the District of Columbia. District laws, therefore, offered the possibility that Congress might expand and extend federal power by chartering national agencies based in the District. Congress might organize, for example, a national bank in the District with power to operate in any state. A broad construction of the Constitution and later political and constitutional developments made the expansion of federal power by this method unnecessary, but in 1821, congressional power over the District offered what might have been an important grant of federal power. The broad bi-partisan opposition in the Virginia legislature to the interpretation, combined with a lack of congressional support for the construction, made it possible that a decision upholding the District's lottery law over Virginia's new lottery statute might have provoked a constitutional amendment.

I

Before examining the arguments presented to the Supreme Court and the Court's decisions in greater detail, it is important to review quickly the chronology of the case and backgrounds of the lawyers appearing before the Court. Virginia's two counsels, Philip P. Barbour and Alexander Smyth, appeared before the clerk of the Court February 6, 1821, to be admitted to practice before the Court, and then waited as bad weather and deep snows delayed the justices and the opening of the new session.[1]

The Cohens case was among the first called up, and after an examination of the Norfolk Court record, formal arguments began February 13, 1821. Barbour and Smyth presented a motion to dismiss the case because of a lack of jurisdiction, and then spent most of the day arguing against the Court's right to hear the case. Philip P. Barbour, who initiated arguments February 13, 1821, came from a distinguished political family. He was elected Speaker of the United States House of Representatives later in 1821, and was appointed in 1836 to the United States Supreme Court. Fellow House member William Plumer Jr., described Barbour as, "of all men in the House, the most subtle and acute logician--He is never better pleased than when splitting hairs

---

[1]"Minutes of the Supreme Court of the United States of America," February 6, 1821, Minute Book C, 151-152, National Archives. See also Richmond Compiler, January 26, 1821, Alexandria Gazette, January 27, 1821.

and indulging in nice metaphysical distinctions--He is however a very able man."[2] Hugh Blair Grigsby, Virginia author and legislator, affirmed Plumer's characterization.

> His appearance is unfavourable, and he is decidely [sic] an ugly man, but he is overpowering in logic. His voice is harsh, his manner tolerable, but his logic excellent. A quick, very rapid speaker; condensing his thoughts much.

He is "almost unrivalled in the powers of his mind, and incorruptible integrity."[3] Alexander Smyth, Virginia's other counsel was also a distinguished lawyer. Born in Ireland, Smyth subsequently served as Inspector General of the United States Army. He represented Southwest Virginia in the House of Representatives, and his views of the Constitution and the powers of the states were even more state rightist than Barbour's.

Nearly a week passed before David B. Ogden and William Pinkney, representing the lottery promoters, answered the Virginia arguments on February 19, 1821. David B. Ogden, who spoke first for the Cohen brothers, was one of the country's most distinguished constitutional lawyers. Ogden did not hold public office, but practiced before the Supreme Court for more than 25 years. William Pinkney, the Cohens' other lawyer, in contrast, held a number of impressive governmental positions. He was elected United States Senator from Maryland, served briefly as

---

[2]William Plumer, Jr., to William Plumer, February 12, 1820, _The Missouri Compromises and Presidential Politics 1820-1825, From the Letters of William Plumer, Junior_ ed. Everett S. Brown (St. Louis, 1926), 9.

[3]Hugh Blair Grigsby, "Sketches of Men of the Constitutional Convention, 1829-30," _Virginia Magazine of History and Biography_, LXI (July 1953), 331.

Attorney General of the United States, and served with distinction as United States Minister to England and Russia. Pinkney, perhaps the most celebrated constitutional lawyer then practicing, often attracted a large following when he appeared before the Court. In his "Hampton" papers reviewing the Cohens case, Charles Hammond critically described the scene.

> If Mr. Pinckney [sic] wishes to play the principal character in an oratorical exhibition, he always makes the hall of the Supreme Court his theatre. The Intelligencer gravely announces that upon such a day Mr Pinckney will make a speech. It is fashionable to hear Mr. Pinckney [sic] make a set speech, so that all the beauty, if not all the intelligence, of the city, crowd the hall. Mr. Pinckney [sic] enters a la dandy, makes his bow to the audience, and then to the court, who sit as kind of managers of the farce. Five or six hours are consumed, part in traversing the bar, part in argument, part in rhodomontade. The ladies go home marvellously delighted.[4]

William Wirt, a long time adversary of Pinkney, was kinder in his final estimation of Pinkney. "Yet Pinkney was a great man--on a set occasion, The greatest I think, at our bar.. . He was an excellent lawyer."[5]

Pinkney's arguments did not end official debate on the Court's jurisdiction. The next day, February 20, 1821, Philip P. Barbour gave Virginia's final rebuttal. His arguments are mentioned in contemporary newspaper accounts, the official docket of the case, and the Court's minutes, but do not appear separately in the case's official report. An examination of the

---

[4]Charles Hammond, Review of the Opinion of the Supreme Court of the United States, in the Case of Cohens vs. Virginia. . . . (Steubenville, Ohio, 1821), 58.

[5]William Wirt to Francis W. Gilmer, March 9, 1822, F. W. Gilmer Collection, University of Virginia Library.

Wheaton report indicates that the last four pages of Barbour's initial argument are, in fact, that rebuttal.[6] Barbour's rebuttal goes beyond the previous discussion of the Court's jurisdiction to examine the merits of the case. Perhaps knowing that his instructions would not allow him to appear before the Court during the argument on merits, Barbour still wanted his arguments made part of the case's record.

Barbour's presentation ended Virginia's participation in the case. Barbour and Smyth followed their instructions to debate only the court's jurisdiction. Barbour and Smyth then waited almost two weeks for the Court's decision. Before delivering a decision on the Court's jurisdiction, the judges agreed to hear arguments on the case's merits. By the time the Court agreed to hear those arguments, many observers had correctly guessed that the Court would uphold both the Court's jurisdiction and the Virginia fine. Alexander Smyth wrote Governor Thomas Mann Randolph on February 27, 1821, that: "It is confidently expected that the court will assume jurisdiction; and decide that there is not error in the judgment rendered by the borrough [sic] court of Norfolk."[7] Charles Hammond, an Ohioan, later wrote that "after

---

[6]Ibid., 349-344, "Minutes of the Supreme Court," Book C., 171, "Dockets of the Supreme Court," Vol. C, 1151, National Archives; Richmond Compiler, February 23, 1821; Virginia Patriot and Daily Commercial Advertiser, February 23, 1821.

[7]Alexander Smyth to Governor Thomas Mann Randolph, February 27, 1821, Executive papers, incoming, Virginia State Library, William Plumer, Jr., wrote the same speculation to his father two days earlier. See William Plumer, Jr., to William Plumer, February 25, 1821, Everett Brown (ed.) Missouri Compromises 41-42.

Mr. Pinckney's [sic] declaration that he would make no argument upon the merits, it seemed to be very well understood that the judgment was to be affirmed."[8] Hammond criticized the Court for ruling on the merits so that "the venders of the lottery tickets [could] know whether they were or were not as supreme as the bank of the United States!" The decision on the merits, Hammond intimated, was also to help "allay the apprehension" that a decision upholding the Court's jurisdiction would excite in Virginia.[9]

Arguments before the Court on the case's merits were brief in comparison with the jurisdiction debates. Daniel Webster, counsel for New York in a similar case defending a New York lottery law, represented the Virginia point of view Friday, March 2, 1821, while Attorney General William Wirt, another new participant, joined David B. Ogden in presenting the lottery vender's position.

The Supreme Court's decision on jurisdiction quickly followed the final pleadings. The Court delivered its opinion March 3, 1821, one day after the arguments on the merits. Chief Justice John Marshall required two hours to read the lengthy decision, which fills fifty-five pages in the Wheaton report. The decision is one of Marshall's most important, and shows the care he spent during the nearly two week period between the

---

[8]Charles Hammond, Review of Supreme Court, 58.

[9]Ibid., 58-59.

jurisdiction arguments and the decision.[10] After "the most deliberate consideration of which we are capable," the Court "unanimously" decided that "the objections to its jurisdiction are not sustained and that the motion ought to be overruled. Motion denied."[11]

With the Court's jurisdiction safely defended, Marshall and the Court quickly resolved the case's merits. Marshall delivered the Court's short decision upholding the state fine the next working day, Monday, March 5, 1821. Marshall's urgency is evident not only by the speed with which the decision was written, but by its delivery on the same day Marshall administered the oath of office to James Monroe as he began his second presidential term. Virginia could prohibit the sale of Washington lottery tickets, the Court said, not because of any weakness in congressional power over the District of Columbia, but because Congress had not stipulated that this particular law superseded state regulation.

II

The central objection Barbour and Smyth raised to the Supreme Court's jurisdiction in the case mirrored a concern expressed many times during the past few months in Virginia--that a state was a party to a suit against its will. Barbour clearly outlined his objections:

---

[10]Robert Faulkner calls the Cohens opinion "the most judicious and eloquent of his [Marshall's] opinions." Robert K. Faulkner, The Jurisprudence of John Marshall (Princeton, 1968), 104.

[11]6 Wheaton, 429.

> It is an axiom in politics, that a sovereign and independent state is not liable to the suit of any individual, nor amenable to any judicial power, without its own consent. All the states of this Union were sovereign and independent, before they became parties to the federal compact; hence, I infer that the judicial power of the United States would not have extended to the states, if it had not been so extended to them, *co nomine*, upon the fact of the constitution.[12]

An examination of the Constitution, he reported, reveals no such whole-sale grant. It grants power to the Supreme Court only in very limited cases when states are involved--controversies between two or more states, between a State and a citizen of another state, and between a state and foreign citizens or states.[13] No provision is made for a citizen to sue his own state in that court.

Smyth agreed. The basic question is one of sovereignty. "Shall the states be denied the power of judging of their own laws?"[14] An essential part of sovereignty is the ability to pass and enforce laws. The states had such power before the Constitution was adopted, and retain it now. The Constitution itself recognizes state sovereignty by providing that treason can be committed against a state. The Constitution, Smyth maintained, unlike the Articles of Confederation, does not allow the general government to act upon the state governments. Both governments now work directly upon the people. Congress has "no power to prescribe to the state legislature a legislative act.

---

[12] *Ibid.*, 303.

[13] *Ibid.*

[14] *Ibid.*, 327.

This government cannot prescribe an executive act to the executive of a state, a legislative act to the legislature of a state, or (as I contend) a judicial act to the judiciary of a state."[15]

Smyth opposed the legality of an appeal from a state court to the Supreme Court. Barbour did not oppose such an appeal in his arguments, even allowing such appeals for the sake of argument at one point. Smyth said the question had not been settled. "Federal judicial power is authorized to correct the errors of federal judicial power. I contend, that in no case can the federal courts revise the decisions of the state courts."[16] While it is true that the Supreme Court can reverse unconstitutional acts of a state executive or legislature, this gives it no power over state courts.

> When the federal courts declare an act of a state legislature unconstitutional, or an act of the state executive unlawful, they exercise no higher authority than the state courts exercise, who will not only declare an act of the state legislature, but even an act of Congress, unconstitutional and void.[17]

The Constitution, Smyth noted, contained no provisions to allow appeals from a state court. The Supreme Court cannot require a state to grant a re-trial or to make a federal reversal of a state decision part of the state's legal record. The Constitution makes no mention of any supervision federal courts

---

[15]Ibid., 314.

[16]Ibid., 314.

[17]Ibid., 321.

can exercise over state courts. State courts, in fact, are not even mentioned. "If it had been intended to give appellate jurisdiction over the state courts, the proper expressions would have been used."[18] Smyth feared a "complete consolidation of the states, so far as respects judicial power," if the appellate jurisdiction over state courts were upheld.[19]

David B. Ogden firmly rejected both Virginia contentions regarding the complete sovereignty of a state. He refused to discuss the legality of an appeal from a state court to the Supreme Court, saying the question had been settled in Martin v Hunter. He then argued vigorously that the states were not immune from all Supreme Court suits. We deny, that since the establishment of the national constitution, there is any such thing as a sovereign state, independent of the Union."[20] The people are sovereign, and they in the Constitution took many powers away from the state governments, "so that they are no longer sovereign and independent in that sense which exempts them from all coercion by judicial tribunals."[21] Whether a state has exceeded constitutional limits is a question the people entrusted to the Supreme Court, not to state legislatures or judiciaries.

William Pinkney spent most of his presentation on other areas, ending with the question, "Does the fact of a state being

---

[18]Ibid., 318.

[19]Ibid., 320.

[20]Ibid., 347.

[21]Ibid.

a party prosecutor in the state court, make this case an exception, and take it out of the general rule?"[22] Pinkney answered no.

> The suability of the states might have been dispensed with, and the constitution still be safe. But the judicial control of the Union over state encroachments and usurpations, was indispensable to the sovereignty of the constitution--to its integrity--to its very existence. Take it away, and the Union becomes again a loose and feeble confederacy--a government of false and foolish confidence--a delusion and a mockery.[23]

If state cases were exempt from appeal, the state could effectively take away from the Supreme Court the examination of almost any area by initiating such actions in state courts. This fact, combined with the Constitution's seeming lack of concern about giving the Supreme Court jurisdiction over cases involving the states, and the respect a writ of error gives state sovereignty by acting only upon a state court and not upon the state itself, convinced Pinkney that the Constitution provided no exemption to the Supreme Court's jurisdiction in this case.

The question of state sovereignty and state immunity to Supreme Court suits became a major section in John Marshall's decision. Marshall agreed with the Virginia contention that a sovereign state cannot be sued without its consent. The Court must therefore examine the Constitution and its background to determine what has or has not been surrendered. Marshall's decision outlined his version of the Constitution's adoption.

---

[22]Ibid., 370.

[23]Ibid., 371.

> The American States, as well as the American people, have believed a close and firm Union to be essential to their liberty and to their happiness. They have been taught by experience, that this Union cannot exist without a government for the whole; and they have been taught by the same experience that this government would be a mere shadow, that must disappoint all their hopes, unless invested with large portions of that sovereignty which belongs to independent states. Under the influence of this opinion, and thus instructed by experience, the American people, in the conventions of their respective states, adopted the present constitution.[24]

The final relationship between the states and the general government is exemplified in the clause making the Constitution and laws of the United States the "Supreme law of the land." The Constitution thus "marks with lines too strong to be mistaken, the characteristic distinction between the government of the Union and those of the states."[25] Marshall then examined national powers and state limitations in a section of the decision which Virginia found particularly upsetting during later newspaper reviews of the decision.

> With ample powers conferred to this supreme government, for those interesting purposes, are connected many express and important limitations on the sovereignty of the states, which are made for the same purposes.

The provisions on war and commerce are two such limitations.

> but in addition to these, the sovereignty of the state is surrendered in many instances where the surrender can only operate to the benefit of the people, and where, perhaps, no other power is conferred on Congress than a conservative power to maintain the principles established in the constitution. . . When we consider the situation of the government of the Union and of a state, in relation to each other; the nature of our constitution; the subordination of the state governments to that constitution; the great

---

[24]<u>Ibid.</u>, 380-381.

[25]<u>Ibid.</u>, 381.

> purpose for which jurisdiction over all cases arising under the constitution and laws of the United States is confided to the judicial department, are we at liberty to insert in this general grant, an exception of those case in which a state may be a party? . . . We think not.[26]

"Marshall had been Chief Justice of the United States for twenty years," Albert J Beveridge wrote in 1919, "and these were the boldest and most extreme words that he had spoken during that period."[27]

Marshall then treated the broad defense claim that the Supreme Court's appellate jurisdiction "cannot be exercised, in any case, over the judgment of a state court."[28] The question Marshall examined is essentially the same as the earlier question in Martin v Hunter's Lessee. That decision had not been enforced, however, and the Virginia Court of Appeals met and formally declared it invalid. Joseph Story's Martin v Hunter's Lessee decision, considered one of his finest decisions, involved more technical disputes than Marshall's Cohens decision, which is a broad statement of the nature of the government containing some of Marshall's most nationalistic pronouncements.[29]

Marshall found no basis for the Virginia counsel's argument that state and federal courts are as separate as the courts of

---

[26]Ibid., 382.

[27]Albert J. Beveridge, The Life of John Marshall (Boston, 919), IV, 349.

[28]6 Wheaton, 413.

[29]James McClellan, a recent biographer of Story, says the Hunter decision "was the most important decision handed down by Story during his entire career." James McClellan, Joseph Story and the American Constitution (Norman, 1971), 246.

two foreign countries. Only a misreading of the Constitution or a misapplication of theories about state and federal relations could sustain such a view. Instead, "the United States form, for many, and for most important purposes, a single nation." The country is one in war', making peace, in commerce, and in "many other respects." "The government which is alone capable of controlling and managing their interests in all these respects is the government of the Union."[30]

> The people have declared, that in the exercise of all powers given for these objects it is Supreme. It can, then, in effecting these objects, legitimately control all individuals or governments within the American territory.[31]

The Constitution and laws of the United States should be interpreted by the United States judiciary, Marshall continued, but if the states are able to hear cases involving the Constitution without any appeals to the Supreme Court, it becomes the state courts, and not federal courts, who interpret the Constitution.

> The necessity of uniformity, as well as correctness in expounding the constitution and laws of the United States, would itself ,suggest, the propriety of vesting in some single tribunal the power of deciding, in the last resort, all cases in which they are involved.[32]

Marshall then used history to substantiate Supreme Court power to review state court decisions. The Constitution was created to give the general government more power. Under the

---

[30]6 Wheaton, 413-414.

[31]Ibid., 414.

[32]Ibid., 416.

Articles of Confederation, national courts could review prize cases appealed from state courts. In addition to the powers possessed by the federal courts under the Articles of Confederation, the Constitution gave the Supreme Court power to hear cases involving the Constitution and laws of the nation, and to exercise that power by appeal.

Marshall gathered contemporary evidence to show that the Supreme Court's appellate jurisdiction was intended to extend to state as well as inferior federal courts. The Federalist recognized the principle: "The object of appeal, not the tribunals from which it is to be made are alone contemplated."[33] The Judiciary Act of 1789 was quoted to show the framers' intentions.

> Not a single individual, so far as is known, supposed that part of the act which gives the Supreme Court appellate jurisdiction over the judgments of the state courts in the cases therein specified, to be unauthorized by the constitution.[34]

Supreme Court judgments upholding that review power have, with one exception, Marshall continued, been universally accepted despite the reversal of several state decisions. "This concurrence of statesmen, of legislators, and of judges, in the same construction of the constitution, may justly inspire some confidence in that construction."[35] An examination of the great purposes for which the Constitution was formed does not reveal

---

[33] Ibid., 419.

[34] Ibid., 420.

[35] Ibid., 420.

anything "extravagantly absurd" in giving the Supreme Court appeals in cases involving the nation. Therefore, the case must rest upon the words of the document itself, Marshall concluded, and these arguments have already been examined in Martin v Hunter.

III

Closely associated with Virginia's central objections to the Supreme Court's jurisdiction in the case--that the state was not liable to be sued against its will and that the Supreme Court could not review decisions from state courts--were a number of constitutional and judicial obstacles to the claimed authority, most of which were ultimately based on a concept of sovereign immunity and a closely balanced federal system. Barbour and Smyth asserted that the Court could not review the case for at least three such reasons. First, a review of the case would violate the Constitution's grant of jurisdiction to the Supreme Court. Second, the review of a criminal case would counter several Supreme Court precedents, and finally the review would violate the spirit of the Eleventh Amendment

Philip P. Barbour objected to the Court's jurisdiction because the Constitution did not give the Supreme Court appellate jurisdiction in cases involving states. In the third article of the Constitution, the Supreme Court is given original jurisdiction in all cases involving ambassadors, other foreign representatives, and states. In all other cases, the Court has appellate jurisdiction. That distinction was the basis for the Court's landmark decision, in Marbury v Madison (1803), declaring a congressional law unconstitutional. In that case, the Court declared invalid that part of the Judiciary Act of 1789 which authorized the Court to issue a writ of mandamas, because the mandamas was an original form used in a case where the Constitution gives the Court only appellate authority.

> If Congress remains at liberty to give this court appellate jurisdiction, where the constitution has declared their jurisdiction shall be original; and original jurisdiction, where the constitution has declared their jurisdiction shall be appellate, the distribution of jurisdiction made in the constitution, is form without substance.[36]

The Court maintained that "the plain import of the words seem to be, that in one class of cases, its jurisdiction is original, not appellate; in the other, it is appellate, not original."[37] The Virginia congressman continued that in this case a state was a party, and the case was brought to the Supreme Court by writ of error, "which is surely appellate jurisdiction." Since the Court has only original jurisdiction in cases involving the states, "this court cannot take jurisdiction in this way, if they could take it at all."[38] The Cohens case, involving a state criminal code can only originate in a state court. Since the Court has no appellate jurisdiction in cases involving the states, the Court

---

[36]Ibid., 300.

[37]Ibid., 301.

[38]Ibid.

can have neither original or appellate jurisdiction, and the case is outside the court's purview.

Court Supporters argued that the Court's power extended to all cases where the subject matter deals with a constitutional question, with no reference to the parties involved. It is, however, possible, Barbour countered, to list specific cases falling within constitutional subject matter which the Court cannot review. He cited two examples: If a state should give titles of nobility or engage in war, the violations to the Constitution would be obvious and great, but the Court could not compel obedience to the Constitution.

> It will be remembered by the court, that the words are not all questions, but all cases. Although, therefore, a question may arise, yet before there can be a case there must be parties over whom the court can take jurisdiction; and if there be no such parties, the court cannot act upon the subject, though the question may arise, though it may be clearly of a judicial nature, and though there may be the clearest violation of the constitution.[39]

Barbour's contention that the Supreme Court had only original jurisdiction in cases involving a state, buttressed by John Marshall's decision in Marbury v Madison, received lengthy review by David B. Ogden and William Pinkney, and in Marshall's decision. The arguments ultimately appealed to the intent of the authors of the Constitution. All the participants, including John Marshall, agreed that a state was not suable without its consent. There was little agreement, however, as to whether.the states intended to surrender their immunity to suits only in those cases

---

[39] Ibid., 305.

involving states specified in the third article of the Constitution, or agreed to make a broader surrender and become subject to "all Cases, in Law and Equity, arising under this Constitution, the Laws of the United States, and Treaties made, or which shall be made, under their Authority."[40]

David B. Ogden was as adamant as Barbour had been. The Constitution, he maintained, gave the Supreme Court jurisdiction in all cases arising under the Constitution and laws of the land. "The term 'all cases,' means all without exemption."[41] Ogden further asserted that the later clause giving the Supreme Court original jurisdiction in cases involving the states "does not limit, but extends the judicial power of the Union."[42] William Pinkney agreed. The "obvious answer" to Barbour's contention was that the present case is based not upon the section of the Constitution giving the Supreme Court original jurisdiction in cases involving states, but upon the Court's auxiliary power to review all cases involving the Constitution and laws of the United States.[43] The arguments about original and appellate jurisdiction, Ogden added, are immaterial because the Supreme Court's limitation to original jurisdiction in cases involving a state was placed in the Constitution only to prevent a state from being sued in an inferior national court. The case is outside

---

[40]Ibid., 380-382.

[41]Ibid., 348.

[42]Ibid.

[43]Ibid., 368.

that concern. Besides, appeals in cases involving United States laws do not subject the states to suits, since such cases originate in state courts, and a state cannot be sued in its own courts. There certainly are, Ogden agreed, cases in which the Constitution may be violated and the Supreme Court remain helpless to remedy the violation. But whenever a case presents itself for deliberation, "or whenever the state tribunals take cognizance of it, whether properly or not, the appellate power of this court may intervene, and protect the constitution and laws of the Union from violation."[44] Under some circumstances, a state can violate the Constitution without being called to account by the Supreme Court, but as soon as they use the state judiciary to enforce such violations, they are subject to the Supreme Court's review. Pinkney added that "Many unlawful things cannot be restrained by judicature; but does it follow that where they can be restrained, they shall not?"[45]

Both sides realized the massive impact the decision would have on the Supreme Court's jurisdiction. The question was much broader than whether cases can be appealed from a state court to the Supreme Court. The Court must decide if it had power to review both civil and criminal cases instigated by a state in a state court. Smyth makes a strong case for the exclusion of criminal cases from the Supreme Court's review. Such review "would degrade the state governments, and devest them of every

---

[44]Ibid., 350.

[45]Ibid., 373.

pretension to sovereignty" and present a number of other problems.[46] Such appeals, involving aliens and citizens of other states, could be made in direct opposition to the Eleventh Amendment. Appeals in jury trials could be included even though federal courts do not permit such appeals because the defendant is guaranteed a trial in the District where the crime is committed. At least one justice of the Supreme Court so ruled, Smyth continued. Justice Johnson wrote that "the courts of the United States are vested with no power to scrutinize into the proceedings of the state courts, in criminal cases."[47]

Ogden countered by denying that the Cohens case was a criminal case. The state had not made the sale of lottery tickets a misdemeanor. They merely imposed a penalty, and the case is an attempt to recover that penalty. But if the case were a criminal one, it would make no difference. The Constitution gave the Supreme Court power in all cases involving the Constitution, laws or treaties of the United States, and all cases includes criminal as well as civil cases.[48] Pinkney's discussion of Supreme Court review of criminal cases is among his least effective. He attempted to explain the Court's decision in the Hunter case, which concluded a section on the problems of examining state criminal prosecutions involving constitutional questions by saying: "in respect to criminal prosecutions, the

---

[46] Ibid., 321.

[47] Ibid., 323; 4 Wheaton, 377.

[48] 6 Wheaton, 351.

difficulty seems admitted to be insurmountable."[49] "What difficulty?" Pinkney asked. "The difficulty of controlling them by the courts of the United States without the aid of a writ of error, because those courts could take no original cognizance of this description of cases, and they could not be removed before judgment."[50]

The major thrust of Ogden and Pinkney's arguments, however, ignored the specific problems involved in allowing appeals in state criminal cases and concentrated on the necessity of such appeals "in order to produce uniformity in the construction of the constitution."[51] Pinkney justified the power because of certain cases, like the present, which must be appealed because they "cannot . . . form the subject of, or create subjects for, its original jurisdiction. The courts of the United States can here exert only a controlling or restraining power for the protection of the rights of the Union, and this can only be done by appeal or writ of error."[52] Pinkney continued that if the Virginians were right that appeals in state cases were unconstitutional, it illustrated clearly the need for a writ of error which is not an appellate action. "Take away both, and the

---

[49]1 Wheaton, 311; 6 Wheaton, 369.

[50]6 Wheaton, 369.

[51]Ibid., 349-350.

[52]Ibid., 368.

constitution, laws, and treaties of the Union lie at the mercy of the state judicatures."[53]

Whether a writ of error constituted a case as defined by the Eleventh Amendment became one of the central issues in the examination of the final objection to the Court's jurisdiction--the Eleventh Amendment. The Eleventh Amendment prohibits "any suit in law or equity commenced or prosecuted against one of the United States by Citizens of another State, or by Citizens or Subjects of any Foreign State." William Pinkney argued that although a writ of error might sometimes technically be called a suit, it was only a suit if something is restored and in this case nothing is being restored. Further, the writ does not act directly upon the state. It is only a notice to the state telling of the case but "leaving it at her option voluntarily to appear."[54] Because the writ works only upon the state court it is no different than the many private suits between individuals which call into question state statutes. Alexander Smyth disagreed. Although there seemed to be some disagreement about whether a writ of error should be considered a suit, "This seems expressly to extend to this writ of error, which, although not a suit in law commenced against a state, is a suit in law prosecuted against a state."[55] This is true legally because "a release of all suits is a release of a writ of error, and

---

[53]Ibid., 356.

[54]Ibid., 366.

[55]Ibid., 135.

consequently, a writ of error is 'a suit in law' and can-not be prosecuted against a state."[56] Ogden and Pinkney argued that the case was not, in the words of the amendment, a suit commenced or prosecuted against a state by the citizen of another state or country, and so the amendment had no application. The amendment, Ogden argued, applied only to jurisdiction based on the character of the parties, and had no effect upon those cases based on treaties, laws, or the Constitution.[57] Philip P. Barbour countered that the amendment did not apply because the power to review the case had never been given to the Supreme Court. Could it be seriously argued that a citizen retained any power to sue his own state? It was true that the Eleventh Amendment mentioned only subjects of another state or foreign country, but the language was not used to retain a citizen's power to sue his own state, but because "it was only to them (citizens of another state or country) that the privilege of being parties in a controversy with a state, had been extended in the text of the constitution." "It was only from them, therefore, that it was necessary to take away that privilege."[58]

John Marshall's decision painstakingly examined the Supreme Court's appellate jurisdiction in order to counter the Virginia view of the third article of the Constitution. The Supreme Court's power, Marshall maintained, can be divided into the two

---

[56]<u>Ibid.</u>, 316.

[57]<u>Ibid.</u>, 341-342, 348.

[58]<u>Ibid.</u>, 306.

categories used during arguments on the case: those arising from the case's subject matter (involving the Constitution, treaties or laws of the United States) and those arising because of the parties involved. The two powers are separate. The provisions giving the Court jurisdiction over the cases involving certain parties is an additional grant of power and cannot limit cases coming to the Court because of their subject matter. The Court's power to hear all cases involving the Constitution and laws of the United States is made without any reference to the parties. "If there be any exception, it is to be implied against the express words of the article."[59] The parties to the case, Marshall continued, generally determine whether the Court can exercise original or appellate jurisdiction. If a case involved both a subject and parties that are fit for adjudication, the "conclusion seems irresistible" that the framers desired to give the Supreme Court appellate jurisdiction when the case came to it by the nature of the case, and original when it came by the identity of the parties. Otherwise, the Court could not hear cases originating in state courts.

> In such a case, the jurisdiction can be exercised only in its appellate form. To deny its exercise in this form is to deny its existence, and would be to construe a clause, dividing the power of the Supreme Court, in such a manner as in a considerable degree to defeat the power itself.[60]

The Court's earlier ruling in Marbury v Madison caused Marshall only momentary embarrassment. Every legal decision, the

---

[59] Ibid., 378.

[60] Ibid., 394.

Chief Justice wrote, can only be followed in the specific points at issue. Other parts are dicta and "ought not to control the judgment in a subsequent suit."[61] The Marbury case decided whether Congress can define the Supreme Court's power without reference to the Constitution. It was claimed that Congress could give the Court original jurisdiction when only appellate was authorized. The Court said Congress could not. The ruling, Marshall admitted, went beyond the case itself when it ruled that the affirmative words in the Constitution give a negative meaning to other jurisdictional grants to the Court. The Court laid down a principle "which is generally correct in terms much broader than the decision, and not only much broader than the reasoning with which that decision is supported, but in some instances contradictory to its principle."[62] The attempt is now made to use that reasoning in another case "in which the negative, or exclusive sense, is to be so used as to defeat some of the great objects of the article."[63] "To this construction the court cannot give its assent." The Marbury case must be understood in its own terms, terms which "in no degree affect the decision in that case, or the tenor of its reasoning."[64] The Constitution gives the Supreme Court appellate power in all cases involving the Constitution and laws of the United States. "The words are

---

[61] Ibid., 399.

[62] Ibid., 401.

[63] Ibid.

[64] Ibid., 402.

broad enough to comprehend all cases of this description, in whatever court they may be decided."[65]

Marshall next countered Philip P. Barbour's argument that there are cases where the Constitution can be violated, but the Supreme Court has no jurisdiction. It is true, Marshall conceded, that the Court cannot stop the states from laying an excise tax or printing paper money, but if a state, in either case, tries to use the judiciary to enforce the collection or acceptance of the unconstitutional act, the case is similar to the one now before the Court and can be appealed. The Supreme Court could not interfere unless a case is presented which turns on the correct interpretation of the Constitution. But just because the Constitution may be violated, and no remedy provided, should not require that "an interpretation more restrictive than the words themselves import ought to be given to this article."[66]

Marshall then examined the final objection to the court's jurisdiction because a state was party to the case--the Eleventh Amendment. That amendment was designed to protect the states from law suits seeking to recover debts against them rather than to protect the state's sovereign immunity. The states showed their lack of concern with state sovereignty when they did not remove state liability to all suits. Cases involving other states were not removed, because there was not much reason to

---

[65]Ibid., 416.

[66]6 Wheaton, 405.

fear that foreign or sister states would be creditors to any considerable amount."[67] The states also allowed jurisdiction in those cases which "might be essential to the preservation of peace."[68] Marshall could not, or would not, concede that sovereign immunity played any part in the amendment. A general state interest might be manifest to avoid debt suits, "but no interest could be felt in so changing the relations between the whole and its parts, as to strip the government of the means of protecting, by the instrumentality of its courts, the constitution and laws from active violation."[69]

The Eleventh Amendment also does not apply to this case, Marshall continued, because the writ of error used in it is not legally a suit. Amplifying Pinkney's argument, he quoted Blackstone and Coke to show that suits are "cases where the party suing claims to obtain something to which he has a right."[70] In a tortuously reasoned section which would later provoke his opponents, Marshall claimed that:

> This suit is not commenced nor prosecuted against a state. It is clearly in its commencement the suit of a state against an individual, which suit is transferred to this court, not for the purpose of asserting any claim against the state, but for the purpose of asserting a constitutional defense against a claim made by a state.[71]

---

[67] Ibid., 406.

[68] Ibid., 407.

[69] Ibid.

[70] Ibid., 408.

[71] Ibid., 409.

> A writ of error, then, is in the nature of a suit or action when it is to restore the party who obtains it to the possession of anything which is withheld from him, not when its operation is entirely defensive.[72]

The writ of error simply brought the record of the lower judgment to a higher court for "re-examination." No claim "of any description is asserted or prosecuted. . . . Essentially, it is an appeal on a single point."[73] The citation to the state was also not a summons, but a notice that the case's record is removed to another court. The party receiving it may appear or not appear. Failure to appear is not "considered a default" and does not bring a penalty.[74] Finally a writ of error was not a suit because a writ of error can be used against the United States, even though a suit cannot. After carefully limiting the definition of a suit, Marshall admitted that the definition was academic. "But should we in this be mistaken, the error does not affect the case now before the court."[75] He agreed with Pinkney and Ogden that if the writ of error were a suit, this suit was still not commenced or prosecuted against the state by the citizens of another state, or the subject of a foreign country.

Both Philip P. Barbour and Alexander Smyth listed a final objection to the Supreme Court's jurisdiction in the Cohens case--that the law authorizing the lottery was not a national law as

---

[72]Ibid., 409-410.

[73]Ibid., 410.

[74]Ibid., 411.

[75]Ibid., 412.

required by the Constitution or the 25th section of the Judiciary Act of 1789. The two Virginians included these arguments even though they were really arguments on the case's merits. Barbour examined the third article of the Constitution outlining the Supreme Court's jurisdiction. The Court is given jurisdiction involving the Constitution, laws, or treaties of the United States. No one, he presumed, would claim the jurisdiction in the Cohens case is based upon a treaty, so it must be based upon the Constitution or a law of the United States. The case does not arise under the Constitution, because it is not specified within the document, and Barbour denied that the lottery law was a law of the United States. "Now, it would sound curiously, to call a law passed for a district, not itself exalted to the dignity of a state, a law of the United States."[76]

Much of the confusion in the case, Smyth maintained, came from two specific constitutional grants of power to Congress. The first applied to all stat-s but gave Congress only specific, enumerated powers. The second power over the District gave Congress all authority over that area. District advocates have confused the two. They have enlarged the act for the District, which is made by the unlimited powers over a limited geographical area to an act of unlimited power over an unlimited geographical area. "Now a law over the states cannot be passed by a power to legislate over Columbia."[77] The power the Constitution grants

---

[76]Ibid., 292.

[77]Ibid., 336.

Congress over the District of Columbia is one allowing the District to establish local codes. These powers resemble those possessed by any state legislature. Such powers, however, are valid only within the jurisdiction of the state. No one would argue that Congress is given power over internal state legislation, and yet, this is what the lottery proponents claim. "The claim set up is a claIm of paramount power over the whole United States."[78]

Much of this debate, Smyth added, is purely academic because not only does Congress not have the power to compel ticket sales in other states, but Congress has not said that the tickets can be sold beyond the confines of the District. The legislation, as written, allows the tickets to be sold anywhere there is no legislation prohibiting such sales. Members of the District corporation "have no power to pass a law authorizing the sale of lottery tickets in Georgetown, much less have they the power to authorize the sale of them in a state, contrary to its laws."[79]

David Ogden, who represented the Cohen interests, admitted that his opponents might be correct--the lottery authorization might be a local ordinance and not a general United States law. But the only way to tell was to examine the Constitution. "If this law be thus limited in its operation, how is this to be discovered but by examining the Constitution? and how is this

---

[78]Ibid., 338.

[79]Ibid., 333, 344.

examination to be had but by taking jurisdiction of the case?"[80] The District is a complete creation of the Constitution, and the laws of Congress in relation to the District must be judged by the Supreme Court. "Are not the extent of the powers vested in Congress, and the manner in which these powers are to be executed, necessarily questions arising under the constitution?"[81] William Pinkney agreed with Ogden that "the question on this motion to dismiss the writ of error; is not whether the act of Congress is valid as against the act of Virginia; but whether that question is presented by the record, so that this court can determine it."[82] Pinkney went further. The Court's jurisdiction, he claimed, was not limited to the Constitution, treaties, or laws of the United States operating throughout the country. "It is a law of the United States, because it is passed by the legislative power of the United States."[83]

Pinkney chided his opponents for not realizing that although a local or territorial body passed a law, the impulse which set it in motion is the power of the nation. Whether this District law can bind the union is not settled, he continued, but "is the very question to be determined, when the merits come to be

---

[80]<u>Ibid.</u>, 345.

[81]<u>Ibid.</u>, 346.

[82]<u>Ibid.</u>, 362.

[83]<u>Ibid.</u>, 364.

discussed."[84] The Virginians discussed the case's merits to show that the jurisdiction should not be upheld. The two questions are distinct, and only the jurisdiction is now being debated.

John Marshall followed many of Pinkney's arguments in his decision. A case, he said, "may truly be said to arise under the constitution or a law of the United States, whenever its correct decision depends on the construction of either."[85] Congress "as the legislature of the Union," is given exclusive power over the District. While it is true that Congress does exercise exclusive powers over some areas and limited authority over other areas, its powers over the District are not completely analogous to a state legislature's powers. The same congressional power when applied to forts, arsenals, and dock yards is the basis for national laws governing the punishment of murder in those areas. These laws establish rules for the criminal's transportation away from the crime's locality, allow trial elsewhere, and provide rules governing executions in areas not controlled by the federal government. Such rules far exceed state authority, which cannot make laws which operate outside the state's confines. "The power vested in Congress, as the legislature of the United States, to legislate exclusively within any place ceded by a state, carries with it, as an incident, the right to make that power

---

[84]Ibid., 365.

[85]Ibid., 379.

effectual."[86] "Congress is not a local legislature, but exercises this particular power, like all its other powers, in its high character, as the legislature of the Union."[87]

Whether any particular law be designed to operate without the District or not, depends on the words of that law."[88] To see if he lottery law operates outside the District, the Constitution, congressional authority, and the specific law must be examined. It may be true, as the Virginians argue, that the law is confined to Washington, but that question concerns the case's merits, not the Court's jurisdiction. Many of the Virginia counsel 's arguments are "calculated to sustain their case upon its merits," rather than to show the lack of jurisdiction of the Court.

IV

Formal arguments on the merits of the case were brief and concentrated on the law establishing the Grand National Lottery and the constitutional provisions giving Congress power over the District of Columbia. David B. Ogden explained that congressional power over the District of Columbia was established to give protection and independence to Congress--certainly a national object. "The district was created only for national

---

[86]Ibid., 428.

[87]Ibid., 429.

[88]Ibid.

purposes, and every law passed for its government is peculiarly a national law."[89]

> The law in question is the expression of the national will on a national object. It is, then, an act of the general legislative power of the Union, and its operation must be co-extensive with the limits of the Union, unless it is limited to the District of Columbia in express terms, or from the nature of the power itself being incapable of acting without the district.[90]

Some provisions of the law in question are local, but not the power to establish lotteries "with the consent of the President." The power is clearly necessary and proper to carry out congressional power over the District of Columbia Congressional power to raise money for the District will be limited if the tickets cannot be sold everywhere. Such limitations may make the revenue raised inadequate, and the states will frustrate Congress in the exercise of a national power.

William Wirt, United States Attorney General, agreed that Congress had "acted in the name of the whole nation, and for a great national object."[91] The power Congress exercised over the District is more than the power exercised by the states controlling the District before it was given to the federal government. It was no longer just the powers exercised by Virginia and Maryland, "but the power of all the states."[92] Can a state, for example, tax other states or borrow money on their

---

[89] 6 Wheaton, 431.

[90] Ibid., 432.

[91] Ibid., 437.

[92] Ibid.

credit for the improvement of a city? Congress can and has done so. Congressional power over the District, it is true, differs from congressional power over the states. Congress' power is all powerful within the District, "yet it is not so circumscribed that it may not incidentally affect the states, although exerted for a local purpose, as it is called."[93] The law in question is for the national object of improving the nation's capital. This is confirmed by a provision of the law which requires the approval of the President of the United States. A purely local act does not require an appeal to higher authority.

Daniel Webster, the lone representative against lottery claims, spoke briefly, without great originality. His remarks did, however, summarize well several points made earlier by the two Virginians. Congress does not have power to establish a lottery extending throughout the nation, and the law in question does not claim to extend beyond Washington. The lottery authorization is included in an act "for the establishment of a local city government, . . . and the clause authorizing the establishment of lotteries is combined with other clauses of a mere municipal character."[94] It is therefore clear that Congress was enacting a local law restricted to the District. The law gives no hint that the lottery portion of the act is expected to extend beyond Washington. "It may be exercised within the city alone, and Congress has not said, and the court

---

[93]Ibid., 439.

[94]Ibid., 435.

cannot intend, that it is to be exercised in other parts of the Union."[95] The Constitution's supremacy clause does not apply to this law. That clause was inserted to provide priorities for conflicting state and federal laws upon the same people. District of Columbia laws, in this case at least, cannot come into conflict with state laws because laws for the District and for the states cannot work upon the same people. The lottery law in question is limited to Washington and does not even apply to other municipalities within the District "A law cannot exceed the authority of the law-giver," Webster concluded, "and that does not extend beyond the district."[96]

Speaking for a unanimous Court, Marshall explained that two questions must be explored concerning the lottery act: does it claim to authorize the sale of lottery tickets beyond Washington, and if it does, is it constitutional? If the law does not claim to give power beyond the District, Marshall continued, no inquiry will be made into Congress' constitutional power to grant such power since that discussion would be "merely speculative."[97] The Court, he continued, can find in this particular law "no expression which looks beyond the limits of the city."[98] The bill's major subject is a local matter-the organization of the city government, and the bill's provisions seem limited to the

---

[95]<u>Ibid.</u>

[96]<u>Ibid.</u>, 437.

[97]<u>Ibid.</u>, 441.

[98]<u>Ibid.</u>

city itself. If it were intended to extend the power beyond Washington's boundaries, "we should expect to find . . . some words indicating such intention."[99] Such positive authorization is especially necessary in this case because the law would supersede a state penal act. Interference with internal laws "is a very serious measure, which Congress cannot be supposed to adopt lightly, or inconsiderately." An act like the present one cannot be construed to thwart such state laws "unless its provisions were such as to render the construction inevitable."[100]

The Court then denied that the sale of lottery tickets outside Washington was essential to the lottery's success. Such power might facilitate ticket sales, but it does not follow that Congress intended to override state penal authority. Washington, "the great metropolis of the natior." is visited "by individuals from every part of the Union." Such visitors may freely purchase lottery tickets in Washington. It is true, Marshall continued, that the states cannot make illegal anything Congress declares may be legally sold, but this does not mean that Congress intended to make these tickets saleable when such sales conflict with local laws. A truly national lottery, the Court noted, would no doubt include presidential appointment of those running the lottery. "The whole subject would be under the control of

---

[99]Ibid., 442.

[100]Ibid., 443.

the government, or of persons appointed by the government."[101] The city government, however, directed the lottery in question and they can establish it or not as they see fit. The proceeds are to be used for local purposes. Presidential approval does not make the lottery a national lottery and the President has no direction of the project aside from his approval or non-approval.

The Court was careful to stress that the laws under consideration were "laws of universal obligation." The law was of universal obligation, but the specific powers given in any law must be determined by examining the law itself.

> Whether we consider the general character of a law incorporating a city, the objects for which such law is usually made, or the words in which this particular power is conferred, we arrive at the same result. The corporation was merely empowered to authorize the drawing of lotteries; and the mind of Congress was not directed to any provision for the sale of tickets beyond the limits of the corporation. That subject does not seem to have been taken into view. It is the unanimous opinion of the court, that the law cannot be construed to embrace it.[102]

John Marshall thus ruled for Virginia while relinquishing little he valued. Virginia, on the other hand, won the case while losing a five year battle with the Supreme Court over the interpretation of the Constitution.

---

[101] Ibid., 443.

[102] Ibid., 445.

CHAPTER V

SUPPORTERS AND OPPONENTS RESPOND

John Marshall's decision in Cohens v Virginia represented a compromise giving the Court jurisdiction while upholding the state's fine of the Cohens. The decision pleased neither state rights Virginians nor those supporting the Washington lottery. Despite such lack of support, there was no immediate outcry against the decision. Most early newspaper articles about the case were, in fact, limited to reports of the decisions or arguments used during the case, with little editorial comment. More partisan articles supporting or opposing the case came within several weeks and were initiated by unsigned political articles supporting the Court's decision on jurisdiction. The massive newspaper attack on the case, which historians and legal scholars have noted, was written in response to these pro-Court articles. Spencer Roane's widely quoted articles, like most newspaper articles criticizing the Court, were not designed to be part of a well-planned attack upon the Supreme Court, but were written in defense of earlier political opinions expressed in newspaper, legislative, and Court debates. The Supreme Court's decision, and newspaper articles supporting the decision, attacked ideals that some Virginians felt compelled to defend. Richmond and Washington newspapers, especially the Richmond Enquirer, Richmond Daily Mercantile Advertiser, National

Intelligencer, and Washington Gazette, filled their columns with a discussion of the decision that quickly escalated into a full constitutional debate, examining in minute detail the decision and the constitutional principles on which it was based. Articles thoroughly examined the decision and then quickly deteriorated into a discussion of political philosophy, including topics such as which side was the rightful heir to the Republican legacy.

The newspaper articles growing out of the Cohens decision continued until the conclusion of the 1821-1822 session of the Virginia General Assembly. The General Assembly's decision not to pass a constitutional amendment, or take official action opposing the decision, marked the effective end of debate on the Cohens decision, although a few pieces about the case were published after that time.

An examination of the chronology of these articles and letters is important to show the action--reaction nature of the debates and to provide an insight into the roles played in the debates by Spencer Roane, John Marshall, Thomas Jefferson and others. The arguments used in this constitutional debate will be discussed in the following chapter.

I

Newspaper articles about the Cohens case reveal several stages in the arguments as Court supporters and opponents reacted to arguments presented by one another. During the first stage which lasted slightly more than two months after the decision, newspapers from Baltimore to St. Louis published the decision or a summary of it.[1] At least ten papers printed, in entirety, one of the case's two decisions.[2] The Richmond Enquirer and the Washington Gazette went further, reprinting Smyth's and Barbour's arguments in full.[3] Most articles maintained a disinterested viewpoint, but several show the partisan spirit which would characterize later discussions. An Enquirer editor penned a short note introducing the reprint of the decision. The decision "flies directly in the face of the constitution: . . . and is a piece with the others that have preceded it . . . these judiciary encroachments upon the rights of the states 'have increased, are increasing, and ought to be diminished.'"[4]

The Richmond Daily Mercantile Advertiser also showed a partisan spirit in its introduction to the decision. The editor observed that the decision does "honor, even to this august and impartial national tribunal," and will "shed a lustre upon the

---

[1]See fn. No. 2 below plus: National Intelligencer, March 2, 1821, American Beacon, March 6, 10, 1821, Richmond Enquirer, March 9, 1821, Alexandria Herald, March 9, 1821, Farmer's Repository, March 14, 1821, Central Gazette, March 16, 1821, and Genius of Liberty, March 20, 1821.

[2]National Intelligencer, March 15, 16, 1821; Baltimore American, March 17, 1821; American Beacon (Norfolk), March 19, 20, 21, 22, 1821; Richmond Enquirer, March 20, 23, 1821; Richmond Daily Mercantile Advertiser, March 20, 21, 1821; Norfolk and Portsmouth Herald, March 21, 25, 1821; Richmond Compiler, March 21, 1821; Washington Gazette, March 22, 23, 24, 1821; Alexandria Herald, April 2, 1821; Louisville Public Advertiser, April 7, 1821; St. Louis Enquirer, April 14, 1821.

[3]Richmond Enquirer, March 3, 6; April 10, 1821; Washington Gazette, April 13, 1821.

[4]Richmond Enquirer, March 20, 1821.

records of American Jurisprudence and the historic annals of the times." It shows, the editor continued, that "federal, state, and individual rights, are always safe in the hands of the Supreme Court." The decision is certainly much better, he concluded, than the Virginia Legislature's resolutions and report.[5]

Perhaps spurred by such Court support, two days later the Richmond Enquirer published a long article strongly opposing the decision. The article examined the opinion which the editor felt would be refuted or "anatomised by some competent critics." The more one examines the decision the clearer becomes the danger to state rights and "the stronger reason there is to fear that the judiciary power, with a foot as noiseless as time, and a Spirit as greedy as the grave, is sweeping those rights to their destruction."[6]

The Richmond Daily Mercantile Advertiser responded in kind. "Pericles'" four long essays, the only series of political essays published during this early period, are as complimentary to the decision as any writings appearing during the entire controversy. Richmond Enquirer articles, the Advertiser proclaimed, are "wholly mistaken, completely confounded, and altogether wrong."[7] Virginia dragged the Cohens to the state bar and must allow them recourse.[8] The Supreme Court must have supervisory power in

---

[5]Richmond Daily Mercantile Advertiser, March 21, 1821.

[6]Richmond Enquirer, March 23, 1821.

[7]Richmond Daily Mercantile Advertiser, March 30, 1821.

[8]Ibid., March 27, 1821.

cases involving the Constitution, or there will be "at _least_ as many _different_ standards of authority, in the shape of precedents and decisions, as we have states!"[9] The Court's opponents, "Pericles" claimed, are those who have opposed every administration and are not interested in principle, but in weakening the federal government. "These are the _seedlings_ of the old _anti-federalists_--men, who would have lost the _nationality_ of this great republic, had their policy prevailed."[10] The decision is "so clear and so conclusive, that it does appear impossible, for the impartial mind, to resist its full force, influence and correctness."[11] It shows "a clearness of perception, an irresistible strength of reasoning and profound jurisdicial knowledge, never surpassed in this or any other country," which "stamps with immortality" the judges and the decision.[12]

When compared with later writing about the case, these early articles are mild, usually limited to reprinting the decision or an argument given in the case. The _Richmond Enquirer_ did publish four articles, including one fairly long one against the decision, but most polemical articles defended the Court, or like some articles in the _National Intelligencer_, opposed the decision because it might harm District of Columbia improvements.

---

[9] _Ibid._, March 29, 1821.

[10] _Ibid._, March 30, 1821.

[11] _Ibid._, March 26, 1821.

[12] _Ibid._, March 30, 1821.

A few newspaper articles, however, noted deepening, behind the scenes, political maneuverings indirectly involving the case. The Richmond Daily Mercantile Advertiser published three articles during the period which hinted at a growing political division within the state. A mid-April article lamented that John Rutherfoord, a local candidate for the state legislature, was using the case as a campaign issue; calling the Court's decision "usurpation." The Richmond paper disagreed and asked why Rutherfoord had not supplied reasons to substantiate his charge. "None, however, was given, and it is presumed, for the best of all possible reasons--none could be given."[13] The same editor complained earlier that a concerted effort seemed to be directed at electing "thorough going Democrats" to the legislature rather than "real Republicans (alias Federalists)," on the theory that the former would better protect state rights. Such a claim is false. All will defend such rights. Support should be given the "unassuming, honest and well-informed candidate, and leave private political opinions out of the question."[14] The newspaper's most intriguing article, however, appeared near the end of April 1821. The editor wrote that the current newspaper controversy involved not only editors, but "High Functionaries" of the state in a semi-official way. No more will be said, he added, unless it became necessary.[15] The charge is not

---

[13]Ibid., April 19, 1821.

[14]Ibid., March 23, 1821.

[15]Ibid., April 27, 1821.

mentioned in any later articles, but the possibilities are intriguing.

Substantial behind the scenes activities can be discovered, but they are not as sinister as the old Federalist paper suggested. Spencer Roane and other Junto members viewed the Court's decision as national usurpation and looked for a pattern to the previous successful experience in opposing such encroachment--the crusade against the Alien and Sedition Acts. Sounding the alarm against those acts, they felt, finally resulted in Thomas Jefferson's election as President and the popular, if not legislative, enactment of his program. All that seemed necessary to stop this new instance of usurpation was to follow the pattern from the earlier conflict, and writers often refer to the precedents of "'98" and "'99." The Court's opponents attempted to enlist the leadership from the opposition to the Alien and Sedition Acts, Jefferson and Madison. Jefferson refused to become publicly involved, declining Thomas Ritchie's request that he endorse John Taylor's new book, Construction Construed. Jefferson praised the book highly, and agreed with its anti-Supreme Court viewpoint; privately, he called the Supreme Court justices a "corps of sappers and miners constantly working under ground to undermine the foundations of our confederated fabric," but he would not enter the public battlefield again, he said, because he longed for the quiet of retirement.[16] A month later on January 19, 1821, he reiterated the point in a letter to Archibald Thweat.[17] While repeating his private praise for Taylor's book, Jefferson encouraged Spencer Roane to oppose the Court, writing Thweat that against the judiciary's consolidating tendencies "I know no one who, equally with Judge Roane himself, possesses the power and the courage to make resistance; and to him I look and have long looked as our strongest bulwark."[18] Spencer Roane, however, was not completely satisfied with Jefferson's replies and made one last attempt to convince the Sage of Monticello. No one, Roane wrote Jefferson, respected Jefferson's repose more than he did, "although therefore, in losing our leader, we run the risk of losing our all."[19] Jefferson's reply, written just after the Supreme Court delivered its decision, seems designed to convince Spencer Roane to lead the opposition to the Court. The letter criticized the judiciary, mentioning the corruption which can occur to institutions over time. Jefferson hoped the new generation would "preserve for their sons the political blessings delivered into their hands by their fathers." He urged Roane to

---

[16]Thomas Jefferson to Thomas Ritchie, December 25, 1820, The Writings of Thomas Jefferson, edited by Andrew Liscomb (Washington, 1904), XV, 295-299.

[17]Thomas Jefferson to Archibald Thweat, January 19, 1821, Ibid., 306-7.

[18]Ibid.

[19]Spencer Roane to Thomas Jefferson, February 25, 1821, "Roane Correspondence," John P. Branch Historical Papers, II (June, 1905), 137-138.

"be not weary of well doing. Let the eye of vigilance never be closed." The elder statesman concluded: "to you I hope many hours will be given; and am certain they will all be employed for the good of our beloved country, I salute you with sentiments of especial friendship and respect."[20] Roane could clearly assume from these letters that Jefferson endorsed him to lead the opposition to the Supreme Court.

Nearly a month later Roane wrote to the other leader of the Revolution of 1800--James Madison. By then the "Pericles" articles had been published, but had not been answered. Roane urged Madison to review the Court's decision.[21] Madison, who was never as hostile toward the Court and the concept of Judicial review as Thomas Jefferson, wrote a lengthy reply in which he urged Roane to undertake a review of the decision.

> Under any circumstances, I should be disposed rather to put such a subject as that to which it [your letter] relates into your hands than to take it out of them. Apart from this consideration, a variety of demands on my time would restrain me from the task of unravelling the arguments applied by the Supreme Court of the United States to their late decision. I am particularly aware, moreover, that they are made to rest not a little on technical points of law, which are as foreign to my studies as they are familiar to yours.[22]

---

[20]Thomas Jefferson to Spencer Roane, March 9, 1821, Jefferson's Writings, XV, 325-326.

[21]Spencer Roane to James Madison, April 17, 1821, Madison Papers, Library of Congress.

[22]James Madison to Spencer Roane, May 6, 1821, Letters and Other Writings of James Madison . . . (Philadelphia, 1865), III, 217-222.

Spencer Roane and other Virginians were working behind the scenes, but they were disorganized, trying to determine what action should be taken and who should take it. Such activities hardly merit the Richmond Daily Mercantile Advertiser's fears. It was, in fact, a Court supporter's series of articles which pushed state rights Virginians to action. Henry Wheaton, United States Supreme Court Clerk, started the second phase of debate about the case May 8, 1821, when the first number of "The Dangers of the Union" by "A Federalist of 1789" was published in the New York American. Wheaton's essay started a veritable avalanche of long, detailed essays examining the case during the late spring and summer of 1821. The first Virginia essay answering Wheaton appeared one week later in the Richmond Enquirer. Peyton Randolph, soon to be the Clerk of the Virginia Court of Appeals, published seven articles, from May to July, examining the case under the name "Somers." One week after the first "Somers" article, the Enquirer started publishing Spencer Roane's five "Algernon Sidney" articles. A third major essay series by "Fletcher of Salton" started near the end of June, two weeks after the "Algernon Sidney" essays stopped in the Enquirer. This unidentified writer is more moderate than Roane or Randolph, but still highly critical of the Court.

The critical review of the Cohens decision was not limited to the Richmond Enquirer, although that paper did publish more articles criticizing the decision than any other newspaper. The Washington Gazette published eleven "Hampden" essays by Charles

Hammond, perhaps the best reasoned essays against the decision. Hammond, who served in both houses of the Ohio legislature and later edited the Cincinnati Gazette, was a lawyer of considerable talent. He would later serve as the first reporter of the Ohio Supreme Court, and presented the state's case in Osborne v. The Bank of the United States. His review of the Cohens case is equal to Marshall's decision. More moderate and less political than Roane, Hammond evidenced a wider familiarity with federal law than did Roane.

These lengthy essays were often reprinted in other papers, and few readers could have read them all. The Roane essays, for example, filled more than one hundred pages when they were later reprinted, and the pamphlet containing the Hampden essays required more than sixty pages of small type.[23] Reading even a single newspaper might require considerable leisure. The June 1, 1821, Richmond Enquirer, for example, used one-half of its news columns to print the third installments of both "Algernon Sidney" and "Somers." Despite the mass of material, it took only a short time for a reader to understand an author's message. Peyton Randolph, for example, in his "Somers" articles wrote that the Court's claimed jurisdiction is a "death blow" . . . "aimed at the very existence of the states."[24] He expressed particular

---

[23]"Algernon Sidney", reprinted in John P. Branch Historical Papers, II (June 1906), 78-183; Charles Hammond, Review of the Opinion of the Supreme Court of the United States in the Case of COHENS vs. VIRGINIA. . . . (Steubenville, Ohio, 1821).

[24]"Somers" No. 1, Richmond Enquirer, May 15, 1821.

concern with the Supreme Court's lack of objectivity and disputed its ability to be an impartial judge between the states and the national government. The Court's esprit de corps explains why "almost every man connected with the federal government is insensible to the dangers of federal encroachment."[25]

Spencer Roane's "Algernon Sidney" essays examine Marshall's decision almost paragraph by paragraph. The articles are not completely legalistic, however, and were written to arouse citizens to re-examine the Constitution and the courts. Beyond Roane's suggestion to repeal the twenty-fifth section of the Judiciary Act of 1789, the specifics of his plan are not clearly defined, but the message is nevertheless clear. Roane addressed the people in their "primary and sovereign character," "under a solemn conviction, that the liberties and constitution of our country are endangered--deeply and vitally endangered, by the fatal effects of that decision."[26] The essays, or parts of them were reprinted in several papers, and stung John Marshall enough that he wrote his fellow Justice Joseph Story: "I think for coarseness and malignity of intention Algernon surpasses all party writers who have ever made pretensions to any decency of character."[27] The "Fletcher of Salton" essays discuss the same questions in much the same tone. "Federalism 'is not dead, but

---

[25]Ibid.

[26]"Algernon Sidney" No. 1. Richmond Enquirer, May 25, 1821.

[27]John Marshall to Joseph Story, June 15, 1821, "Marshall Letters." Proceedings of the Massachusetts Historical Society, 327-328.

it sleepeth,' and well may it revive when called into life by the powerful genius of the chief justice."[28]

Charles Hammond's eleven long articles are different. Hammond, a former Federalist, was more moderate in tone partially because he was not concerned with arousing the public. He opposed the case's constitutional doctrine and meticulously examined the case's legal rulings. Hammond brilliantly examined Marshall's decision discussing precedents and Marshall's alternatives. Spencer Roane used a hatchet against the Court, Hammond used a scalpel against the decision. In his final number, he discussed his purpose in writing the articles.

> I think it probable that the Judges themselves may be among the 'few persons' who will take the pains to read what I have written--They will see that I have understood the subject which I have so far discussed. I am satisfied that they will find some matter worthy of their consideration, and some matter not very palatable.[29]

Henry Wheaton's "Federalist of 1789," the period's major essays supporting the Court, were also emphatic. Wheaton published his first essay in early May 1821, and then suspended publication of his remaining essays when the Virginia essays were published. Wheaton's first article is more moderate than his later numbers but leaves no question about his view of the case. The question is "one of the most vitally important constitutional questions that has ever been discussed since the establishment of

---

[28]"Fletcher of Salton," No. 1, Richmond Enquirer, June 22, 1821.

[29]"Hampden" No. 11, Washington Gazette, August 20, 1821, also reprinted in Richmond Enquirer, August 28, 1821.

the present national government," and the Virginian's doctrines are "most pernicious heresies, although supported by the subtlety of acute and ingenious minds." The union's supremacy is at stake, and if the Supreme Court does not have the contested power, the Constitution is "something less or worse than the old confederation," "a mere treaty between independent powers." Wheaton claims that opposition to the decision is an attempt by New York Governor Clinton to gain political support in Ohio, and that Clinton is gaining applause in Virginia from leading politicians, "from whom we might have expected better things."[30]

Wheaton resumed his series in early July, after most Virginia essays had concluded and published seven additional numbers during July and August. Wheaton no longer talked of Virginia politicians who should know better, but of the disgust he felt while reading the "Algernon Sidney" essays. Wheaton charged that "Algernon Sidney" "scattered opprobrious epithets throughout these extra-ordinary, I had almost said fantastic, accusations, with the heedless profusion of an unthinking prodigal."[31] Wheaton's remaining seven numbers are used to critically examine the "Algernon Sidney" essays.

The constitutional conflict growing out of the Cohens case entered a third phase of discussion even before the second one ended. Thomas Jefferson, bowing to pressure from John Taylor,

---

[30]"A Federalist of 1789" New York American, May 8, 1821.

[31]"A Federalist of 1789" No. 2, New York American, July 10, 1821.

Roane, and his son-in-law Governor Thomas Mann Randolph, at last agreed to enter the contest. A public statement about the case, he cautioned, would impair his future serenity, forcing him to comment on every public issue. Jefferson, therefore, combined two earlier letters praising Taylor's *Construction Construed* into a new letter which he allowed them to publish with the understanding that he would deny having given that permission.

Jefferson's letter, which appeared in the June 16, 1821, *Richmond Enquirer* does not mention the *Cohens* case specifically, but directs itself to some of the case's basic issues. Jefferson praised Taylor's book which he felt should be given to all officials, "as a standing instruction and true exposition of our constitution, as understood at the time we agreed to it." Without mentioning the *Cohens* case, Jefferson strongly supported Virginia's arguments against the Supreme Court's jurisdiction in the case.

> If is a fatal heresy to suppose that either our state governments are superior to the federal, or the federal to the states. The people, to whom all authority belongs, have divided the powers of government into two distinct departments, the leading characters of which are *foreign* and *domestic*, and they have appointed for each a distinct set of functionaries. They have been made co-ordinate, checking and balancing each other, like the three cardinal departments, in the individual states: each equally supreme as to the powers delegated to itself, and neither authorized ultimately to decide what belongs to itself, or to its coparcener in government; as independent in fact as different nations. A spirit of forbearance and compromise, therefore, and not of encroachment and usurpation, is the healing balm of such a constitution: and each party should prudently shrink from all approach to the line of

> demarcation, instead of rashly overleaping it, or throwing grapples ahead to haul to hereafter.[32]

Jefferson's letter caused immediate reaction and soon became the cause of a heated argument between the Richmond Enquirer and the National Intelligencer over which paper really represented "correct republican principles." The focus of the Cohens debate quickly enlarged to a general discussion of constitutional principles and priorities. Jefferson's letter marked the end of effective discussion of the Cohens decision because it diffused the narrower focus of earlier essays, which had concentrated on issues arising from the case.

The National Intelligencer responded to Jefferson's letter with amazing quickness. The Intelligencer reprinted Jefferson's letter four days after it appeared in the Enquirer.[33] Jefferson's letter, the Intelligencer insisted, was not written to caution the Supreme Court. In fact, the Intelligencer asserted, Jefferson wrote the letter to oppose Ohio's conduct during that state's disagreement with the Bank of the United States. The former President was telling conflicting states to "Abstain!, Pass not the Rubicon! In a spirit of forbearance and compromise was this constitution formed. By that spirit only can it be maintained."[34]

---

[32] Richmond Enquirer, July 16, 1821.

[33] National Intelligencer, July 20, 1821.

[34] Ibid.

The Intelligencer's speed in responding to the letter reflected political as well as philosophical reasons. John C. Calhoun attempted to have Henry Wheaton's articles republished in the National Intelligencer. The Intelligencer's editors wanted to publish the essays, but did not feel they could without reprinting the opposing Virginia essays. Calhoun informed Wheaton of the editor's decision July 15, 1821, the day before Jefferson's letter was published in the Enquirer.[35] Jefferson's letter, thus, came at an opportune time. It allowed the National Intelligencer's editors to enter the dispute without appearing to be partisans.

The Intelligencer's view of Jefferson's letter was also challenged. That same evening, the Washington Gazette published a rebuttal entitled "GROSS MISREPRESENTATION." Jefferson, the Gazette's editors countered, always sought to limit the judiciary. "Yet Mr. Jefferson's words are twisted to give an unlimited license to the assumptions of the judiciary over the Congress!"[36] A week later the Richmond Enquirer reprinted the Gazette article with additional comments. "Was it possible for any man to mistake the particular pity of these remarks?" Anyone who had read Taylor's book would recognize that the book Jefferson praised in his letter did not take the Intelligencer's

---

[35]John C. Calhoun to Henry Wheaton, July 15, 1821, Wheaton Papers, Pierpont Morgan Library, Also published in W. Edwin Hemphill (ed.), The Papers of John C. Calhoun 8 vols. (Columbia, 1959--) VI, 259-260.

[36]Washington Gazette, July 20, 1821.

position. The Enquirer then challenged the Intelligencer. Although not at liberty to furnish more facts, the editor offered to "decide the matter . . . by laying any wager, in the Virginia style."[37]

The newspapers quickly became more personal. The Intelligencer asserted that someone was no doubt trying to draw an opinion from Jefferson and asked what more the former President could say "to one whose opinions were known to be on the side of the Courts of Virginia and against that of the United States, than that each party should prudently *shrink* from even an *approach* to the line of demarcation." It is foolish, the Washington paper continued, to think that Jefferson at this time of life and high station would promote collision between the state and federal authorities. As a final jab at the Enquirer the Intelligencer wrote that it was not a "friendly part" to the former President to put "him forth as the chief of a new party."[38]

The charge that the Virginians were attempting to create a new political party became the central argument in numerous newspaper articles during the next eight months. On the surface the argument appears at times to degenerate into a meaningless squabble over the right to use Jefferson's name. At heart, however, the argument ran much deeper. It was a struggle for political legitimacy. The Enquirer felt that it was following

---

[37] Richmond Enquirer, July 27, 1821.

[38] National Intelligencer, July 31, 1821.

the doctrines of the "Old Republican party of '98 . . . the very doctrine which is held forth in Madison's Report of '99." "We will not say to which of the old parties the Intelligencer belongs. It is clearly not that of Mr. J."[39] The Intelligencer was just as insistent that its view of the controversy and of Jefferson's letter was correct. If the Editor of the Enquirer "supposes he is holding the language, and supporting the doctrines, of the Republican party, he never was in his life more mistaken."[40] The Intelligencer went further:

> In medical practice, the case has sometimes occurred of the mind of a man becoming on one point totally deranged, whilst on all others he enjoys his wonted sanity and serenity of mind. Such appears to us to be, in a political sense, the case of the Editor of the Richmond Enquirer. He is in sound mind in regards every thing but the Supreme Court; and quo ad that subject, he appears to labor under an unaccountable delusion. If he does not, we certainly do.[41]

The two papers continued their conflict through September. They argued over the Supreme Court's exact role in relations to the state courts, about whether the Judiciary Act of 1789 had been thoroughly examined before passage, and about the best method to end the continuing constitutional crisis. A few concessions were made on each side, but on the basic questions no agreement proved possible. The Enquirer's editors agreed that the Supreme Court should have some role in maintaining a uniform system of law, but would not agree that the Court was "the sole

---

[39] Richmond Enquirer, August 3, 1821.

[40] National Intelligencer, August 8, 1821.

[41] Ibid.

expositor of the constitution in the last resort."[42] What could the states do if Congress passed an unconstitutional law? What role should the states take in relation to such a law?[43]

The Intelligencer refused to engage in a technical discussion of the case but feared "that the aggrandizement of the particular states, and a reduction of the authority of the general government, is at least the inclination, if not the wish of the Enquirer."[44] The debate soon further diffused into a general discussion of the federal government's powers. The discussion touched not only the Bank of the United States but Congress' right to construct roads and canals, and issue pensions.

The discussion reached an impasse by October 1821, when both sides grew silent. Neither newspaper had convinced the other, but it became evident that further comment would produce only additional conflict. October's relative calm was rudely shattered in early November--by a Richmond Enquirer article. The paper printed a "proposed law" under its November 6, 1821, editorial head for consideration of the approaching legislature. It proposed a $1,000 to $10,000 fine for anyone found guilty of enforcing a United States Supreme Court decision reversing a

---

[42]Richmond Enquirer, September 4, 1821.

[43]Ibid., September 25, 1821.

[44]National Intelligencer, September 19, 1821.

Virginia state court's decision, or for anyone enforcing a District of Columbia law in opposition to a Virginia law.[45]

The Intelligencer responded four days later. The proposed law is a "proposition to declare war against the Judiciary of the United States--in other words, against the Union itself " The Washington editors opposed the bill but were glad to see the "new lights" finally reveal their purpose--opposition to the "FOREIGN GOVERNMENT" of the United States. Perhaps, they continued, the law came from "him whose talents, zeal, and influence, justly place him at the head of the New School." The only thing the bill lacks, they continued, is an additional provision that "hereafter the Laws and Treaties of the United States shall have no force or effect in the state of Virginia."[46] The Enquirer cried misrepresentation. The law had not been proposed by the editors, nor had it been enacted by the legislature as some papers claimed when they reprinted the article. The Intelligencer, the Virginia editors continued, seemed more concerned with creating animosity than with discussing ideas.[47]

The proposed Virginia law received wide circulation but did not become the overriding issue Jefferson's letter had been. The Enquirer's editors attempted to disassociate themselves from those urging violence, if necessary, against the Court, while

---

[45]Richmond Enquirer, November 6, 1821.

[46]National Intelligencer, November 10, 1821.

[47]Richmond Enquirer, November 16, 1821.

Supreme Court supporters saw the law as one more attempt to oppose the Court's legitimate power by state sanctioned force.[48]

The approaching legislative session prompted several new articles. The *Enquirer* published a letter from Thomas Jefferson to William C. Jarvis concerning his book, *Republicans*. Jefferson praised the book, but disagreed with a section intimating that the Supreme Court has the final decision on the constitutionality of federal laws. All branches of government retain that right. The Court can declare a law unconstitutional, but so can and should the President and Congress. "The constitution has erected no such single tribunal; knowing that, to whatever hands confided, with the corruptions of time and party, its members would become despots."[49]

The *National Intelligencer* increasingly relied on reprints from other newspapers to answer the *Enquirer*. The editors continued to reply to specific articles, but the brunt of their political comments were found in reprinted articles from other papers. "The Constitutionalist," a section reprinting such essays, appeared six times in the *Intelligencer* during late November and early December 1821.[50]

---

[48]See: *National Intelligencer*, November 10, 19, 21, 24, 1821; February 18, 1822; *Richmond Enquirer*, November 6, 16, 20, 30, 1821; January 22, 1822; *Richmond Daily Mercantile Advertiser*, November 17, 22; December 5, 1821.

[49]*Richmond Enquirer*, November 20, 1821.

[50]*National Intelligencer*, November 16, 19, 21, 28, 30; December 5, 1821.

The Virginia legislature's new session, however, became the focal point for both sides. The Supreme Court's decision in the _Cohens_ case was delivered after the Virginia legislature adjourned, and this new session was the legislators' first opportunity to take an official position on that decision. Governor Thomas Mann Randolph's opening address to the legislature, given December 3, 1821, deals extensively with the _Cohens_ case and the state's remaining options.

> The commonwealth has undergone the humiliation of having endeavoured in vain to vindicate and assert her rights and and sovereignty at the bar of the Supreme Court of the United States, and now endures the mortification, . . . of having altogether failed to procure a disavowal of the right, or the intention, to violate that sovereignty and those rights, by the procedure which was announced to the last legislature.[51]

The decision gave Congress any power it desired, and the Supreme Court became the ultimate judge of any law's constitutionality. The only solution was an amendment, or as Governor Randolph further suggested, a new constitutional convention to resolve the question. Virginia's earlier experience in 1798, 1799, in leading the nation to the "legitimate remedy," justified the state in "making an endeavor, alone, to rouse the other states of the union, to a proper consideration of the importance of the crisis."[52]

The Governor's message was widely reprinted, supported, and opposed, but it failed to inspire the Virginia legislature to

---

[51]_House of Delegates Journal_, 1821-1822 (Richmond, 1822), 7-8.

[52]_Ibid._

action.[53] No amendments or resolutions were introduced. One reason for the legislature's inaction was a constitutional amendment introduced in the United States Senate. The Kentucky legislature, upset over a Supreme Court decision, Green v. Biddle, which threatened to throw state land titles into confusion, passed a resolution asking Kentucky's congressmen to introduce an amendment to create a new tribunal to decide disputes between state and federal judiciaries.

Senator Richard M. Johnson, who would later serve as Martin Van Buren's Vice President, quickly introduced a bill giving the Senate itself power to settle such conflicts. Johnson's amendment evoked immediate and sometimes bitter responses.[54] Neither the Richmond Enquirer nor the National Intelligencer supported the bill. The Enquirer liked the separate tribunal but voiced serious doubts about the lack of separation of powers in the bill. Congress hotly debated the bill, but, as an unidentified Enquirer writer observed, it gained little support because, although many congressmen were concerned about the

---

[53]Richmond Enquirer, December 4, 1821; Richmond Daily Mercantile Advertiser, December 4, 1821; Central Gazette (Charlottesville), December 7, 1821; National Intelligencer, December 11, 1821 (excerpts); Herald of the Valley, December 17, 1821.

[54]Richmond Enquirer, November 23; December 11, 18, 20, 28, 1821; January 5, 22; May 14, 1822; Kentucky Gazette (Lexington) November 29, 1821; National Intelligencer, December 13, 1821; January 1, 14; March 13, 14; August 10, 14, 17, 1822; Alexandria Gazette, December 15, 1821; Washington Gazette, December 19, 1821.

Supreme Court's power, no two minds could agree upon a solution.[55]

As it became apparent that the Senate would not limit the Supreme Court, the Enquirer began to prod the assembly. The paper followed its pattern from a year before, and did little to advise the legislature in official editorials but printed several letters addressed to the legislature urging them to uphold the state's honor. "Fabricius" reminded the legislature that they have always taken the lead in defending state rights. "This crisis appears to me to be all important to the existence of the sovereignty of the states. The ground taken by the Supreme Court produces the crisis, . . . The states must make a stand, or must abandon their rights for ever."[56] The states cannot stop defending such rights because they fear creating new political parties. Such parties have always been part of a free government, the current lull in party activity may, in fact, be caused by a loss of Republican principles. The author's solution, repeal the 25th section of the Judiciary Act of 1789 to help "put at rest" these collisions which so constantly arise."[57]

One week later, January 10, 1821, "Nestor" addressed the legislature as part of a series of articles on state rights. The Court's decision, he protested, had been "sufficiently discussed

---

[55]Richmond Enquirer, January 19, 1822.

[56]Ibid., January 3, 1822.

[57]Ibid.

and canvassed." The current legislature may become "one of the most important in the annals of Virginia," because the legislature "will be called upon to record her declaration, relative to a subject of vital importance to the prosperity of the individual states." He did not suggest a specific course of action.

> We only beg leave to protest, against any more futile 'protests.' Let your ACT be such a one, as shall convince the supreme court of the U. S., Congress, your sister states, and the whole world, that Virginia in the year 1821 was as FREE, SOVEREIGN AND INDEPENDENT, as she was in the year 1788; when she ratified the constitution of the United States.[58]

The Enquirer's editors quickly disclaimed support for any form of violence, urging only a "forcible appeal to the understandings of the country by means of argument."[59]

Two weeks later on January 26, 1821, "Franklin" penned a final letter to the legislature reminding the delegates that they are the "successors to the distinguished legislators of 1765, and of 1799; of those illustrious legislatures, which equally bearded and overthrew British and American tyranny."[60] The present danger, although different, is as real as those earlier ones. "Franklin" urged the legislators to neglect other business if necessary but not to neglect this state rights question. "Your country expects it at your hands: and, believe me, your constituents are neither indifferent, nor uninformed, on this

---

[58]Ibid., January 10, 1822.

[59]Ibid.

[60]Ibid., January 26, 1822.

great subject." He suggested some "_declaratory_ amendments to the constitution," and a "periodical council of censors or arbitrators, to adjust the collisions." Council members would be framers like Jefferson and Madison, not current office holders.[61]

The legislature finally moved toward official reaction on the case on February 2, 1822, as Richard Epps introduced five amendments into the House of Delegates. The five amendments, written by Spencer Roane, sought to limit the power of Congress and the Supreme Court. The first amendment limited congressional powers to those "expressly granted to Congress by the constitution, or _absolutely_ necessary and proper, for carrying the same into execution." The second would prohibit the United States government from binding "_conclusively_, the claims of the states composing the Union, to rights contested between the general and state governments under the constitution." The third withdrew Supreme Court jurisdiction in "_any_ case in which a state shall be a party, except in controversies between two or more states, and in any other controversies involving the rights of a state, and to which such state shall claim to become a party." The fourth provided "that no appeal shall be construed to lie to any court of the United States from any decision rendered in the courts of a state." The last specified that no law for the District of Columbia, state, or a territory "shall be construed to have force, within any other state, which shall conflict with

---

[61]_Ibid._

justice, with the principles of morality, with rights claimed under such state, or with the systems of policy or revenue of such states."[62]

Together the amendments are the legislative culmination of Spencer Roane's principles. They are uncompromising and Epps no doubt knew they had little chance of passage when he introduced them. Roane, to be sure, admitted that fact saying he wrote the amendments partially to influence the United States Senate.[63] The proposed amendments received enough legislative support that a motion to permanently postpone the amendments lost, 72 to 78, but for whatever cause, they were not called up again during the session and the vote proved to be an indefinite postponement.[64]

The Virginia legislature's adjournment on March 4, 1822, ended most active discussion of the Cohens decision. The Virginia legislature had leisurely examined the case and done nothing. The prospect of a state officially opposing the nation had ended. An Intelligencer editorial needled the Enquirer that

---

[62]House of Delegates Journal, 1821-1822, February 2, 1822, 162, Richmond Enquirer, February 5, 1822, National Intelligencer, February 20, 1822. The wording of the last amendment was apparently patterned after the Virginia Court of Appeal's decision in Lewis v. Fullerton. "It decides that the laws of one country attempted to be asserted in another, are with an exception, that they do not violate any moral principle in that other, or the of that other, or any right or interest derived under the law of that other." Richmond Enquirer, December 11, 1821, Washington Gazette, December 13, 1821. Some newspapers incorrectly reported that the amendments had been introduced by John W. Eppes, Thomas Jefferson's son-in-law. See Richmond Enquirer, March 2, 1822.

[63]Spencer Roane to Archibald Thweat, December 24, 1821, Branch Papers, II, 141-142.

[64]Richmond Enquirer, February 5, 1822.

the resolutions did not pass and "the session has passed away without the discharge of another battery of words at the general government. The Editors of the Enquirer have indeed been 'deserted at their utmost need.'" If the legislature possessed the disposition exhibited by the Enquirer's writers, the Washington paper continued, "we might have expected some substantial act of resistance" to the Supreme Court.[65]

> It is now evident, however, that the project has miscarried. The next Legislature, it is hinted by the Enquirer, must be composed of men of better metal--of more 'talent'. The signs cannot be mistaken, which indicate a decay of the excitement into which the minds of the people of Virginia had been lately wrought. The new 'crisis' is postponed, for the present at least, and we hope 'until further notice.'[66]

Four days later, March 12, 1822, the Enquirer replied:

> Triumph not too soon, gentlemen--the crisis is, in truth, only postponed--it has not passed away.--We hope yet to see the usurpations of the Supreme Court and of Congress itself, discountenanced by the voice of an indignant nation, roused to a just sense of its rights.
>
> For our part we do not yet despair of the republic. The states or rather the people, will gradually awaken to the truths which Virginia has endeavored to support. She is actuated by no other consideration than an attachment to the constitution. She is yet firm to her faith. But she forbears at present pressing her opinions, and especially as the doctrines which she has most at heart, are not without their advocates in other quarters.[67]

The battle, at least in Virginia, was over, and national attempts to limit the judiciary proved to be no more successful. Senator Johnson's amendment creating a new tribunal was debated

---

[65]National Intelligencer, March 8, 1822.

[66]Ibid.

[67]Richmond Enquirer, March 12, 1822.

and quickly tabled. Andrew Stevenson, a Junto member recently elected to the House of Representatives, introduced a series of constitutional amendments in the House of Representatives in the spring of 1822, but because of the lateness of the session, they were postponed until the next session.[68]

Articles about the Cohens case were published after the legislature adjourned, but they were written with a new spirit of compromise; without the rancor of earlier articles. Both the Enquirer and the National Intelligencer, in fact, soon published articles supporting their opponent's point of view. The Enquirer published a series of three articles by David Watson, a member of the Virginia legislature, supporting the Court, but only after much pressure and the appearance of the articles elsewhere.[69] The National Intelligencer also published an anonymous article by another member of the Virginia legislature supporting the state's stand. The editors of the Intelligencer invited other correspondents to answer their arguments, then carefully explained that, although they had opposed the Virginians, they had never imputed their motives. Not quite candidly, they reported they had felt compelled to label their opponents "new

---

[68]National Intelligencer, April 27, 1822, Francis F. Wayland, Andrew Stevenson, Democrat and Diplomat, 1785-1857 (Philadelphia, 1949), 58.

[69]"Justinian" Richmond Enquirer, April 16, 19, 23, 1822, see note at the end of the series, See also Richmond Daily Mercantile Advertiser, June 21, 25, 29, 1822, and undated memorandum, Watson Papers, University of Virginia.

lights" only when talk turned to defense of rights with blood, and of official actions against the national government.[70]

II

The conflict over the *Cohens* case provides an excellent opportunity to examine the Richmond Junto's role in Virginia politics. Spencer Roane and other group members felt strongly that the *Cohens* decision provided a chance to return the country to correct political principles and attempted to bring the issue to the public's attention, hoping, thereby, to help enact permanent guarantees for state rights. Roane quietly tried to convince others, especially Thomas Jefferson and James Madison, to join the conflict, and finally helped obtain Jefferson's letter praising John Taylor's book. Spencer Roane enjoyed a close relationship with his cousin, Thomas Ritchie, and no doubt helped direct the newspaper articles about the case. However, the *Enquirer* was not as cooperative as Roane wished. Thomas Jefferson and others wanted Roane's "Algernon Sidney" essays reprinted as a pamphlet like Charles Hammond's "Hampden" essays had been.[71] Archibald Thweatt circulated a subscription list for the pamphlets which Roane gave to the *Enquirer's* editors through an intermediary. Roane expressed his pessimism that Ritchie would undertake such a non-profitable job. For whatever

---

[70] *National Intelligencer*, March 20, 1822.

[71] Thomas Jefferson to Spencer Roane, June 25, 1821, *Branch Papers*, II, 138-139.

reasons, Ritchie did not reprint the essays as a pamphlet but did reprint additional copies of the essays which Roane sent to national leaders such as Jefferson, Madison, Monroe, and Martin Van Buren.[72]

Spencer Roane also sought to help direct the Virginia legislature's examination of the case. He wrote the constitutional amendments that Richard Epps introduced in the 1821-1822 session. He hoped that the amendments would influence national discussions. "With a view to aid them, the United States Senate or rather to lead, on this important subject, I have prepared some amendments to the Constitution to be adopted by our assembly."[73] Two weeks earlier he had asked Archibald Thweatt to seek Jefferson's help to influence the legislature, adding that he would write John Taylor himself. No record remains of such letters or any answers received, but three weeks later an anonymous letter, which has many characteristics of John Taylor's writing, appeared in the Richmond Enquirer.[74]

---

[72]Spencer Roane to Thomas Jefferson, June 25, 1821, Branch Papers, II, 138-139, James Madison to Spencer Roane, June 29, 1821, Letters of James Madison (Philadelphia, 1865), III, 222-224, Spencer Roane to James Monroe, "Letters of Spencer Roane, 1788-1822," Bulletin of the New York Public Library, X (1906), 179, Notes on the Algernon Sidney articles are found in the Van Buren papers, Van Buren Papers, 1821 Misc. Library of Congress.

[73]Spencer Roane to Archibald Thweat, December 24, 1821, Branch Papers, II, 141-142.

[74]"Fabricius" Richmond Enquirer, January 3, 1821, shows the same lack of concern with paragraphing and discusses the same issues in much the same manner as Taylor's Construction Construed.

Despite such activities, Spencer Roane failed to influence the legislature. His amendments were introduced in the House of Delegates, but postponed and never brought to a vote. This is perhaps the best evaluation of the Richmond Junto's supposed "secret control" over the legislature. Roane used his influence, but could not bring the amendments to a vote, much less gain a victory on an issue he considered vital.

It should be noted that other politicians also attempted to use the case politically. John C. Calhoun hoped Wheaton's essays could combat the "radicals" in New York and Virginia, and, of course, improve his chances for the presidency.[75] Even John Marshall used his influence. When Marshall learned that Spencer Roane's essays would, at Jefferson's request, be reprinted in The Journal of Jurisprudence, he wrote Joseph Story that if Hall insisted on publishing Roane's articles and did not wish to appear as a partisan, he should also publish Henry Wheaton's essays on the subject. We do not know how effective Marshall's lobbying was because Hall's journal suspended publication before the next issue.[76]

---

[75]John C. Calhoun to Henry Wheaton, July 15, 1821, Wheaton papers, Pierpont Morgan Library, also Calhoun Papers, Henry Wheaton also had political motives to oppose the Virginians. He was very disappointed at not having received a position from President Monroe. See Henry Wheaton to Levi Wheaton, April 8, 1821, Wheaton Papers, Pierpont Morgan Library.

[76]The Journal of Jurisprudence which succeeded Hall's American Law Journal (1808-1817) published only one issue (1821) before ceasing publication.

Equally unclear is Jefferson's role in the controversy with the Supreme Court. By December 1821, Roane felt that Jefferson and Madison hung back too much in the great crisis.[77] Marshall, on the other hand, was certain the former President was directing opposition to the Court.

> The attack upon it the court therefore is a masked battery aimed at the government itself. The whole attack, if not originating with Mr. Jefferson, is obviously approved and guided by him. It is therefore formidable in other states as well as in this, and it behooves the friends of the union to be more on the alert than they have been.[78]

Marshall's view is certainly too severe, and yet, Jefferson played an important part in opposing the Court. In his letters to Roane and others, he declined to lead, but encouraged Roane to do so. When pressed, he allowed publication of his letters praising John Taylor's book. According to John Marshall, Jefferson attempted to have Roane's essays published in the leading national law journal, The Journal of Jurisprudence. Perhaps more importantly, however, are the numerous letters he wrote during the period criticizing the Court and John Marshall.[79] He usually requested his correspondents not to publish the letters, but his position was widely known and

---

[77]Spencer Roane to Archibald Thweat, December 24, 1821, Branch Papers, II, 141-142.

[78]John Marshall to Joseph Story, September 18, 1822, Marshall Correspondence, 329-331.

[79]See, for example, Thomas Jefferson to Thomas Ritchie, December 25, 1820, Jefferson's Writings, XV 295-299; Thomas Jefferson to Spencer Roane, March 9, 1821, Ibid., 325-326; Thomas Jefferson to Nicholas, Ibid., 350-352; Thomas Jefferson to Charles Hammond, August 18, 1821, Ibid., 330-333.

explicit. In fact, many of Jefferson's oft quoted anti-judicial statements were written during the Cohens controversy rather than during his earlier fight with the Supreme Court while President. Jefferson may have been even more directly involved in the case. In February 1821, just before the case went to the Supreme Court, Roane wrote Jefferson, "I congratulate you on the resolutions of our Assembly produced by the citation of the Commonwealth into the Federal Court."[80] It would be interesting to know why Spencer Roane, supposed leader of the resolutions' passage, congratulated Jefferson on their passage. Obviously Jefferson was more than an interested bystander, but no evidence remains directly connecting the former President with either the writing of the resolutions or the legislative struggles involved in their passage.

---

[80]Spencer Roane to Thomas Jefferson, February 25, 1821, Branch Papers, II, 137-138.

CHAPTER VI

THE CONSTITUTION--TWO VIEWS

I

The detailed newspaper debate over the _Cohens_ decision discloses far more than the constitutional arguments used by Supreme Court supporters and opponents. Collectively the articles reveal concerns and motivations as well as arguments. A careful reading of the arguments is especially important in a case like the _Cohens_ case where the specific constitutional arguments are often secondary to the basic hopes and fears which prompted them.

The newspaper articles about the _Cohens_ case channeled the frustration arising from the economic dislocations of the Panic of 1819, and changing social and political conditions, into constitutional arguments. The debates are, in many ways, a continuation of revolutionary debates which turned economic, social, and political pressures into constitutional questions. Most of the participants in the debates were members of the revolutionary generation who had become accustomed to viewing many political questions in constitutional terms.

Both the state rights Virginians and their nationalist opponents felt the other group was about to subvert the government. The use of constitutional arguments when discussing the Eleventh Amendment or state rights, then, reflects not only the specific questions raised in the Cohens case, but larger concerns about the future of the American system of government. Their fears that the government might be easily changed are more understandable when it is realized that the Constitution had been in operation for only thirty years, and that many of the debaters had seen several fundamental changes in the government during their lifetime. The thirty year existence of the Constitution, brief as it was, was a lengthy period for a constitutional government because of the high mortality rate of earlier constitutional governments.[1] Almost all Americans in positions of power could remember the ratification process and the myriad proposals for the new government, and had participated in the political events surrounding the Alien and Sedition Acts and Jefferson's election in 1800. Most political writers discussing the Cohens case viewed these events as current affairs rather than sanctioned history and many hoped or feared that the Constitution might be easily changed again.

It is possible that the debates were mere rhetoric covering a more fundamental motivation such as the protection of slavery or the advancement of personal political fortunes. A careful examination of newspaper articles about the case, and letters written during the period, leads to the conclusion that, although a defense of slavery, and personal political ambition may have

---

[1]A National Intelligencer article in September 1821 praised the Constitution as "the only Constitution of government in Christendom, one excepted, that has stood for thirty years unchanged," National Intelligencer, September 19, 1821.

motivated some individuals, the major thrusts of their arguments were motivated by a fear that the Constitution, was about to be changed drastically by their opponents.

The defense of slavery, however, might logically be seen as motivation for many Virginians rather than an abstract defense of the Constitution. The _Cohens_ case did occur at the same time as the debates over the admission of Missouri and the resulting debates over slavery. The arguments for a strict construction of the Constitution might have been an attempt to protect slavery from adverse rulings by the Supreme Court. Personal political and economic ambition may also have been major motivations for the debates over the _Cohens_ case. Several individuals, such as John C. Calhoun, seem to have used the _Cohens_ case for private political goals, as was discussed in the last chapter. There is, however, little evidence to show that individual political goals were more than political reactions to the public discussion of the case rather than a fundamental motive which caused the case to become a public issue. Public interest in the case was also increased by the hard economic conditions resulting from the Panic of 1819. Many Americans were forced by the Panic to search for causes for their economic troubles at the same time they were forced to examine their basic economic and political beliefs. The harsh times helped heighten differences and clarify political stands, but usually confirmed and intensified earlier political and constitutional views, rather than influencing participants to see the case as a vehicle for personal political or economic advancement.

Individuals within Virginia were beginning to defend slavery, using the Biblical and wage-slave arguments which would later become so popular.[2] Certainly some politicians within the state reasoned that allowing the Supreme Court to decide cases in which state and national power collided might endanger slavery, and therefore opposed the Court's ruling. However, such support for slavery was never enunciated. No citation can be found in articles about the case in the Enquirer or in private correspondence dealing with the case which mentions a concern with protecting slavery. Indeed, many references show an uneasiness about the institution. Spencer Roane refused to use a defense of slavery to rally support for his attack, and at least one historian has blamed the defeat of his campaign on this reluctance.[3] Governor Randolph asked for some gradual emancipation, or at least exportation of slaves, in the same message which cautioned legislators about the possible dangers of the Cohens case.[4] An editorial in the Enquirer, apparently written by Thomas Ritchie, agreed with a newspaper attack against

---

[2]New York Evening Post, January 20, 1820; Richmond Enquirer, July 17, 1821.

[3]Harry Ammond, "The Republican Party in Virginia, 1789-1824" (Unpublished Ph.D. dissertation, University of Virginia, 1948), 429.

[4]Journal of the Virginia House of Delegates, 1821-22 (Richmond, 1822), 7-8.

slavery, and asked for suggestions for emancipation.[5] James Madison wrote a fable defending the Southern reluctance to emancipate, but showed little sympathy for the institution.[6] John Randolph freed his three hundred slaves.[7] Circumstantial evidence therefore indicates that protection of slavery was not the main reason Virginians opposed the Supreme Court.

II

Those who had labored hard to establish a federal government with powers independent of local and state prejudices viewed the furor over the Cohens case as part of an attempt to limit the power of the federal government or to establish a new system giving more power to the states. Fear that the Virginians and their allies wanted to change the basic nature of the government is found both in period newspaper articles and in private letters.[8] Marshall wrote a fellow Supreme Court Justice that Roane wanted to be known as a champion of state rights "instead

---

[5]Richmond Enquirer, November 27, 1821.

[6]James Madison, "A Fable of Jonathan and Mary Bull," Letters of James Madison (Philadelphia, 1865), III, 249-256.

[7]Hugh Garland, John Randolph of Roanoake (New York, 1850), Vol. II, 150-151.

[8]See Richmond Daily Mercantile Advertiser, March 30; April 7; June 1, 1821, New York American, May 8; July 23, 1821, Washington Gazette, August 23, 1821, Richmond Enquirer, May 25; June 22, 1821; November 9, 1821, National Intelligencer, September 19; November 21, 27, 1821.

of being what he really is, the champion of dismemberment."[9] The National Intelligencer claimed "the petty question about lotteries was too insignificant in itself to have created any commotion; it served as an occasion only for a display of feelings previously existing." The article continued that the doctrines of Virginia "must have some object," adding that the inclination, if not the wish, of the Enquirer is "the aggrandizement of the particular states and a reduction of the authority of the general government."[10] Henry Wheaton admitted that he could not read "Algernon Sidney" without thinking there was a plan to radically change the Constitution into a league.[11] Justice Story feared Virginia sought to reduce the government to "a confederacy," "a petty charter granted to a paltry corporation for the purpose of regulating a fishery or collecting a toll."[12] The National Intelligencer's editor's expressed their fear of the Virginia position in the case. "If the power to enforce laws be not given, the power to make them is nugatory, and all our forms of government, House of Representatives, Senate, and President,

---

[9]John Marshall to Joseph Story, June 15, 1821, "Letters of Chief Justice Marshall," Proceedings of the Massachusetts Historical Society, 2nd Ser. Vol. XIV (1900-1901), 327-328.

[10]National Intelligencer, September 19, 1821. See also "Pericles" No. 4 Richmond Daily Mercantile Advertiser, March 30, 1821.

[11]New York American, August 16, 1821.

[12]Joseph Story to John Marshall, June 27, 1821, Charles Warren (ed.), "The Story-Marshall Correspondence," William and Mary Quarterly, 2nd Ser., XXI (January 1941), 6-8.

are merely costly mummery--the sooner abolished, the better."[13] "A Native of Virginia" saw state jealousy of the union behind the attack upon the Court, but his comments also indicate strong feelings about the states.

> All confederacies have been destroyed from the component parts. History does not present an exemption, and if our well poised government shall perish, it will be from the mad ambition and jealousy of the states. They are so prone to misrule, and to mismanagement of their reserved powers, there is reason to apprehend they will not only destroy themselves, but also the union.[14]

It was not, however, just state ambition which concerned most Court supporters, but personal ambition. Henry Wheaton admitted that the line between the federal and state governments was often not clearly marked. "There are points in it on which the soundest understandings may receive different impressions, and the most upright minds take different directions."[15] Disagreement on such points could be used to further political ambitions. John Quincy Adams felt the Cohens case agitation was motivated by "'close ambition varnished o'er with zeal'" and noted that Jefferson and Madison had earlier gained power using state rights and state sovereignty as issues.[16] Justice Story even professed a willingness to give up the presidency to satisfy Virginians' political goals in the case if that would protect the

---

[13]National Intelligencer, September 19, 1821.

[14]National Intelligencer, October 10, 1821.

[15]New York American, July 23, 1821.

[16]The Diary of John Quincy Adams, . . . Allan Nevins (ed.), (New York, 1928), October 20, 1821, 266.

Supreme Court. He wrote John Marshall that he would rather allow Virginia "exclusive possession of the Executive power for a half a century than witness the prevalence in other States of any of her constitutional dogmas."[17]

The debates over the Cohens case elicited similar fears among state rights Virginians. The arguments of the Court's supporters indicated to the Virginians that their opponents were seeking to consolidate all governmental powers in a powerful national government. The Virginians viewed the American government as an experiment in federalism--an attempt to divide power and check ambition. If the federal government became a truly national one the experiment was over--it had failed. The American government would then be like any number of other national governments open to despotism and monarchy.

Writer after writer echoed the fear of consolidation. Roane declared that the decision was based on "principles which go the full length of destroying the state governments altogether and establishing on their ruins, one great, national, and consolidated government."[18] He later claimed the case's principles would lead to non-resistance by the states "until their confederacy was completely overthrown and a consolidated

---

[17]Joseph Story to John Marshall, June 27, 1821, William and Mary Quarterly XXI, 6-8.

[18]Richmond Enquirer, May 25, 1821, see also: Richmond Enquirer, June 29, 1821, Washington Gazette, June 29, July 27, August 20, 1821.

government erected."[19] "Somers" cautioned that if the American people are wise, they "will forever regret the idea of a great national consolidated government."[20] The Washington Gazette reprinted a letter from Ohio Governor Brown expressing concern about the "progress of the Supreme Court of the United States in subverting the federative principles of the Constitution and introducing on their ruins a mighty consolidated empire, fitted for the scepter of a great monarch."[21] "Marcus Brutus" informed Richmond Enquirer readers that the danger was at hand. The present situation was "not a 'precipice' which threatens them at a distance,--but a gulph (sic) which is already yawning to swallow up the liberties and constitutions of the states."[22]

Both Supreme Court supporters and Court opponents saw the Court as central to their fears. John Marshall felt that the Court was being attacked because it was the federal government's weakest department. "The attack upon the judiciary is in fact an attack upon the union. The judicial department is well understood to be that through which the government may be attacked most successfully, because it is without patronage, and of course without power."[23] Court opponents, on the other hand,

---

[19]Richmond Enquirer, June 1, 1821.

[20]Ibid., May 15, 1821.

[21]Washington Gazette, June 29, 1821.

[22]Richmond Enquirer, November 20, 1821.

[23]John Marshall to Joseph Story, September 18, 1821, Proceedings, XIV (1900-1901), 329-331, New York American, July 23, 1821.

viewed the Court as the central figure in the plot to consolidate governmental power. The Philadelphia Democratic Press wrote that "infringement of the rights by the judiciary is more likely to effect a consolidation of the Union than any other cause or causes which exist."[24] The Enquirer cautioned that the judicial power "with a foot as noiseless as time, and a spirit as greedy as the grave, is sweeping those rights to their destruction."[25] Thomas Jefferson was adamant: "The judiciary branch is the instrument which, working like gravity, without intermission, is to press us at last into one consolidated mass."[26] "The judiciary of the United States is a subtle corps of sappers and miners constantly working under ground to undermine the foundations of our confederated fabric. They are construing our Constitution from a co-ordination of general and specific government to a general and supreme one alone."[27] The Washington Gazette quoted Vattel in cautioning against slight constitutional changes, "'changes that insensibly happen by a long train of steps that are but slightly marked.'" The Supreme Court, the Washington editor continued, is now taking such steps.

---

[24]Reprinted in Ibid., February 22, 1821.

[25]Ibid., March 23, 1821.

[26]Thomas Jefferson to Archibald Thweat, January 19, 1821, The Writings of Thomas Jefferson, Andrew A. Lipscomb (ed.), 20 vols. (Washington, 1903), Vol. XV, 306-307.

[27]Thomas Jefferson to Thomas Ritchie, December 25, 1820, Ibid., 295-299.

"The United States judiciary have climbed from a station subordinate to the law, to the height of lawgivers."[28]

Court supporters were certainly correct in observing hostility and a change in tactics against the Court. While earlier articles against the Court had often been general in nature, the Cohens decision unleashed a barrage of specific attacks against the Supreme Court and John Marshall. Stung by the unanimous decision against Virginia on the question of the Court's jurisdiction and by the Court's use of its own precedent in Martin v. Hunter's Lessee and other cases, authors of several articles about the Cohens decision included lengthy discussions of specific charges against the Court. Without mentioning the Martin case by name, "Somers" lamented that, "one error becomes the parent of many others and fixes the law irrevocably for all future judiciaries, however they may be disposed to retrace their steps."[29] "The precedents which are set to-day, amidst a conflict of jarring opinions, are acquiesced in as unquestioned axioms on the morrow," "Fletcher of Salton" added, "and the ground which has been once gained is never lost, unless it be reconquered by some rival jurisdiction."[30] The continued use of such precedents, "Somers" claimed in another essay, would bring a time when a man could not interpret the Constitution without

---

[28]Washington Gazette, June 21, 1821.

[29]Richmond Enquirer, May 15, 1821.

[30]Ibid., May 25, and June 22, 1821, Washington Gazette, June 21, 1821.

consulting a learned counsel, and his ability to obtain justice might depend upon the fortunate selection of his counsel, or his ability to pay.[31]

The Court's undemocratic nature and the lack of public control over the Court received an indepth review. Believing that the judiciary was the weakest federal branch, the framers of the Constitution provided safeguards which now frustrated popular control over a judiciary which had not proven to be the weakest branch.[32] Periodic elections provided popular control over the other branches, but no controls exist over the judges. This lack of control, "Somers" claimed, makes judicial errors more dangerous than the errors of other branches. Impeachment provides no real control and "does not apply to the honest errors of the judiciary."[33]

More frustrating to Court opponents than the lack of public control over the Court was John Marshall's internal control over the Court. A majority of the Court's judges had now been appointed by Republican Presidents, and yet each new judge seemed to be assimilated into the Court without making any discernable change in the Court's decisions. Marshall's influence was increased by the unanimous decisions the Court issued in most cases, rather than following an earlier precedent of separate decisions. "Somers" decried the unanimous Cohens decision,

---

[31] Richmond Enquirer, May 22, 1821.

[32] Ibid., May 25, 1821.

[33] Ibid., May 15, 1821.

claiming that so many disputed points could not have been unanimously resolved "without resorting to some other supposition than the free exercise of independent judgments."[34] Spencer Roane declared it "would be a miracle if the former Republicans actually agreed in all points on his [John Marshall's] opinions."[35] Earlier Roane maintained such unanimous opinions resulted not just from discussion, but must "be ascribed to a culpable apathy in the other judges, or a confidence, not to be excused, in the principles and talents of their chief."[36] Thomas Jefferson was even more critical: "An opinion is huddled up in conclave, perhaps by a majority of one, delivered as if unanimous, and with the silent acquiescence of lazy or timid associates, by a crafty chief judge, who sophisticates the law to his mind, by the turn of his own reasoning."[37]

A Court _esprit de corps_ caused judges with strong state rights records, "Somers" added, to change philosophies after a Supreme Court appointment. "He looks back with indifference on the scenes of his juvenile exertions; discards his former allegiance; and enters with all the enthusiasm of a new convert into the cause which he has embraced."[38] Constitutional

---

[34]_Ibid._

[35]_Ibid._, June 1, 1821.

[36]_Ibid._, May 25, 1821.

[37]Thomas Jefferson to Thomas Ritchie, December 25, 1820, _Writings of Thomas Jefferson_ XV, 295-299.

[38]_Richmond Enquirer_, May 15, 1821.

interpretation, the author continued, is too important to be left to a few men who cannot be supposed to have all or even the greater part of the country's judicial wisdom. "The people made the constitution, and the people can dissolve it; the same people alone can construe it."[39] The New York Times Democrat agreed.

> The great mass of the people in more than twenty separate and independent states are much less liable to err in the construction of their rights, than are four fallible men (making a majority of the national judiciary) exposed to the temptations of power, and surrounded by a thousand circumstances to bias and mislead their judgments.[40]

Several authors, especially "Somers," seem to be attacking the Court and its judges directly to lesson the authority of the Court's pronouncements.[41] Perhaps if citizens realized the judges' fallibility they would be more likely to take action against this decision. George Hay, President Monroe's son-in-law, voiced the problem frustrating several opponents of the Court. "All that I fear is, that even error, when it comes from such a tribunal as the S[upreme] C[ourt] will be too powerful for truth unless supported by the nation itself."[42]

III

For both Supreme Court supporters and state rights Virginians, the concept of sovereignty was basic to the Cohens

---

[39]Ibid., May 15, 1821.

[40]Reprinted in Richmond Enquirer, August 31, 1821.

[41]National Gazette, June 28, 1821, reprinted in Washington Gazette, July 2, 1821, Southern Recorder (Milledgeville, Georgia), July 10, 1821, Richmond Enquirer, May 15, 1821.

[42]Published in Richmond Enquirer, September 28, 1821.

case, and both sides spent a great deal of space discussing their quite opposite views of the subject. Most articles printed after the decision repeated earlier arguments, but some explored more fully the origins of the United States government. The National Intelligencer started one of the most informative exchanges when it reprinted an article from the Southern Patriot arguing that the Constitution was established by the people of the United States rather than by the states themselves, and asked if less than a majority of the people of the United States could declare the Constitution violated? "Let the people resume the power granted whenever it be abused, but let no single state assume the extravagant pretension of judging of such abuse under the plea of defending the sovereignty of the states."[43] Since the Supreme Court is a creation of the people, "a single state, therefore, or any number comprising less than a majority of the people of the United States, can have no right, in good faith, to release themselves from the compact by which the whole are bound to submit in certain cases to the decisions of that tribunal."[44]

Enquirer writers quickly disagreed and debated the question which would be settled only by the Civil War. "Agrestis" examined the Constitution to show that the states, and not the people in their individual sovereign capacity, founded the government. The title, he noted, is important. It is a Constitution of the United States. The wording indicated a

---

[43]Reprinted in National Intelligencer, September 12, 1821.

[44]Ibid.

singular, sovereign existence for each state separately. It is the states and not the people who are united. The nation's legislative power is vested in a Congress of the United States--not a congress of the people of the United States. When the document referred to the people of the United States, it referred to them in their pre-existing political capacity as citizens of the states. "The union which it declares is of the states--not of individual persons. It is ordained by the states and for the states; but being a fundamental law, it is referred for its authority to the highest, the primary sovereign authority of each state, the people."[45]

> It does not mention the people.--The notion of independent sovereignties, uniting and united to form a constitution for themselves as such, is never departed from in any of its details. Maintaining its character of a pure public fundamental law throughout, individuals or natural persons are not otherwise regarded by it, than they are by the law of nations.[46]

The National Intelligencer and the Richmond Enquirer continued their debate while elaborating their views of the Constitution 's creation. A National Intelligencer article claimed that the founders sought to organize a national government independent of the states. House of Representatives' voting is therefore done by individuals, not states, and even the use of state legislatures to select United States Senators was an accident. The convention, in fact, struggled before deciding to retain the states. The Enquirer's editors quickly doubted any

---

[45]Richmond Enquirer, September 14, 1821.

[46]Ibid.

convention debate about eliminating the states--certainly there had been no such debate in the Virginia ratification debates, and the states were assigned important functions in the workings of the national government. Constitutional changes are still made by a majority of the states. Using the _Federalist Papers_, the _Enquirer_ noted that the first seven states ratifying the Constitution contained less than one-third of the United States population. Even adding New York and Connecticut, the Constitution could have been ratified by less than a majority of the people of the United States. The _Federalist_ itself, they added, was clear: "The assent and ratification of the people, not as individuals composing one entire nation, but as composing the distinct and independent states to which they belong, are the sources of the constitution. It is therefore not a _national_, but a _federal_ compact." That same view had been presented in the Virginia ratifying convention by James Madison. Ratification was not by the people composing one great body, "but the people as composing thirteen sovereignties.[47]

The arguments about the formation of the United States government and the sovereignty of states are important not only because they help explain the hopes and fears of the Court supporters and their state rights opponents, but also because the concepts were basic to several specific arguments resulting from Marshall's decision. The arguments about a state's sovereign

---

[47]_Ibid._, September 25, 1821.

immunity and the Eleventh Amendment were based in large part upon differing concepts of the formation of the United States.

State rights Virginians, such as Spencer Roane, felt that a state's immunity to suits without specific consent was basic to a state's sovereignty. John Marshall agreed in the _Cohens_ decision and then went on to explain that the required consent had been given when the states ratified the Constitution, giving the Supreme Court the right to hear all cases involving the Constitution, laws, or treaties of the United States, even if such cases involved a state. Spencer Roane at first ignored Marshall's statement and spent most of his second "Algernon Sidney" essay arguing that a state is immune from suits unless it specifically surrendered that authority.[48] Henry Wheaton, a Court supporter, called Roane's arguments a straw man, noting that the Supreme Court had already conceded the theoretical immunity in the _Cohens_ decision.[49]

Other Court opponents violently objected to Marshall's contention that the states gave permission to be sued by ratifying the Constitution. Ratification discussions contain no mention of a general surrender of sovereignty, "Hampden" wrote, and thirty years have passed without any mention of the power, leading to the strong presumption "that none of the parties intended to make the _surrender_ in question in the case supposed,

---

[48]_Ibid._, May 29, 1821, see also _Ibid._, March 23; June 5, 22; July 3, 1821.

[49]_New York American_, July 26, 1821.

and that they did not understand it to have been made." The Ohio Bank case, Hammond continued, involved the state treasurer only because neither the lawyers nor the judge believed such action could be taken against the state.[50] "Fletcher of Salton" claimed that even Hamilton's most zealous followers did not dream of such a construction, "which, if it had not been promptly and universally disavowed would have annihilated every hope of the adoption of the contemplated form of government.[51] "Fletcher of Salton" likened the situation to two people signing a contract after agreeing that the document did not cover a certain area and then, after the signing, having one party institute a lawsuit to enforce the document contrary to the earlier understanding.[52] He repeated that "the scheme of the federal constitution would have vanished like the baseless fabric of a vision, if such a pretension had been avowed."[53] "It would require the strongest and most explicit language on the part of the states to convey a right to sue themselves, when no such right had ever existed even in their own tribunals."[54]

"Fulton" carried the argument further, claiming that if the Constitution's framers intended to create a power to sue a state, they would have designated methods to enforce the attendance of

---

[50]Washington Gazette, June 23, 1821.

[51]Richmond Enquirer, June 22, 1821.

[52]Ibid., June 26, 1821.

[53]Ibid.

[54]Ibid., July 3, 1821.

the sovereign power, determined who represented the state, and have designated who in the state is responsible to enforce the Supreme Court's judgment. Such enforcement would not have been left undefined, "or relied upon the marshall and the posse of one state to enforce the judgments of the Supreme Court against the sovereignty of another."[55]

State rights Virginians quickly understood that the Cohens decision not only opened the right to sue a state, but, as importantly, allowed the Supreme Court to review a state's criminal jurisdiction. "Fletcher of Salton" thundered that "there is no scintilla of sovereignty, where the state is not supreme in the administration of its criminal jurisprudence."[56] Charles Hammond carefully examined the problems involved in allowing federal appeals in state criminal cases, citing with particular relish several Supreme Court decisions denying such appeals. He quoted Justice Johnson that "'at present, the uncontrollable exercise of criminal jurisdiction is most securely confided the state tribunals. The courts of the United States are vested with no power to scrutinize into the proceedings of the state courts, in criminal cases.'"[57] The Chief Justice ruled similarly in U.S. v. Moore (3 Cranch 169), which denied an appeal in a District of Columbia criminal case on grounds that the Judiciary Act of 1789

---

[55]Ibid., see also June 5, 1821.

[56]Richmond Enquirer, July 3, 1821, see also Washington Gazette, August 8, 14, 1821.

[57]Washington Gazette, August 8, 1821.

permitted appeals only in civil cases. Hammond finally cited U.S. v. Simms (1 Cranch, 252), in which the Supreme Court assumed jurisdiction in the criminal case by writ of error, but after jurisdiction arguments declined to proceed, saying it would review only those judgments "'a power to review which is expressly given by law.'"[58]

Charles Hammond then carefully examined the Judiciary Act and concluded that even if the Constitution authorized the Court's jurisdiction in the Cohens case, it did not necessarily follow that Congress had given the Court power to review this case--or any criminal case. The 25th section of the Judiciary Act provides for writ of error appeals from the highest state court under conditions applicable to federal courts. The Judiciary Act's 22nd section provides for federal writs of error but limits them to civil suits over $2,000 appealed within a limited number of days. The Court cannot disregard any of these provisions, he claimed, including the limitation to civil suits. The Judiciary Act also made no provisions for criminal suits and made no mention of several problems which must be resolved if criminal jurisdiction is exercised. No provisions were made for sending a case back to a state court for reconsideration, for juries, or for who retained custody of a defendant until he is brought to trial.[59] Congress, Hammond quickly conceded, could

---

[58]Ibid., August 14, 1821.

[59]Washington Gazette, August 14, 1821, see also "Pericles" #2, Richmond Daily Mercantile Advertiser, March 27, 1821.

change the judiciary act to include criminal appeals, but until it does, the Cohens appeal is not a suit under the definition in the 25th section of the Judiciary Act. This argument, Hammond admits, was not advanced by the Virginia counsel, but the Court should have taken notice of it as they did in U.S. v. Moore when it was also not mentioned by defense counsel. These cases are important. "That they should have been overlooked is a matter of astonishment: . . . that they should have been disregarded, lead to reflections which I cannot permit myself to suggest."[60]

The discussion of Supreme Court appeals in state criminal cases expanded earlier arguments. The allied discussion of the Supreme Court's jurisdiction, as established by the third article of the Constitution, produced fewer new arguments, although a great deal of space was used arguing whether the Constitution established Supreme Court jurisdiction based on the parties involved, or the subject matter of the case, as John Marshall ruled in the Cohens case, or divided jurisdiction into two mutually exclusive categories-original and appeallate jurisdiction--as the Virginians claimed. Spencer Roane complained that it was "not a natural construction to reach a case by appellate jurisdiction of the court, which was withheld from it in its original character."[61] Peyton Randolph charged that the Court had created a new type of jurisdiction.[62] It was Charles

---

[60]Washington Gazette, August 14, 1821.

[61]Richmond Enquirer, June 1, 1821.

[62]Ibid., June 29, 1821.

Hammond, however, who again provided the most complete legal analysis of Marshall's decision. The Cohens decision, he noted, not only went against the Constitution but against the Supreme Court's earlier opinion in Marbury v. Madison, in which Marshall ruled that:

> If Congress remains at liberty to give this court appellate jurisdiction where the constitution has declared that their jurisdiction shall be original and original jurisdiction where the constitution has declared it shall be appellate, the distribution of jurisdictions made in the constitution is form without substance. . . . the plain import of the words seems to be that in one class of cases its jurisdiction is original, and not appellate in the other it is appellate, and not original.[63]

Hammond cited Justice Johnson's opinion in Ex parte Bollman and Startout to show that Marshall's distinction had been precedent in other federal cases which placed state cases in the original jurisdiction category.

Hammond strongly opposed several other arguments Marshall used in the Cohens decision to justify dividing jurisdiction into parties and subject matter rather than original and appellate jurisdiction. Marshall begged the question, Hammond complained when asserting that without jurisdiction based on subject matter, the Supreme Court could not review many cases involving federal laws. The power to review those cases is the power which must be proven. That jurisdiction is also not necessary, Hammond asserted, to protect foreign ambassadors against adverse state decisions, as Marshall maintained. Other safeguards protect ambassadors, such as a 1790 law which prohibits a state from

---

[63]Washington Gazette, June 30, 1821.

fining or imprisoning ambassadors or foreign delegates. The Supreme Court could also use a writ of prohibition, Hammond countered, which stops, but does not review such cases. Hammond even took the unpopular position that a state could not sue an individual in an inferior federal court because the Constitution gave federal jurisdiction involving states to the Supreme Court and limited that jurisdiction to original jurisdiction.[64] Hammond's position on the Supreme Court's jurisdiction was slightly more strict constructionist than most Virginians, but he summarized well their feelings that the Supreme Court had ignored the words of the Constitution and the intent of those writing and ratifying the document to allow an expansion of the Court's jurisdiction.[65]

IV

One of the most interesting sections of the newspaper dialogue over the Cohens case concerned the Eleventh Amendment to the Constitution. The Cohens case provided the first opportunity for the Supreme Court to review a case involving the Eleventh Amendment, which had the potential to severely limit the Supreme Court's jurisdiction, until Marshall's decision in the Cohens case interpreted the amendment very narrowly. The Cohens case has long been one of the fundamental decisions used to interpret the Eleventh Amendment although most authors have not used the

---

[64]Ibid.

[65]See Richmond Enquirer, June 19, 1821.

newspaper debate to understand the amendment and its origins. State rights Virginians disagreed with Marshall on most of his decision relating to the Eleventh Amendment, and the resulting debate included topics ranging from the reasons behind the amendment's ratification to Marshall's definition of a suit.

The sections of the newspaper debate discussing the origins of the Eleventh Amendment are particularly important. Courts and legal scholars have examined those origins in an attempt to determine why the amendment was ratified, so that later judgments based on the amendment would reflect the intent of the amendment. A lack of contemporary discussion on the amendment has hampered such efforts. As Clyde E. Jacobs, one of the scholars examining the amendment, has noted: "the debates in Congress and in the state legislatures were not reported, and consequently direct documentary evidence as to the intention of those who proposed and ratified the amendment is meager."[66] The hitherto largely ignored newspaper debate over the Cohens case contains one of the most complete discussions about why the amendment was enacted.

The Eleventh Amendment was not discussed in any detail until the Supreme Court's Cohens' decision claimed that the amendment was instituted to stop debt suits pending against the states, not to shore up their sovereign immunity. If the states wished to protect their sovereignty, they would have stopped suits by foreign governments and other states as well. Virginians viewed

---

[66]Clyde E. Jacobs, The Eleventh Amendment and Sovereign Immunity (Westport, Connecticut, 1972), 92.

such arguments as artificial attempts to obscure the real reason for the amendment's adoption. Spencer Roane objected that the Court had not even shown that the states were in debt when the amendment was adopted. Some states were, but others were not. By the time of the amendment's adoption, only three states had been sued in federal court. Virginia's case was a land claim and not a debt case, and had earlier been decided in the state's favor.[67] Ohio's Governor Brown questioned the Supreme Court's constitutional right to hear debt cases. Governor Brown quoted Alexander Hamilton's statement in the Federalist Papers that state debts could not be recovered by litigation, thus allowing the states to pay their debts in any manner they thought proper.[68] Charles Hammond said all agreed that the states gave up some sovereignty against suits with the Constitution's adoption, but did not make themselves liable to individuals' suits. When the Supreme Court interpreted the Constitution as allowing individual's suits against a state, the states initiated the Eleventh Amendment, not to limit the document, but to limit the document's construction to eliminate "any suit commenced or prosecuted against the states by individuals."[69]

Roane detailed his version of the Amendment's adoption. The Amendment was approved "because the states claimed to be

---

[67]Richmond Enquirer, June 8, 1821.

[68]Washington Gazette, July 13, 1821.

[69]Ibid., June 23, 1821, see also July 13, 1821, and Richmond Enquirer, July 13, 1821.

sovereign and independent states, . . . and not on the sordid ground of an unwillingness to pay debts which are not shown to have had any existence." He cited a 1793 Virginia legislative resolution directing the state's senators and representatives to seek a constitutional amendment protecting the state's sovereignty.

> Resolved that a state cannot, under the constitution of the United States, be made a defendant at the suit of any individual, and that the decision of the supreme federal court, that a state may be placed in that situation, is inconsistent with, and dangerous to, the sovereignty and independence of the individual states, as the same tends to a general consolidation of these confederate republics.

The resolution requested the senators to work for an amendment to "'remove or explain any clause or article of the said constitution, which can be construed to imply or justify a decision that a state is compellable to answer, in any suit, by an individual or individuals, in any court of the United States.'" This view, Roane continued, is consistent with an earlier October 1792 legislative pronouncement concerning a suit against Virginia in a federal court. The legislature resolved: "'that the state cannot be made a defendant in the said court at the suit of any individuals.'"[70]

Two other specific portions of Marshall's decision dealing with the Eleventh Amendment received vigorous review: his definition of a suit and his contention that the amendment did not apply to appealed cases. Marshall argued that the Cohens case did not fall under the Eleventh Amendment because the case

[70] Richmond Enquirer, June 8, 1821.

was appealed under a writ of error which was not a suit as required by the amendment, because it allowed a court' s record to be examined by another court without placing demands upon the original plaintiff. Roane totally disagreed with Marshall's definition. The Cohens, as defendants in error, did seek to recover something--the one hundred dollar fine. "In substance therefore this writ of error is entirely a suit. It is also undoubtedly a suit, technically speaking and in point of law." "If this be not a suit, I cannot conceive what is."[71] "Somers" agreed. The Court claimed the writ was not a suit and yet they cannot define what it is. It has all the elements of a suit. The Cohens were attempting to have a right restored to them, and "Somers" quoted Blackstone that a release of all action will release a writ of error if a plaintiff may recover or be restored to anything.[72] Governor Brown of Ohio, in a letter published in the Washington Gazette, claimed that the Court's definition was merely a play on words. The Cohens certainly sought to recover something--their original condition.[73] "Somers" ridiculed a definition which would have Virginia prosecuting the case in the Supreme Court even though she had done everything in her power to avoid it.[74]

---

[71]Ibid.

[72]Ibid., July 13, 1821.

[73]Published in Washington Gazette, July 13, 1821.

[74]Richmond Enquirer, July 13, 1821.

Charles Hammond also adamantly disagreed with Marshall. "I deny that this definition of a case in law is a correct one." Hammond cited an earlier Marshall definition of a suit which included a writ of error. "'It was a controversy between parties that had taken a shape for judicial decision. . . . There must be parties to come into court, who can be reached by its process, and bound by its power; whose rights admit of ultimate decision by a tribunal to which they are bound to submit.'"[75] Peyton Randolph called the Cohens definition

> indefensible. It is an insult to the understanding of the American people. The only question is, whether the suit of Cohens vs. the state of Virginia comes under the description of 'any suit'? If it does not, then language is only calculated to mislead, and the distinguished gift of heaven to man, is a curse sent in its wrath. . . . The supreme court were unanimously of the opinion that the amendment does not embrace such a case! although the words are as comprehensive as the English language can afford; yet six grave judges have decided without a dissenting voice, that the expression any suit does not include a particular class of suits! This event is now a new era in judicial history.[76]

Henry Wheaton gamely supported the Court's definition. A writ of error is not a suit. The Cohens were only defending themselves. They were not seeking anything. A writ of error and an appeal are not suits under the Constitution's definition and it is a uniform court practice to uphold them where suits would not be upheld.[77]

---

[75]Washington Gazette, June 27, 1821, and June 23, 1821.

[76]Richmond Enquirer, June 19, 1821.

[77]New York American, August 2, 1821.

The Supreme Court admitted that it might be mistaken about the definition of a suit, but cautioned that the case would still not fall under the Eleventh Amendment because it was not a suit commenced or prosecuted against a state by a citizen of another state or country. Peyton Randolph voiced his amazement at the ruling. "The silence of the amendment as to a citizen suing his own state, is well accounted for, by the silence of the original constitution. It was not necessary to take away a power, which had never been given."[78]. The Richmond Enquirer wrote that the contention did not deserve an answer.[79] "Algernon Sidney," however, examined the question. "There never was any pretence to say that it ought to be granted to the courts of the general government in any form, . . . The most feverish and unwarrantable jealousy of the State tribunals never apprehended any want of impartiality in them toward their own citizens."

> The proposition would have been indignantly spurned, if made at the time of adopting the constitution. The idea is but newly stated.--I had almost said trumped up.[80]

Henry Wheaton countered in his fifth "Federalist of 1789" essay that the Constitution lists cases and controversies--not suits. Wheaton attempted to show that in the first category it does not matter who are the parties, and in the second who is plaintiff and who defendant. "If the amendment had been intended to be co-extensive with the section amended, it is reasonable to

---

[78]Richmond Enquirer, June 19, 1821, and June 1, 1821.

[79]Ibid., March 23, 1821.

[80]Ibid., June 8, 1821.

suppose that the same terms would have been used." The matter "must have been too well considered, for any material change of language to be attributed to chance." The Constitution is amended only to the extent that the words are changed. It is evident that the amendment was not intended to apply to the Court's jurisdiction in cases arising under the Constitution and laws of the United States, "because in such cases, if a state were a party, a citizen of the same state would be almost always, the other party." The wording "goes very far to prove" that the amendment limits only jurisdiction based on the character of the parties, and not that resulting from the nature of the case.[81]

An equally fundamental difference of interpretation existed over the Eleventh Amendment's prohibition against suits "commenced or prosecuted against one of the United States." The Court interpreted the phrase as applying to any suit then in process, or which should later be commenced against a state, but claimed it did not include cases appealed to the Supreme Court. Spencer Roane denied that the amendment was intended to limit pending suits against the states, although the Court later ruled that it did limit such suits. Commenced or prosecuted, he explained, is disjunctive, and thus applied to any case commenced against a state, or one, like the _Cohens_ case, which although commenced elsewhere might through appeal be prosecuted against a state.[82]

---

[81] _New York American_, August 2, 1821.

[82] _Richmond Enquirer_, June 8, 1821.

To many Virginians the issue was clear. The Eleventh Amendment, adopted to protect state sovereignty, had been emasculated by the Court. "Somers" vocalized his frustration; "the court resort[s] to the most attenuated distinction of philosophy and law to prove that the amendment means one thing and speaks another."[83]

V

The newspaper articles about the Cohens case also examined anew an old state rights opponent--the 25th section of the Judiciary Act of 1789. Among the Richmond Enquirer's earliest reactions to the decision were three articles in March 1821, calling for the "repeal or modification of the 25th section of the Judiciary Act."[84] Spencer Roane, who had written the Virginia Court of Appeals' opinion in Martin v. Hunter's Lessee declaring the section unconstitutional, attacked the section in three of his "Algernon Sidney" essays.[85] It is "founded upon the most unwarrantable jealousy of the state judiciaries, and finds nothing to warrant it in the constitution."[86] Roane labeled the act "absurd and ridiculous" and claimed that it had not been examined carefully before being "passed in great haste by congress, and amidst a vast mass and pressure of other

---

[83]Ibid., July 13, 1821.

[84]Ibid., March 23, 1821, see also March 6, 9, 1821.

[85]Ibid., June 1, 5, 8, 1821.

[86]Ibid., June 1, 1821.

business."[87] The Supreme Court itself, Roane continued, declared part of the act unconstitutional in Marbury v. Madison, and "none who read that decision, can for a moment, doubt that it would have been very grateful to the court to have sustained its jurisdiction."[88]

Henry Wheaton's seventh "Federalist of 1789" answered Roane. The Judiciary Act is a contemporaneous exposition of the constitution of very great weight." How can the bill's consideration be considered hasty? The act went to committee early in the session, which lasted from March to September, and was not passed until September 24--certainly time for thorough consideration. It is no "reflection upon the sagacity of the framers of the bill," that they considered a mandamus, which is generally an appellate process, to be so in all cases. That mistake cannot "be urged as a foundation on which to rest the condemnation of a great and well-considered measure." The act received additional consideration in the short-lived Judiciary Act of 1801, which contained a similar section, and later, when no objection was made to the 25th section when the Judiciary Act of 1789 was reinstated later in 1801.[89] The argument continued

[87]Ibid.

[88]Ibid., June 8, 1821.

[89]New York American, August 9, 1821.

through the series of newspaper articles with no resolution and little agreement.[90]

Not only did state rights Virginians attack the Judiciary Act, but used the act to show that the Cohens appeal had been premature. The Judiciary Act allowed an appeal from the highest state court to the Supreme Court. There are, the Enquirer noted shortly after the decision, two Virginia courts higher than the Norfolk Borough Court.[91] Later Spencer Roane objected that the borough court was not, as the Supreme Court claimed, the highest state court having cognizance of the case and the case had been "prematurely carried into the Supreme Court of the United States." The case could have been appealed to the county court, perhaps to the general court. As a civil suit to recover money, it is even possible that the case could have gone to the Virginia Supreme Court of Appeals. Roane, however, quickly dismissed the premature appeal argument. "Probably, however, this point may have been conceded by counsel, or, possible, it may have been feigned by the court."[92] Roane's essay impressed at least one reader--John Marshall. Four days after the essay appeared he wrote Henry Wheaton on the subject. If Wheaton's report of the case did not mention that an appeal had been made but refused, Marshall suggested inserting an asterisk at the point where the

---

[90]National Intelligencer, August 27, 1821, Richmond Enquirer, August 17, 1821.

[91]Richmond Enquirer, March 23, 1821.

[92]Ibid., May 29, 1821.

borough court is called the highest court where the case could be heard, saying: "'Cohens prayed an appeal from his judgment but it was refused on the principle that there was no higher tribunal which could take cognizance of the case.'"[93] Wheaton did, or already had, included the information in a slightly different form at the end of the borough court record.[94] But he went further. In his third "Federalist of 1789" essay, Wheaton examined Virginia state law. The Virginia Court of Appeals, he claimed, ruled in Becinger v. the Commonwealth that no appeal existed in cases like the Cohens case, and since that decision, no criminal case had been appealed in the state. The Supreme Court record also shows that the Cohen brothers attempted an appeal but were turned down, and no objection was made that the appeal was premature during the Virginia legislative debates or by Virginia's counsel before the Supreme Court. Wheaton felt that if there were grounds for this objection, which, "if well founded, would have been fatal" they would have been mentioned earlier.[95]

Two weeks later, on August 7, 1821, the Enquirer published an editorial and an essay assuring the "Federalist of 1789" that the objection did not escape the legislature's notice. Last October in Norfolk it was noted that the borough court was not

---

[93]John Marshall to Henry Wheaton, June 2, 1821, Wheaton Papers, Pierpont Morgan Library.

[94]6 Wheaton 290.

[95]New York American, July 23, 1821.

the highest state court to which the Cohens case could be appealed. The point was made in the legislative debates and was known by the State counsel in the Supreme Court but Virginia

> wished to take the bull at once by the horns.--They were determined at once to meet the question as to the power of the court, and not to skirmish on any subordinate point. They contested the jurisdiction of the court on broad grounds--and therefore they avoided raising this point.[96]

An unsigned essay followed examining Virginia appellate procedures in great detail, concluding that although no appeals had taken place in Virginia since the Becinger case, that borough court judgments could still be reversed by a superior court writ of error, and the superior court judgment could be examined by a general court writ of error.[97]

VI

Two areas received less attention in the newspaper discussions after the decision than they had received during the legislative debates: the Supreme Court's right to exercise appellate jurisdiction over state courts and the nature of District of Columbia laws. Both sides did, however, reiterate arguments made in earlier debates and in Martin v. Hunter. Henry Wheaton repeated the necessity for the power to review state

---

[96]Richmond Enquirer, August 7, 1821.

[97]Ibid., Herbert Alan Johnson sees the concern of the Virginians as an attempt to block appeals to the Supreme Court by limiting appeals to the highest state court. There does not appear to be any evidence in the documents to indicate this. Herbert Alan Johnson "John Marshall" in Leo Friedman and Fred L. Israel (ed.) The Justices of the United States Supreme Court, 1789-1969, Their Lives and Major Opinions (New York, 1969) Vol. 1, 296.

decisions or "the constitution, laws, and treaties of the Union may be violated with impunity by the state tribunals." Supreme Court review of state decisions, he declared, was "essential to the preservation of the Union."[98] The Supreme Court's examination of the subject in Martin v. Hunter, Wheaton continued, was so thorough "that no new argument remains to be urged upon it," raising "the expectation that the question would never be raised again."[99] Spencer Roane quoted earlier arguments and modestly claimed that Virginia's Court of Appeals' arguments in Martin v. Hunter "cannot be answered. They certainly have not been answered in the case in Wheaton referred to by the supreme court."[100] While the question was discussed briefly by the two sides, neither entered into a detailed examination of the subject.

The status of congressional legislation for the District of Columbia had been an almost universal objection to the Cohens case before the decision. Marshall defused the issue, however, when he ruled that the congressional authorization for the National Lottery did not supersede state regulation. Yet the danger was not over, Roane reminded his readers. The District law had been judged "to be an act of the United States, in the case in question." A differently worded law would have

---

[98]New York American, August 8, 1821.

[99]Ibid.

[100]Richmond Enquirer, June 8, 1821.

superseded state regulation.[101] "The court has sanctioned the right of the legislature of the District of Columbia, to act by deputy; and has exalted to the dignity of a statute of the United States an ordinance of the Common Hall of the city of Washington."[102] Roane's fifth "Algernon Sidney" essay quotes many historical precedents mentioned during earlier legislative debates. The power of the "petty corporation of the city of Washington" is, he said, of effect only within the District. "Virginia is independent of _it_ and them, as she is of the small island of Malta."[103]

An article in Clinton's New York _Times Democrat_ noted the lack of discussion on the topic, erroneously reporting that "'as this question has not been discussed, it was probably deemed unworthy of notice.'"[104] The article guessed that this lack of discussion was prompted by Virginia's desire to oppose the Court's jurisdiction on broad principles. A few other articles mention the status of District laws but the topic did not become the popular cause it had been the winter before.[105]

The essays and letters examined the _Cohens_ decision from almost every possible angle. The _Richmond Enquirer's_ editors noted

---

[101] _Ibid._

[102] _Ibid._, May 25, 1821.

[103] _Ibid._, June 8, 1821.

[104] Reprinted in _Richmond Enquirer_, August 31, 1821.

[105] _Washington Gazette_, November 30, December 4, 1821.

> The subject which has engrossed so much of the attention of this paper, has lately become a sort of leading topic in many of our public prints. Since '98 and '99, when the alien and sedition laws were tried, condemned and executed by an indignant people, the discussion of constitutional principles has not been so general or animated as it is at this moment.[106]

The decision's opponents, however, wished to do far more than just examine the case as an academic or legalistic exercise. They wanted to arouse American citizens against a consolidation of governmental powers. They sought to limit the Supreme Court's power or at least deny that the Court is the Constitution's ultimate arbiter. If the Supreme Court gained that power, Court opponents feared that dual sovereignty, the imperium in imperio, would be ended and the sovereignty of the states become a mere fiction. The national government might grow under such conditions, but it would not be the federal system established by the Constitution's founders.

---

[106] Richmond Enquirer, August 31, 1821.

CHAPTER VII

CONCLUSION

FAILURE AND LEGACY

Organized opposition to the Cohens decision gradually ended after a year and a half. Court opponents had mounted perhaps the most vociferous attack on the Supreme Court during Marshall's tenure as Chief Justice and participated in a significant political and constitutional dialogue. They did not, however, protect the state's sovereign immunity by passing a constitutional amendment to change the Court's jurisdiction or organize a new tribunal to hear cases involving disputes between states and the federal government. The agitation over the Cohens decision brought to the surface widespread popular discontent but state rights Virginians were not able to channel that discontent into action. The National Intelligencer was essentially correct when it declared that the Virginia campaign had failed.[1] The reasons for that failure are as instructive in understanding the Supreme Court and American society in 1821 as the reasons for popular discontent are instructive about why the Cohens case captured wide attention.

The Virginians failed because they failed to understand political and constitutional changes that had taken place since 1789. They were unable to formulate a positive program to unite

---

[1]National Intelligencer, March 8, 1822.

those groups unhappy with the Supreme Court, and they underestimated the political skill of John Marshall. Most Virginians participating in the _Cohens_ discussions had also taken part in the debates over the Constitution or had come of age during those debates. Most of those Virginians developed their personal political philosophies during the constitutional debates and continued to view politics in those terms. A majority of Americans living in 1821, however, had not been alive in 1790, and many others who were alive in 1790 had grown up under the Constitution and had known no other governmental system. To such citizens, Roane's fears about a plot to consolidate all governmental powers in the federal government were distant at best. The federal government had not destroyed liberty as many cynics had predicted, and many fears aroused during the Constitution's ratification no longer seemed frightening. Nationally many, if not most, of the new generation coming to power were willing to give the federal government the benefit of the doubt, or at least did not share Roane's view that the American form of government could be easily changed. This general acceptance of the Constitution is illustrated in the amendments added to the Constitution. After the Eleventh and Twelfth Amendments were quickly ratified in 1798 and 1804, the country waited 61 years before another formal change was made in its basic charter of government. There were many reasons for this long period between the 12th and 13th amendments, but one the reasons was a general acceptance of the Constitution, despite some basic disagreements over how it should be interpreted.

The growth of the United States from just under four million citizens in 13 states in 1790, to almost 10 million citizens in 24 states in 1821, presented additional problems to Court opponents. The enlarged territory increased the number of state and local interest groups. This expansion made an individual state less important, and made it harder to unite diverse economic, social, and geographic areas. Charles Hammond incidently touched on this problem in his eleventh "Hampden" essay.

> It is true, lamentable true, that '<u>north of the Potomac</u>; few persons take any interest in discussions growing out of the constitution. New York, Pennsylvania and Maryland are rent with factions, who take a much deeper interest in the appointment of a sheriff, an auctioneer, or a justice of the levy court, than in the correct understanding of constitutional doctrines. In New England, the old-fashioned federalists adhere more consistently to their ancient notions of accumulating power to the government of the union. And, for the rest, of whom it may be fairly enquired, <u>cujum pecus</u>? the most of them only wish to know the opinion of the President and the heads of Departments, that they may adopt the same.[2]

Such varied interest groups not only prevented Roane and Ritchie and others opposing the Court from solidifying Virginia against the Court, but also impeded union with those states that had been involved in recent disputes with the Court. Three states were likely prospects. Maryland had lost her right to tax the Bank of the United States in <u>McCulloch v Maryland</u>. Unwilling to accept the Maryland decision as binding, Ohio was fiercely contesting

---

[2]<u>Washington Gazette</u>, August 20, 1821.

for similar powers in Osborn v The Bank of the United States. Kentucky was involved in Green v Biddle, a case state leaders feared would disrupt most land titles in the state.

Despite the McCulloch decision, little opposition to the Court remained in Maryland. Individuals who opposed the federal bench could certainly be found, but not enough to support a crusade. Perhaps, as Hammond claimed, state politicians were so concerned with internal conflicts that they had no energy left to oppose the Supreme Court. On the national scene, the Maryland legislature shifted to other projects, including a proposal to give school land to the original thirteen states, a proposal Virginia leaders could not accept.[3]

The withdrawal of taxes from the Bank of the United States and the resulting suit against the Ohio state treasurer created much Ohio opposition to the Supreme Court. Virginia and Ohio, however, could not agree on united action. The Virginians were reluctant to accept Ohio's unilateral action against the Bank, and the Virginia Legislature could not agree on what action to take on the Ohio Legislature's resolutions on the case. The resolutions were finally tabled because the Virginia legislators could not agree on whether the federal government could bring suit against a state official for enforcing an unconstitutional law. Ohio said no! The Virginians were not sure.[4] The refusal of Virginia to endorse the resolutions illustrates clearly how

---

[3]See: "Fabracious," Richmond Enquirer, January 3, 1822.

[4]Richmond Enquirer, June 12, 1821.

seemingly minor differences over methods and constitutional theory kept two states that opposed the Court from cooperating.

Similar problems existed when an attempt was made to unite with Court opponents in Kentucky. The major obstacle to that unity came because most of the contested Kentucky land titles in the Supreme Court case involved disputes between Virginians and Kentuckians. A tentative compromise was worked out, but the Virginia Legislature refused to ratify it, making further cooperation increasingly difficult. Contested land titles thus prevented the two states from joining wholeheartedly together to oppose the Supreme Court as they had joined together to oppose the Alien and Sedition Acts.

Although the Virginians looked to the successful campaign against the Alien and Sedition Acts for their model, they did not understand differences between the two campaigns which severely limited their chances for success. The election of 1800 was not a plebiscite on the Alien and Sedition Acts and "correct" political principles, as some Virginians believed, but the acts were a major issue in the highly contested presidential election between Jefferson and John Adams. The Cohens case did not have the support of a major political party during a presidential election. The case did coincide with James Monroe's re-election effort, but because much of the controversy over the case developed after the electoral vote took place, it played no part in the election. This is not, however, to say that the case was uninfluential in presidential politics. The case became an issue in the early campaigning for the election of 1824, which started even before Monroe was inaugurated. The case, however, became an issue in a way which was unlikely to help, and could seriously hurt, the case in other states.[5] At least one presidential candidate in 1824 viewed the agitation over the Cohens case as a tactic to test support for a new candidate from Virginia--perhaps Spencer Roane. John Quincy Adams characterized Roane's opposition as "'close ambition varnished o'er with zeal.' Jefferson and Madison did attain power by organizing and heading a system of attack upon the Washington administration, chiefly under the banners of State rights and State sovereignty."[6] Adams concluded that Roane wished to follow Jefferson and Madison. Many of the politicians opposing the Virginia position in the Cohens case alluded to the Virginian's political motives but few were as explicit as the Southern Patriot:

> Those spirits who cannot expect to rise to public honors, except under the State governments, find this sphere too narrow for their ambition. The magic words, state rights and state sovereignty, are those by which they hope successfully to work their spells.[7]

John C. Calhoun's use of the case has already been mentioned. He hoped Henry Wheaton's writings about the case would counter the "radicals" in New York and Virginia who he viewed as political

---

[5]For contemporary discussions about the election see: Richmond Enquirer, July 19, 26; August 13, 27, 30; September 13, 27; January 10, 15, 19, 26; April 16, 1822.

[6]John Quincy Adams, The Diary of John Quincy Adams, edited by Allan Nevins (New York, 1928), 226.

[7]Reprinted in National Intelligencer, September 12, 1821.

opponents. Other Court supporters questioned their opponents' loyalty, comparing their actions to the Hartford Convention, and Ohio's seizing funds from the Bank of the United States.

The accusation that Virginians were using the Cohens case to promote a Virginian for President was correct to the extent that some Virginians, feeling keenly their loss of political and economic power, would have welcomed a continuation of the Virginia dynasty. Robert Carter Nicholas wrote to Samuel Smith in February 1822, that "it would not surprise me if the nation be forced to tax once more Virginia. Much as her stores are reduced and great as her relative population is diminished, she could certainly yet, if urged to it furnish a more competent man than either of those yet named."[8] John Hampden Pleasants, who later became a leading member of the Whig party in Virginia, wrote in his Lynchburg newspaper that Spencer Roane would be his first choice for the Presidency.[9] John Randolph and Thomas Ritchie reportedly agreed with the choice.[10] It is now apparent that election objectives were not the main motivation for the Court's

---

[8]Robert Carter Nicholas to Samuel Smith, February 21, 1821, Samuel Smith Papers, Library of Congress.

[9]Lynchburg Press, January 18, 1822.

[10]John Randolph to James M. Garnett, March 22, 1820, Randolph-Garnett Papers, University of Virginia; also John Randolph to John Brockenbrough, January 5, 1821, quoted in Hugh Garland, The Life of John Randolph of Roanoke, 2 vols. (New York, 1850), II, 143-144. The evidence that Ritchie wanted Roane to become President is less definite. Charles H. Ambler makes the claim, but does not document it. Charles H. Ambler, Thomas Ritchie (Richmond, 1913), 87.

opponents, and yet there was enough truth in the charges to concern some, and provide others with ammunition.

Virginia's presentation of the case did little to overcome these problems; in fact, it often contributed to the problem. The position of opponents to the decision was usually included in long legalistic arguments which few readers then, or since, have digested. A National Gazette writer complained that the discourses "move on with a course in extent like that of the Mississippi or Amazon. Few persons, we fear, north of the Potomac, will have the courage and patience to navigate their endless stream of discussion."[11] Others echoed the sentiment. The Philadelphia Franklin Gazette wrote of "'mock Hampdens and Sidneys, who so laboriously and with so much dullness fill the columns of certain newspapers.'"[12] The Richmond Daily Mercantile Advertiser described Roane's articles as being of a "most unreasonable length," showing "much labor and many words."[13] "Senex," answering the "Hampden" articles, complained that he had "perused him with attention, and shown a patience, which few I believe possess."[14]

It was not just the great length of the Virginia articles, however, which limited their impact. The articles lacked focus

---

[11]National Gazette, June 28, 1821, reprinted in Washington Gazette, July 2, 1821.

[12]Reprinted in Richmond Enquirer, August 14, 1821.

[13]Richmond Daily Mercantile Advertiser, June 5, 1821.

[14]Washington Gazette, August 23, 1821, and Richmond Daily Mercantile Advertiser, June 1, 1821.

and contained no united plan of action. The articles discussed a wide variety of subjects and individual authors generally treated several subjects in a single article. The result was a potpourri of arguments, often expressed in legalistic language, which inspired few uncommitted readers to more than periodic intellectual agreement. Even those who might be convinced of the correctness of the Virginia position were given little direction for future action. The inability of opponents to the *Cohens* decision to formulate a clear program for action was one of the Virginians' major flaws. Without a specific program, discontent might surface, but would dissipate without being directed toward some action. The basic problem seems to have been the same one which faced Richard M. Johnson's amendment to make the Senate a court to hear conflicts between the states and the federal government--even among those who agreed that something should be done, no one could agree on the solution.[15] Without such agreement no lasting action could be expected--and none was forthcoming.

A final reason for the Virginia failure was the skill of Chief Justice John Marshall. In fact, the *Cohens* case illustrates Marshall's blend of jurist and politician better than the more widely known case of *Marbury v. Madison*. In the *Cohens* decision, in fact, Marshall followed the pattern established in *Marbury v. Madison*. He upheld major Court powers while ruling for his opponents on the merits of the case. In the face of

[15] *Richmond Enquirer*, January 19, 1822.

severe political opposition, Marshall's opinion and timing of the opinion defused a potentially dangerous situation while protecting the Court. Marshall first divided the questions involved in the case and scheduled a full examination of the Court's jurisdiction. Marshall then limited opposition to the jurisdiction, ruling in favor of the Court by hearing arguments on the merits of the case before announcing the jurisdiction decision, and then ruling for Virginia on the merits of the case three days after ruling for the Court on the jurisdiction question. Marshall's decision on merits further calmed the situation. Marshall upheld the theoretical right of Congress to legislate for the nation through their power over the District of Columbia, but granted that Congress had not wished the present lottery law to extend beyond District boundaries. Marshall's skillful timing, however, went beyond orchestrating the relationship of the two decisions. Either by coincidence or perhaps, by design, the Court's two decisions came just as the United States Congress and the Virginia General Assembly were adjourning. This insured that any official examination of those decisions by either body would have to wait almost a year--surely enough time for some of the furor to die down. Finally, Marshall showed a keen interest in the review of the decision. He may have influenced the Henry Wheaton articles upholding the decision, and at least attempted to get them published in the nation's leading law journal to counter the proposed publication of Spencer Roane's articles critical of the decision.

Participants understood some of the difficulties posed by Marshall's skillful handling of the decision. "Franklin," in a letter to the Virginia General Assembly, compared the present situation to the Alien and Sedition Acts. The threat in the *Cohens* case was less obvious than the jailings and political restrictions of the Alien and Sedition laws. "We deal not with the frantic swaggerings of *John Adams*, or with the open and unblushing tyrannies of *Judge Chase*. We have now to deal with a . . . cooler set of men than these."[16] It had been much easier for Jefferson and Madison to characterize Alexander Hamilton and John Adams as evil archetypes than to cast John Marshall in that role.

The failure of the Virginia campaign against the *Cohens* decision does not mean the case and the debates over the decision were unimportant to later American history. The *Cohens* case left an important historical legacy, ranging from the case's legal rulings to an important political and constitutional debate, illustrating American political thought and practice in 1821.

John Marshall's nationalistic pronouncements in the *Cohens* case are the case's most lasting legacy. In one case, Marshall was able to define the jurisdiction of the Supreme Court, give the major interpretation of the Eleventh Amendment, amplify an earlier decision that cases could be appealed from state courts to federal courts, and keep open the possibility that Congress could enact laws for the District of Columbia which would

[16] *Ibid.*, January 26, 1822.

overrule state legislation. It is amazing that these rulings, highly disputed at the time, have been accepted by most later jurists with little or no question. Marshall's ruling that the Constitution granted the Supreme Court jurisdiction in all cases involving an interpretation of the Constitution or laws of the United States, regardless of the parties involved, went against earlier Supreme Court precedents in Marbury v. Madison and several rulings which limited the Court's jurisdiction to civil cases. The ruling also went against the understanding of some, if not all, state ratifying conventions. Similarly, Marshall's view that the Eleventh Amendment was ratified to escape state debts rather than to protect state sovereignty does not correspond with contemporary understanding.[17] Marshall's interpretation that the amendment applied only to cases originated as suits against a state, and not to state actions against individuals, appealed to the Supreme Court, allowed federal courts to establish a unified interpretation of the Constitution, and solidified the supremacy of the federal government. The ruling has been an important element in the growth of out present legal system. The ruling was not, however, in accord with the understanding of those who ratified the amendment. Finally, Marshall's careful protection of the right of Congress to legislate for the nation through legislation for the District of Columbia seems unimportant today. That power

---

[17]Clyde E. Jacobs, The Eleventh Amendment and Sovereign Immunity (Westport, Connecticut, 1972), 69.

might, however, have been a major avenue for the expansion of federal power if Roane and other state rights Virginians had succeeded in limiting the power of the federal government to those powers absolutely necessary and proper. The Cohens case thus shaped much of our present legal system and established basic definitions about the relation of federal and state courts.

The Cohens case also left an important political and constitutional legacy. The case is particularly helpful in illustrating several political relationships. First, the case clearly shows the acceptance of the Constitution in 1821. Although the stability of the Constitution by 1821 seems obvious today, neither the state rights Virginians nor the supporters of the Supreme Court seem to have recognized the almost universal acceptance of the Constitution. Each side was motivated to enter the Cohens discussions, in part, by a fear that the Constitution was a malleable instrument which could be easily changed by designing men like their opponents. This mistrust is more easily understood when it is remembered that those political leaders who had been active during the Revolution not only remembered the past thirty years under the Constitution, but the three governmental systems during the previous twenty years. It is clear, however, that by the time of the Cohens decision, most Americans had accepted the Constitution. During the debates over the Cohens decision, for example, both sides pictured themselves as the defender of the Constitution. Differences still existed as to how the Constitution should be interpreted, but the document was considered inviolable by the vast majority of American citizens.

The general acceptance of the Constitution, and the failure of any proposed Constitutional amendments following the _Cohens_ decision, helped change state rights thought by shattering the confidence of state rights supporters in the successful pattern of the events surrounding Virginia's opposition to the Alien and Sedition Acts and the election of Jefferson as President. Whether correctly or not, most state rights Virginians felt that their earlier efforts had fundamentally changed the federal government. They felt that the political process had been responsive not only politically, but constitutionally as well. Such men felt that they had changed the government when it had strayed from correct principles and that they could do so again anytime the occasion arose. State rights Virginians did not fully understand the elements which brought success in 1798-1800 or the elements involved in the current failure. They did understand that the earlier model had not worked for them and that new solutions must be found. Those solutions would not be found in the political arena and ultimately had to be settled on another kind of battlefield.

The _Cohens_ case also illustrates, as few other episodes can, the overestimation by historians of the Richmond Junto's power in Virginia. Long viewed as a political faction which had virtual control over every facet of Virginia government, the _Cohens_ case both shows their importance in state politics and lays to rest the myth of Junto control of the state. The Junto was able to help bring to the surface the dangers they saw in the _Cohens_ case and the decision of the Supreme Court. They were not able, however, to bring to a vote in the Virginia legislature a series of constitutional amendments authored by Junto leader Spencer Roane to limit the jurisdiction of the Supreme Court. If the Junto had been as powerful as historians have later claimed, they might not have been able to change John Marshall's decision, but they certainly could have passed Roane's amendments.

Finally, the _Cohens_ case shows the importance of understanding the local background of cases like the _Cohens_ case. The _Cohens_ case is in large part a product of such local economic, political, and social forces, which provided both the reasons the case became controversial and the reasons for the Virginians' failure. Even the case's major legal rulings were largely shaped by state concerns, such as the Supreme Court's right to hear the case, which had little to do with the extent of congressional laws for the District of Columbia. Without the local element, it is possible that the Supreme Court might have upheld the superiority of the District's lottery law without making an examination of the Court's jurisdiction. It is ironic that the jurisdiction decision, which gave the federal government important precedents in establishing the supremacy of the Supreme Court, came at the urging of Virginia's counsels, and that many of the specific provisions upholding the Court's power came in answer to arguments presented by the Virginians. The case's background, however, is often forgotten when the case is cited or examined. The Court's nationalistic pronouncements in the case are used as precedent, without the tempering effect provided by the opposing arguments. Perhaps Marshall's constitutional view was best for America, but it was not the only valid interpretation available. Perhaps in the end John Marshall was just the better politician.

BIBLIOGRAPHY

Manuscripts

Ambler Papers, University of Virginia Library (U.Va.)

Anderson Family Papers, U.Va.

James Barbour Papers, U.Va.

Barbour Family Papers, U.Va.

Barbour Papers, Library of Congress (LC).

Barbour Papers, Virginia Historical Society Library (VHS).

Bryan Family Papers, U.Va.

Cabell Papers, U.Va.

Cabell-Carrington Papers, U.Va.

John C. Calhoun Papers, Pierpont Morgan Library (PM).

Campbell Papers, Duke University Library (DU).

Carr-Cary Papers, U.Va.

Carter Papers, U.Va.

Henry Clay Papers, U.Va.

James Hartwell Cocke Papers, U.Va.

Cohen Papers, Maryland Historical Society Library (MdHS).

Cohens v Virginia, mss, Norfolk County Courthouse.

Cohens v Virginia mss file, Records of the United States Supreme Court, National Archives (NA).

Council Minutebook, Virginia State Library (VSL).

Isaac Davis Papers, U.Va.

Dockets of the Supreme Court of the United States, NA.

Executive Letterbook, VSL.

Executive Papers, VSL.

Garnett-Randolph Papers, U,Va.

Francis W. Gilmer Papers, U.Va.

Gooch Family Papers, U.Va.

Grinnan Family PaPers, U.Va.

Charles Hammond Papers, Ohio Historical Society Library (OHS).

Harrison-Tucker-Smith Collection, U.Va.

Heath-Selden Manuscripts, U.Va.

Robert T. Hunter Papers, U.Va.

Irving-Saunders Papers, U.Va.

Journal of the Council of State, VSL.

Legislative Petitions, VSL.

Benjamin Watkins Leigh Papers, U.Va.

Benjamin Watkins Leigh Papers, VHS.

James Madison Papers, LC.

James Madison Papers, U.Va.

James McDowell, Jr. Papers, DU.

James McDowell Papers, University of North Carolina Library (UNC).

Minutes of the Supreme Court of the United States of America, Minute Book C, NA.

Wilson Cary Nicholas Papers, LC.

Nicholas Papers, U.Va.

Preston-Radford Papers, U.Va.

Edgehill-Randolph Papers, U.Va.

John Randolph of Roanoake (combined papers), U.Va.

Randolph Family Papers, U.Va.

Thomas Ritchie Papers, LC.

William C. Rives Papers, LC.

Rives Family Papers, U.Va.

Roane, Harrison, and Williams Papers, VHS.

Frank G. Ruffin Papers, UNC.

"Session Day Book," Wheaton Papers, PM.

Samuel Smith Papers, LC.

Smith Papers, U.Va.

Stuart-Baldwin Papers, U.Va.

Andrew Stevenson Papers, LC.

Archibald Stuart Papers, VHS.

Creed Taylor Papers, U.Va.

Tazewell Papers, VSL.

Terrell Family Papers, U.Va.

Nicholas Trist Papers, LC.

Tucker Coleman Papers, William and Mary Library (W&M).

Henry St. George Tucker Papers, UNC.

Martin Van Buren Papers, LC.

Washington Monument Papers, MdHS.

Watson Family Papers, U.Va.

Webb-Prentis Papers, U.Va.

Henry Wheaton Papers, PM.

William Wirt Lettergook, LC.

William Wirt Papers, UNC.

Wirt Papers, MdHS.

Wirt Papers, U.Va.

NEWSPAPERS

Alabama

Mobile Commercial.

Connecticut

Connecticut Journal (New Haven).

Georgia

Milledgeville Times and State Rights Advocate.

Southern Recorder (Milledgeville).

Illinois

Illinois Gazette (Shawnestown).

Kentucky

Argus of the Western World (Frankfort).

Kentucky Gazette (Lexington).

Kentucky Reporter (Lexington).

Louisville Public Advertiser.

Louisiana

The Asylum and Felicia Advertiser (West Francisville).

Maryland

American and Commercial Advertiser (Baltimore).

Cohens Gazette and Lottery Register (Baltimore).

The Maryland Gazette and Political Intelligencer (Annapolis).

The Maryland Herald and Hagerstown Weekly Advertiser.

Niles Register (Baltimore).

The Torch Light and Public Advertiser (Hagerstown).

Massachusetts

The Pittsfield Sun.

Missouri

Independent Patriot (Jackson).

Missouri Gazette and Public Advertiser (St. Louis).

The Missourian (St. Charles).

St. Louis Enquirer.

New Jersey

The Herald and Gloucester Farmer (Woodbury).

New York

The Albany Argus.

The American (New York).

Commercial Advertiser (New York).

Norwich Journal.

Rochester Gazette.

Rochester Telegram.

North Carolina

The Cape Fear Recorder (Willmington).

Carolina Centinel (New Bern).

Edenton Gazette and North Carolina General Advertiser.

Hillsborough Recorder.

Raleigh Minerva.

Raleigh Register and North Carolina State Gazette.

The Star (Raleigh).

West Carolinian (Salisbury).

Ohio

Scioto Gazette and Fredonia Chronicle (Chillicothe).

The Supporter and Scioto Gazette.

Western Star (Lebanon).

Pennsylvania

Easton Centinel.

South Carolina

Carolina Gazette (Charleston).

Charleston Courier.

Tennessee

The Clarion and Tennessee Gazette (Nashville).

Knoxville Register.

Nashville Whig.

Tennessee Watchman (Clarksville).

Virginia

The Alexandrian.

The Alexandria Gazette and Daily Advertiser.

The Alexandria Herald.

American Beacon (Norfolk).

Central Gazette (Charlottesville).

Farmer's Repository (Charles Town).

The Genius of Liberty (Leesburg).

Herald of the Valley (Fincastle).

The Lynchburg Press.

Norfolk and Portsmouth Herald.

Palladium of Liberty (Warrenton).

Petersburg Republican.

Richmond Commercial Compiler.

Richmond Mercantile Advertiser.

Richmond Enquirer.

The Virginia Herald (Fredericksburg).

Virginia North-western Gazette (Wheeling).

Wellsburg Gazette.

Washington, D. C.

City of Washington Gazette.

National Intelligencer.

Washington Republican and Congressional Examiner.

Published Primary Works

Ambler, Charles H. (ed.). "Unpublished Letters of Thomas Ritchie," *John P. Branch Historical Papers*, III (June 1911).

Annals of the Congress of the United States, 43 vols. Washington, 1834-1856.

Barbour (James) Papers. *New York Public Library Bulletin*, VI, 22-34.

Brown, Everett Somerville (ed.). *The Missouri Compromises and Presidential Politics 1820-1825, From the Letters of William Plumer, Junior*. St. Louis, 1926.

Cohens v. Virginia. 6 Wheaton (U.S.), (1821), 264-448.

A Collection of All Such Acts of the General Assembly of Virginia. . . . as Are Now in Force; . . . Richmond, 1803.

Commonwealth v. Chubb. 5 Randolph (Va.), (1827).

Cralle, Richard Kenner (ed.). *The Works of John C. Calhoun*, 6 vols. New York, 1854-1858.

Fitzpatrick, John C (ed.). *The Writings of George Washington*, 39 vols. Washington, 1939-1944.

Hamilton, Stanislaus M. (ed.). The Writings of James Monroe, . . . , 7 vols. 1902, Reprint New York, 1969.

Hammond, Charles. Review of the Opinion of the Supreme Court of The United States, in the Case of Cohens v. Virginia: Originally Published in the Washington (City) Gazette; . . . . Stubenville, Ohio, 1821.

Hening, William W. The Statutes at Large; Being a Collection of all the Laws of Virginia . . . , 13 vols. Richmond, 1821.

_____, The Virginia Justice . . ., 4th ed. Richmond, 1825.

Hopkins, James F. The Papers of Henry Clay, 3 vols. Lexington, 1963.

Lee, Henry. Letters on the Richmond Party, By a Virginian, Originally Published in the Washington Republican. Washington, 1823.

Letters and Other Writings of James Madison, Fourth President of the United States, 4 vols. Philadelphia, 1865.

"Letters of Chief Justice Marshall." Proceedings of the Massachusetts Historical Society, 2nd Ser. Vol. XIV (1900-1901), 320-360.

Liscomb, Andrew (ed.). The Writings of Thomas Jefferson, 20 vols. Washington, 1904.

"Macon Papers," John P. Branch Historical Papers, III (June 1909).

M'Duffie, George. National and State Rights Considered . . . Columbia, 1821.

Maryland, General Assembly. Laws Made and Passed by the General Assembly of the State of Maryland . . . Annapolis, 1815-1835.

Nevins, Allan (ed.). The Diary of John Quincy Adams, 1794-1845 . . . New York, 1928.

The Revised Code of the Laws of Virginia, 2 vols. Richmond, 1820.

Roane, Spencer. "Roane Correspondence," John P. Branch Historical Papers, II (June 1905), 123-142.

_____, "Letters of Spencer Roane, 1788-1822," Bulletin of The New York Public Library, X (Feb. 1906), 167-180.

_____, "Virginia Opposition to Chief Justice Marshall," John P. Branch Historical Papers, II (June 1906), 78-183.

Taylor, John. Tyranny Unmasked . . . Washington, 1822.

Tucker, George Holbert (comp.). Abstracts from Norfolk City Marriage Bonds . . . n.p., 1934.

Virginia, Constitutional Convention. Journal, Acts and Proceedings of A General Convention of the State of Virginia. . . Richmond, 1850.

Virginia, General Assembly. Journal of the House of Delegates of Virginia . . . Richmond, 1820-1852.

_____, Acts Passed at a General Assembly of the Commonwealth of Virginia . . . Richmond, 1810-1852.

The Virginia Report of 1799-1800 . . . reprint Richmond, 1850.

Warren, Charles. "The Story-Marshall Correspondence," William and Mary Quarterly (W&MQ), 2nd ser., XXI (Jan. 1941), 1-26.

West, Elizabeth H. (ed.). Calender of the Papers of Martin Van Buren. Washington, 1910.

Wheaton, Henry. Reports of Cases Argued and Adjudged in the Supreme Court of the United States, 12 vols., 4th ed. New York, 1883.

Articles

Aitkin, Hugh G. J. "Yates and McIntyre: Lottery Managers," The Journal of Economic History, XIII (Winter, 1953), 36-56.

Ammon, Harry. "James Monroe and the Election of 1808 in Virginia," W&MQ, 3rd ser. (January 1963), 33-56.

_____, "The Richmond Junto, 1800-1824," Virginia Magazine of History and Biography (VHMB), LXIV (October 1953), 395-418.

Baroway, Aaron. "The Cohens of Maryland," Maryland Historical Magazine (MHM), XVIII (December 1923), 355-376; and XIX (March 1924), 54-77.

Beach, Rex. "Spencer Roane and the Richmond Junto," W&MQ, 2nd ser. XXII (January 1942), 1-17.

Burnette, Allen Lawrence. "Peter V. Daniel: Agrarian Justice," VHMB. LXII (1954), 289-305.

Cohen, Mendes. "Mr. Mendes Cohen on 'the Cohen Collection of Egyptian Antiquities,' and its Collector, Colonel Mendes I. Cohen," Johns Hopkins University Circulars, vol. IV, no. 35 (December 1884), 21-23.

Dodd, William E. "Chief Justice Marshall and Virginia, 1813-1821," American Historical Review, XII (July 1907), 776-787.

Grigsby, Hugh Blair. "Sketches of Men of the Constitutional Convention, 1829-1830," VHMB, LXI (July 1953), 319-332.

Harrison, Joseph H. Jr. "Oligarchs and Democrats: The Richmond Junto." VHMB, LXXVIII (April 1970), 184-198.

Hartogenis, Benjamin H. "Unequal Religious Rights in Maryland Since 1776," Publication of the American Jewish Historical Society, XXV (1917), 93-107.

Hackett, Homer C. "Rufus King and the Missouri Compromise." Missouri Historical Review, II (1908), 211-220.

"James City County Petitions," Tyler's Quarterly Historical and Geneological Magazine, II (January 1921), 177-193.

Jefferson, Thomas. "Thoughts on lotteries," In Andrew A. Lipscomb (ed.). The Writings of Thomas Jefferson. Washington, 1903, 448-465.

Johnson, Herbert Alan. "John Marshall," In Leon Friedman and Fred L. Israel (ed.). The Justices of the United States Supreme Court 1789-1969 . . . , vol. I. New York, 1969, 285-355.

Johnson, Robert C. "The Lotteries of the Virginia Company, 1612-1621," VHMB, LXXIV (July 1966), 259-292.

_____, "The Running Lotteries of the Virginia Company," VHMB, LXVIII (April 1960), 156-165.

Ketcham, Ralph L. "James Madison and Judicial Review," Syracuse Law Review, VIII (Spring, 1957).

Larsen, Henrietta. "S & H Allen, Lottery, Exchange, and Stock Brockerage," Journal of Economic and Business History, III (1930-1931), 424-445.

"Letters and Other Papers, 1705-1829," VHMB, VIII (October 1915), 353-370.

Letters of Thomas Adams, 1768-1775," VHMB, VIII (January 1915), 52-65.

"Lotteries in the District of Columbia," American State Papers, Class X (misc), vol. II. Washington, 1834.

Luce, W. Ray. "The Cohen Brothers of Baltimore: From Lotteries to Banking." MHM, LXVIII (Fall, 1973), 288-308.

Mays, David J. "Judge Spencer Roane," Reports of the Virginia State Bar Association, XL (1929), 446-464.

Morton, Richard L. "The Virginia State Debt and Internal Improvements, 1820-1838." Journal of Political Economy.

Nagel, Paul C. "Virginia Debates National Destiny," VHMB, LXIII (October 1955), 427-439.

"Notes on the Career of Colonel William Tatham," VHMB, (April 1917), 198-199.

O'Brien, Terence. "The London Livery Companies and the Virginia Company," VHMB, (April 1960), 137-155.

"The Preston Papers," VHMB, XXVI (October 1918), 363-379.

Riley, Henry C. "Sketche of William H. Cabell," Reports of the Virginia State Bar Association, XLI (1930), 581-612.

Stockbridge, Henry. "Baltimore in 1846," MHM, VI (March 1911), 20-34.

Upton, Anthony F. "The Road to Power in Virginia in the Early Nineteenth Century," VHMB, LXIII (July 1954), 259-280.

"Virginia Gazette Extracts," W&MQ, XII (October 1903), 73-83.

Walne, Peter. "The Running Lottery of the Virginia Company in Reading, 1619, and in Chester, 1616." VHMB, (January 1962), 30-34.

Warren, Charles, "Legislative and Judicial Attacts on the Supreme Court of the United States. A History of the Twenty-fifth Section of the Judiciary Act." American Law Review, XLVII (January-February 1913).

"Will of Colonel William Byrd 3d," VHMB, IX (July 1901), 80-88.

"Williamsburg Lodge of Masons," W&MQ, I (July 1892), 1-33.

Books

Ambler, Charles H. Sectionalism in Virginia from 1776 to 1861. Chicago, 1910.

_____. Thomas Ritchie, A Study in Virginia Politics. Richmond, 1913.

Anderson, Dice Robins. William Branch Giles: A Study in the Politics of Virginia and the New Nation from 1790 to 1830. Reprint Gloucester, 1965.

Armes, Ethel. Stratford Hall, The Great House of the Lees. Richmond, 1936.

Asbury, Herbert. Sucker's Progress . . . New York, 1938.

Bender, Eric. Tickets to Fortune . . . New York, 1938.

Beveridge, Albert J. The Life of John Marshall. 4 vols. Boston, 1916-1919.

Blau, Joseph L., and Salo W. Baro. The Jews of the United States, 1790-1840, A Documentary History. 3 vols. New York, 1963.

Bruce, Philip Alexander. History of the University of Virginia, 1819-1919. 5 vols. New York, 1920-1922.

Bruce, William Cabell. John Randolph of Roanoke, 1773-1833. 2 vols. New York, 1922.

Cabell, Nathaniel Francis (ed.). Early History of the University of Virginia as Contained in the Letters of Thomas Jefferson and Joseph C. Cabell. Richmond, 1856.

Calendar of the Correspondence of Thomas Jefferson, Part II, Letters to Jefferson. Bulletin of the Department of State, VIII (November 1894), Washington, 1895.

Carpenter, Jesse T. The South as a Conscious Minority, 1789-1861, A Study in Political Thought. New York, 1930.

Corwin, Edward S., et al. (ed.). The Constitution of the United States of America, Analysis and Interpretation . . . Washington, 1964.

Corwin, Edward S. The Doctrine of Judicial Review . . . Princeton, 1914.

Dabney, Virginius. Virginia, the New Dominion. Garden City, 1971.

Ezekiel, Herbert T., and Gaston Lichtenstein. The History of the Jews of Richmond From 1769 to 1917. Richmond, 1917.

Ezell, John Samuel. Fortune's Merry Wheel, the Lottery in America. Cambridge, 1960.

Falkner, Robert K. The Jurisprudence of John Marshall. Princeton, 1968.

Frank, John P. Justice Daniel Dissenting . . . Cambridge, 1964.

Gaines, William H. Jr. Thomas Mann Randolph, Jefferson's Son-in-Law. Baton Rouge, 1966.

Garland, Hugh. The Life of John Randolph of Roanoke. 2 vols. New York, 1850.

Gordon, Armistead C. William Fitzhugh Gordon . . . New York, 1909.

Gray, Lewis C. History of Agriculture in the Southern States to 1860. 2 vols. New York, 1941.

Grigsby, Hugh Blair. The History of the Virginia Federal Convention . . . 2 vols. Richmond, 1890.

Grossman, Joel B., and Richard S. Wells. Constitutional Laws and Judicial Policy Making. New York, 1972.

Haines, Charles G. The Role of the Supreme Court in American Government and Politics, 1789-1835. Los Angeles, 1944.

Hall, Claude M. Abel P. Upshur: Conservative Virginian, 1790-1844. Madison, 1964.

Hendrick, Burton J. The Lees of Virginia: Biography of a Family. New York, 1935.

Hughes, Robert W. Editors of the Past. n.p. n.d.

Jackson, Robert H. The Struggle for Judicial Review. New York, 1941.

Jacobs, Clyde E. The Eleventh Amendment and Sovereign Immunity. Westport, Connecticut, 1972.

Kennedy, John P. Memoirs of the Life of William Wirt. Philadelphia, 1849.

Kutler, Stanley. Privilege and Creative Destruction. Philadelphia, 1971.

Leggett, M. D. Subject Matter Index of Patents for Inventions. Washington, 1874.

McClellan, James. Joseph Story and the American Constitution. Norman, 1971.

Nagel, Paul C. One Nation Indivisible: The Union in American Thought, 1776-1861. New York, 1964.

Palmer, W. P. et al. (ed.). Calendar of Virginia State Papers and Other Manuscripts. 11 vols. Richmond, 1875-1893.

Risjord, Norman. The Old Republicans, Southern Conservatism in the Age of Jefferson. New York, 1965.

Royall, William I. A History of Virginia Banks and Banking Prior to the Civil War. New York, 1907.

Scharf, J. Thomas. The Chronicles of Baltimore . . . Baltimore, 1874.

Schmidhauser, John R. The Supreme Court as Final Arbiter in Federal State Relations, 1789-1957. Chapel Hill, 1958.

Simms, Henry. The Rise of the Whigs in Virginia, 1824-1840. Richmond, 1929.

Standard, Mary Newton. Colonial Virginia, Its People and Customs. Philadelphia, 1917.

Starnes, George T. Sixty Years of Branch Banking in Virginia. New York, 1931.

Swem, Earl G., and John V. Williams. A Register of the General Assembly of Virginia, 1776-1918 . . . Richmond, 1918.

Tresolini, Rocco J., and Martin Shapiro. American Constitutional Law 3d ed. New York, 1970.

Tucker, Beverly Randolph. Tales of the Tuckers . . . Richmond, 1942.

Tyler, Lyon G. The Letters and Times of the Tylers. 3 vols. Richmond, 1884-1896.

Warfield, Ethelbert Dudley. The Kentucky Resolutions of 1798, An Historical Study. New York, 1894.

Warren, Charles. The Supreme Court in United States History. 3 vols. Boston, 1923.

Wayland, Francis Fry. Andrew Stevenson, Democrat and Diplomat, 1785-1857. Philadelphia, 1949.

Wheaton, Henry. Some Account of the Life, Writings and Speaches of William Pinckney. New York, 1826.

Wiltse, Charles M. _John C. Calhoun Nationalist, 1782-1828_. Indianapolis, 1944.

Secondary Sources: Theses and Dissertations

Ammon, Harry. "The Republican Party in Virginia; 1789 to 1824." Unpublished Ph.D. dissertation, University of Virginia, 1948.

Beach, Rex. "Judge Spencer Roane: A Champion of State Rights." Unpublished Master's thesis, University of Virginia, 1941.

Bell, Claudia F. "_Green v. Biddle_." Unpublished Master's thesis, University of Virginia, 1970.

Gerback, Clyde C. "Spencer Roane of Virginia, 1762-1822, a Judicial Advocate of State Rights." Unpublished Ph.D. dissertation, University of Pittsburgh, 1955.

Harrison, Joseph Hobson. "The Internal Improvements Issue in the Politics of the Union, 1783-1825." Unpublished Ph.D. dissertation, University of Virginia, 1954.

Horsnell, Margaret Eileen. "Spencer Roane: Judicial Advocate of Jeffersonian Principles." Unpublished Ph.D. dissertation, University of Minnesota, 1967.

Jordan, Daniel Porter Jr. "Virginia Congressmen, 1803-1825." Unpublished Ph.D. dissertation, University of Virginia, 1970.

Lowery, Charles D. "James Barbour, A Politician and Planter of Anti-Bellum Virginia." Unpublished Ph.D. dissertation, University of Virginia, 1966.

Roberts, Edward Graham. "The Roads of Virginia, 1607-1840." Unpublished Ph.D. dissertation, University of Virginia, 1950.

Schmidhauser, John R. "The Role of the Supreme Court as Arbiter in Federal-State Relations." Unpublished Ph.D. dissertation, University of Virginia, 1954.

Sutton, Robert P. "The Virginia Constitutional Convention of 1829-1830. . . ." Unpublished Ph.D. dissertation, University of Virginia, 1967.

Tanner, Carol Minor. "Joseph C. Cabell, 1778-1856." Unpublished Ph.D. dissertation, University of Virginia, 1948.

Treon, John A. "_Martin v. Hunter's Lessee_: A Case History." Unpublished Ph.D. dissertation, University of Virginia, 1970.

Weeder, Elinor Janet. "Wilson Cary Nicholas, Jefferson's Lieutenant," Unpublished Master's thesis, University of Virginia, 1946.